Susan Hayward

Susan Hayward

Her Films and Life

KIM R. HOLSTON

McFarland & Company, Inc., Publishers

Jefferson, North Carolina, and London

The present work is a reprint of the illustrated case
bound edition of Susan Hayward: Her Films and Life,
first published in 2002 by McFarland.

Frontispiece: 20th Century–Fox publicity portrait, ca. 1952.

LIBRARY OF CONGRESS CATALOGUING-IN-PUBLICATION DATA

Holston, Kim R., 1948–
Susan Hayward : her films and life / Kim R. Holston.
p.   cm.
Includes bibliographical references and index.

ISBN 978-0-7864-4334-5
softcover : 50# alkaline paper ∞

1. Hayward, Susan, 1918–1975.
2. Motion picture actors and actresses—United States—Biography.
I. Title.
PN2287.H378 H65   2009   791.43'028'092—dc21   2002009784

British Library cataloguing data are available

On the cover: Hayward in the film *Smash-Up: The Story of a Woman*
(Universal-International, 1947)

Manufactured in the United States of America

*McFarland & Company, Inc., Publishers
Box 611, Jefferson, North Carolina 28640
www.mcfarlandpub.com*

For Nancy Spellman

To be a star, yes, you have to have talent, and my God, do you
ever have to be lucky, but riding alongside is this: desire.
—William Goldman, Which Lie Did I Tell?
More Adventures in the Screen Trade (2000)

Contents

PREFACE

Susan Hayward is a rather unusual individual to have become my favorite female movie star. I generally favor Jessie Matthews, Terry Moore, Mitzi Gaynor, Janet Munro, all those who possess that rarest of physical attributes: genuine cuteness. Although she had a cute (if rarely heard) squeal, Susan Hayward was not cute. She was beautiful, and her characters were tough, pugnacious, belligerent, brash.

My crush on Susan Hayward began in May 1956. I was seven years old and my mother took me up High Street to the Warner Theater in West Chester, Pennsylvania. We saw *The Conqueror*, the maligned "Mongolian western" in which John Wayne played Temujin, aka Genghis Khan. Early in the film Temujin and his tribesmen waylay a caravan whose prime cargo is Bortai (Hayward). Temujin approaches her open carriage, gives her the once-over, and rips the coverlet from her body. Of course there was no nudity in 1956, but the flash of flesh—even if it was only bare shoulders—left me with an indelible memory of a ravishing redheaded goddess. Nor was I the only spectator to be impressed. Bronte Woodward of the *Los Angeles Times* gushed, "Susan never looked lovelier, red hair and pale skin against the desert sand and sky, exercising her Divine Right as a Movie Star—being all things to all people."

My familiarity with Susan Hayward increased in 1961. Perhaps other baby boomers became fans of hers at that time, as they would of Tyrone Power, Richard Widmark and Clifton Webb. It was on September 23, 1961, that NBC-TV premiered *Saturday Night at the Movies*. This was the first time fairly recent theatrical movies were presented on TV in prime time. That first season of *Saturday Night at the Movies* featured 20th Century–Fox films of the '50s, and Susan Hayward starred in five: *The Snows of Kilimanjaro, Garden of Evil, Demetrius and the Gladiators, Soldier of Fortune* and *With a Song in My Heart*. I thank my parents for allowing me to stay home some Saturday nights to watch those films rather than accompany them to my grandparents' house.

Appreciation for more recent help on this project goes to Sandy Bowman, Ed Colbert, Laurie Higgins, Kristine Krueger of the Academy Foundation/National Film Information Service, Milton T. Moore, Jr., Eduardo Moreno, *Movie Star News*, James Robert Parish, Stephen Sally, and Dianne Thomas. My wife Nancy was an invaluable sounding board and a consultant on photo selection.

Introduction

Susan Hayward was sometimes called "The Sphinx" because she rarely talked about herself.[1] More so than most stars, she would be known to the public—and her movieland peers—as much through her reel as her real life.

Hayward's career was unique among the big stars. "Susan Hayward's career was in certain respects quite curious. Few stars of her stature have appeared in so few interesting films or worked so seldom with distinguished directors (*Canyon Passage*, *The Lusty Men*) ... except from the viewpoint of Hayward's intrinsic interest there is really not much else to salvage."[2]

As for acting,

> The keynote of Susan Hayward's acting style is her pugnacity, which has become more marked over the years. This has not made her one of Hollywood's most attractive heroines, though in movies like *White Witch Doctor* and *Untamed*, her spirit of rugged determination is very fitting. Just occasionally her personality has been harnessed to effect, though not in her Oscar-winning style of the late fifties. She was at her best under Nicholas Ray in *The Lusty Men*.... Verbally and physically on the offensive against the rodeo's camp followers, she is for once sympathetically aggressive.[3]

Hayward's characters certainly smacked of pugnacity. "For women to have a long career in films requires superhuman energy, guts and determination. The longest surviving ladies usually betray in their performances something of their off-screen battles."[4] She was "earthy, a product of the soil. She's remindful of a slightly unripe and hard-core persimmon. Acrid. Fresh. But refrigerator-chilled."[5]

Chilled or not, and more accurately a product of the sidewalks of New York City, Hayward had charisma—and something besides professionalism:

1

As Bortai in *The Conqueror* (RKO, 1956).

There was another, equally important factor in Hayward's appeal. With few exceptions, most forceful women on the screen were dynamic and independent at the expense of their femininity. Joan Crawford, Bette Davis, Katharine Hepburn and Barbara Stanwyck, for example, could never be described as sex symbols in the strictest sense. Susan was different. She was perhaps the first star ever to pull it off. She was full-breasted, softly enticing, and yet at her best was as powerful a feminist as any of the others. There was never a picture in which Susan was anything but All Woman.[6]

Hayward furnished her own take on her allure:

I keep my head lowered and look up at a man. Sort of sideways out of the corner of my eyes. Especially when he's lighting my cigarette. That'll get him. A pouting lip helps, but then mine pout naturally. I've always tried to play scenes with a superior air, too. That gives the impression of trying to seduce someone.[7]

Versatility was also a Hayward hallmark. When she began making films in the late 1930s, the classical Hollywood studio system was operating at peak efficiency. Great numbers of films were made, and there was no onus placed on performers who made films in various genres. Even if those actors objected, they were under contract and nixed roles at the peril of suspension. Throughout her career Hayward proved her worth as Biblical femme fatale, Roman temptress, hearty pioneer (on two continents), antebellum aristocrat, resilient torch singer, brazen B girl, and street-smart denizen of the modern urban jungle. It all began in Brooklyn.

Chapter 1

Brooklyn

EVE (Anne Baxter): *Erasmus Hall. It's in Brooklyn, isn't it?*
PHOEBE (Barbara Bates): *Well, lots of actresses come from Brooklyn. Barbara Stanwyk and Susan Hayward. Of course, they're just movie stars. You're going to Hollywood, aren't you?*

—All About Eve *(20th Century–Fox, 1950)*

Of Hollywood leading ladies, Brooklyn has supplied its fair share, including Clara Bow, Barbara Stanwyck, Veronica Lake, Gene Tierney, Barbra Streisand—and Susan Hayward, born Edythe Marrenner.

Edythe's father, Walter Marrenner, had been a Coney Island barker when he met her stenographer mother, Ellen Pearson. Ellen had been born on October 10, 1888.[1] Walter was a bit older.[2] The Marrenner family traced its ancestry to Ireland, the Pearsons to Sweden. After the Pearson-Marrenner marriage on August 14, 1909, Walter became a lineman for the Interboro Rapid Transit Company.[3] Later he worked in the office.

Edythe was the third of three children born to Walter and Ellen. Sister Florence had arrived on May 29, 1910, and her brother, Walter, Jr. (Wally), on December 8, 1911.[4] Edythe was born in the family's 3507 Church Avenue apartment.[5]

The actual birthdate of Susan Hayward, née Edythe Marrenner, has been a minor mystery, as has been the spelling of her maiden name, often incorrectly given as Marrener. The most frequently specified birthdate is June 30, 1918, but seemingly reliable sources cite 1917 to 1919. As late as 1949 columnist Sidney Skolsky muddied the waters by making it 1923.[6]

Hayward's crypt in Carrollton, Georgia, reads, "Mrs. F. Eaton Chalkley, 1919–1975."[7]

The truth? In the first issue of the *Susan Hayward Collectors' Club Newsletter*, club president Dianne Thomas wrote that Hayward's son Timothy Barker told her his mother had been born on June 30, 1917.[8] Hayward's death certificate has that same date. Birth records in New York are not public records, but a phone conversation on September 6, 2000, confirmed Edythe Marrenner's birthdate as June 30, 1917.

The Marrenners were poor but not downtrodden in spirit. Evidence of Edythe's spunk lies in a youthful adventure involving the "borrowing" of a neighbor boy's bicycle. When she returned it, "I greeted him, all smiles, for it was a beautiful bike … but he was so mad he didn't say a word. He just reached over and pushed me off the machine into the gutter. Then, when I got up, he punched me in the nose." At home, her father told her to return the favor.[9]

Edythe followed in brother Wally's footsteps and delivered newspapers.

> I earned my first dollar selling newspapers at the age of 12, and was the only girl who had a route for the *Brooklyn Eagle*. When I was 14, I supplemented the family income by modeling. Dresses for fat 14-year-olds. When I slimmed down I did a lot of "the skin you love to touch" routines and passionate kisses for cigar manufacturers, inferring that the men who smoke them had really dined on chloryphyll [sic].[10]

When she wasn't delivering papers or attending Public School 181, Edythe spent her free time with Wally. They attended films and between double features participated in vaudeville routines. They even won an amateur dancing contest.[11] But Edythe's sister Florence was the true terpsichorean. Entering competitions at age seventeen, Florence demonstrated a talent that landed her in Broadway chorus lines. For a time she was the Marrenner with the most potential for success. Florence's income allowed the family to move to a larger apartment at 2568 Bedford Avenue.[12]

As the years and decades progressed, Edythe became estranged from her older sister. She probably exaggerated the degree of favoritism her mother had shown Florence. Florence recalled their childhood in 1961:

> There are so many things I'd like to forget and some I enjoy remembering, like the time when Susan and I were kids back in Flatbush. Everything was so happy then. My father, Walter Marrenner, worked for the subway company. He didn't make much money, but he and my mother, Ellen—she was a stenographer before she married my father—gave us a lot of loving care and attention. We lived in a five-bedroom apartment. It was just a plain place, but it was home.

My brother, Walter, Jr., and I went to ordinary high schools, but Susan went to a girl's commercial school. We never had any parties at home because we didn't have money for parties, but we went a lot of places together. We'd go to the beach and to shows and sometimes we'd take a plane ride or go somewhere and play tennis.[13]

One cannot ignore the importance of the irrational in human affairs. Late in her life, Edythe, now Susan, described her relationship with her sister and mother to close friend Ron Nelson, who said:

Susan was very critical of her mother. She used to tell me that she was an emasculating, cold-hearted woman. She told me, "I could never get over the way she treated my father; it was just ridiculous. She was selfish and cold and cruel, and she wanted what she wanted and didn't give a damn how she got it." She said that her mother had never given her encouragement, never told her that she loved her, that she was pretty. It was always "Florence is pretty, Florence is the one." She told me that she thought her mother was frigid and that she never wanted anything but money.[14]

Confirmation of Nelson's recollection came from Hayward's son Timothy Barker, who said his grandmother was "very cold, very angry."[15]

Edythe was closer to her father but would not be in New York when he passed away on March 16, 1938, of a heart attack and kidney failure. He was fifty-six. Ironically, Edythe's life would not be much longer in duration.

An accident that would give the future actress a distinctive gait occurred when Edythe was seven. In 1924 on Snyder Avenue[16] she was hit by a car and suffered broken legs and a broken hip. She recuperated in traction at home. Because of such cursory medical treatment, she retained a slight limp.

The Great Depression had begun in 1929, and times remained tough. The Marrenners were used to it. Florence said, "There were times when we didn't have enough to eat. I remember once, when I was about eleven, I only had bread to eat for three days."[17] Wally recalled that at Christmas they'd wait till the trees were reduced in price to get one. "Our parents gave us what presents they could…. As we got older, we got less and less. We used to get apples, oranges, candy and nuts."[18] Later they received gift-wrapped coal lumps.[19]

After P.S. 181, Edythe chose to attend Girls Commercial High (which later became Prospect Heights High). She acted in school plays, securing the lead in *Cinderella in Flowerland*[20] and graduated in June 1935. She was designated "Most Dramatic" in the yearbook.

Looking for work, preferably in the acting realm (though she had precious little experience or training), Edythe crossed the East River to Manhattan. She attended the Feagin School of Dramatic Arts but discovered that modeling jobs generated immediate income. Redheads were at a premium, and the Walter Thornton Agency signed her up. She modeled Luralace foundation garments and Noxzema, among other items. She was pictured in the October 30, 1937, *Saturday Evening Post* "Merchant of Venus" article as the girl in "A Day in the Life of a Model." She had also appeared in a Vitaphone Pictorial Short in 1936.[21] Hollywood beckoned. Sort of.

Chapter 2

Hollywood or Bust

She is, in fact, Hollywood's ablest bitch-player.
—Time *review of* The Hairy Ape[1]

Like her birthdate, Edythe Marrenner's first journey to Hollywood is cloaked in mystery. Seemingly reputable sources indicate that director George Cukor spotted Edythe's October 30, 1937, *Saturday Evening Post* cover and considered her a Scarlett possibility for *Gone with the Wind*.[2] But Edythe Marrenner was not on that cover, which featured Halloween artwork of two children staring at a figure wearing a pumpkin. Edythe *was* pictured inside but only identified as "a model" in an article about Walter Thornton's modeling agency. She was in all seven color photos by Ivan Dimitri, however.[3] A 1958 Paramount press release was probably closer to the truth when it indicated Cukor "happened to thumb through the magazine."[4]

Whatever brought her to the attention of Hollywood's moviemakers, Edythe and her sister Florence took the train to California on November 18, 1937. Edythe had a screen test on December 6, 1937.[5] Surviving footage reveals that she was "Edith Marrener" on the Hollywood screen-test clapboard. She may also have been screen-tested before leaving New York.[6]

It's quite possible that Hayward was never seriously considered for the plum role of the decade—Scarlett O'Hara in *Gone with the Wind*. Rather, her inexperience fitted her merely as a stand-in with whom that film's prospective male actors could work.[7] *Gone with the Wind*'s first director, George Cukor, said, "She was very young and not too experienced, in fact, completely inexperienced. It would have been stupid to get a twenty-year-old girl to play a most demanding part. We thought, David [O. Selznick] thought, 'This girl may have some possibilities. Let's bring her out and use her for tests and put her under contract.'"[8]

A year later David O. Selznick wrote: "I think we can forget about Susan Hayward because we don't even need her any more as a stand-in for Scarlett [other Scarlett contenders were Paulette Goddard, Doris Jordan (Davenport), Jean Arthur, Katharine Hepburn and Loretta Young[9]] or to work with people we are testing for the other roles, what with others around...."[10]

According to a 1951 article, "George [Cukor] recalled yesterday that he and David Selznick met Susan on the train with her sister.... David wanted her tested for *Gone with the Wind*, but she was too young and too inexperienced to qualify. However, she did continue to make tests with about one hundred other actors who were up for parts in *Gone with the Wind*."[11]

Neither a choice role nor a contract with Selznick had come her way, but Edythe Marrenner decided to tough it out. Later on she recalled those days when she, her sister and mother lived in Los Angeles while she sought film work.

> I can remember those horrible months when we always had to rush to make payments.... That's the reason why you'll never hear me crying about taxes or about what the Government takes out of my salary. Those days were too grim to forget. I admit I was stupid, but I was exposed to the whole routine in too much of a hurry. I think that then the young people shot up too fast and I defy any newcomer not to believe his or her publicity at the very beginning. It's only natural. At least it was for me.[12]

1938

In 1938, Warner Bros. gave Edythe Marrenner her first film roles. Warner Bros., studio of such stars as James Cagney, Edward G. Robinson, Bette Davis, Errol Flynn, Olivia de Havilland, and the emerging Humphrey Bogart, was the maker of such gritty urban gangster films as *The Public Enemy* (1931), Depression era musical pick-me-ups like *42nd Street* (1934), and swashbuckling adventures like *Captain Blood* (1935).

When 1938 dawned, Warner Bros. talent agent Max Arnow came up with the Susan Hayward name.[13] Arnow was conducting business with agent Leland Hayward at the time and liked the name Hayward. He didn't recall where the "Susan" came from.[14]

One apocryphal report says a bicycle played an important part in Hayward's success in Hollywood. She is said to have lost control, jumped a curb, crossed a lawn and fallen through an open ground-floor window of agent Ben Medford![15]

Medford *did* become her agent and in February 1938 negotiated her Warner Bros. term contract. Hayward was to get parts in *The Clarion* and *The Sisters*.[16] There is no Warner Bros. movie titled *The Clarion*, and as for *The Sisters*, Hayward's role would be miniscule at best.

When Hayward later signed with Paramount, that studio made light of her previous credits while admitting she'd signed a six-month contract with Warner Bros. "Susan made many pictures for Warners, but they were all still pictures in bathing suits and shorts, which newspaper editors and readers duly appreciated."[17]

Posing for "cheesecake" photographs was indeed one of Hayward's tasks at WB, as it would be for decades to come for starlets and even stars. But Hayward did get some film work after attending Frank Beckwith's Warner drama school, along with, among others, Ronald Reagan and Jane Wyman.[18] MGM's elocution coach helped her learn to speak from the diaphragm.[19]

Bit Parts

Hollywood Hotel (Warner Bros., 1938) was filmed late in 1937 and released in January 1938. When Allyn Joslyn inspects a line-up of young women in hopes of selecting a double for Lola Lane, the last girl in line on the right may be Hayward. One biographer says she's in the finale.[20] *Hollywood Hotel* is of interest as a lower-level Busby Berkeley–directed musical comedy about saxophonist Ronnie Bowers (Dick Powell) called to Hollywood by a major studio. Booked into the Hollywood Hotel, he is assigned to be the date of Virginia Stanton (Rosemary Lane) at a film premiere. Virginia is posing as the film's absent star, Mona Marshall (Lola Lane). Returning, Mona gets Ronnie and Virginia fired. Later Ronnie is overheard singing and lands a wonderful deal with the film studio courtesy of some fast thinking by Virginia.

One biographer says Hayward had a few lines at the beginning of *The Amazing Dr. Clitterhouse* (1938),[21] another that she's a patient in that film,[22] and a third that this part did not materialize.[23] Neither *The American Film Institute Catalog* nor *The Motion Picture Guide* lists her in the credits.

Hayward is often registered as a bit player in *The Sisters* (1938), a

Warner Bros. publicity photo, ca. 1938.

high-class Warner Bros. film starring Bette Davis and Errol Flynn. She is supposed to be one of the switchboard operators seen near the end of the picture. But they are all viewed from the back as their room is entered. There are no close-ups of those backs. It is impossible to identify Hayward.

Some sources indicate Hayward had a bit part in another Edward G.

Warner Bros. publicity photo, ca. 1938.

Robinson film, *I Am the Law* (1938). But there are bit parts where the subject can be identified and bit parts in which the subject cannot be positively recognized. Sometimes an actor or actress was announced for a film and either the film was never made or the actor did not appear in it for any number of reasons (e.g. tied up in another movie).

Released on December 3, 1938, *Comet Over Broadway* (1938) was another Busby Berkeley–directed film (not a musical) with the Broadway theater as background. It starred Kay Francis and John Litel. One biographer says Hayward's face is shown in one scene and that she has one line of dialogue.[24] In *The American Film Institute Catalog* Hayward is listed with Alice Connor and Fern Barry as "Amateur actors."

Susan Hayward did have a bit part in the two-reel Vitaphone/Warner Bros. short, *Campus Cinderella*. It was released December 23, 1938.[25]

Girls on Probation (Warner Bros., 1938)

The story: Connie Heath (Jane Bryan) loses her job at the Avery Todd Company Cleaners & Dyers in Irvingdale, New York, after borrowing a dress from co-worker Hilda Engstrom (Sheila Bromley). Unknown to Connie, that dress belonged to a customer, Gloria Adams (Hayward). Gloria sent the dress in for cleaning, then saw Connie wearing it at the Hula House dance. The next day Gloria went to the shop to retrieve it and noticed that it had been ripped and repaired. While interviewing Connie at the Detention Center, Gloria's boyfriend, Attorney Neil Dillon (Ronald Reagan) of the Empire Insurance Company, learns that Hilda is the real culprit. But Hilda's left town. Nevertheless, Neil pays the claim and lets Connie make restitution payments to him. After her overbearing father (Sig Ruman) slaps her, Connie leaves Irvingdale for Ardmore, becomes a secretary and begins sending $10 checks to Neil. One day Connie stumbles into Hilda and finds herself in the midst of the Union Bank robbery, committed by Hilda's boyfriend Tony Rand (Anthony Averill). All three are arrested. Sympathetic probation officer Jane Lennox (Dorothy Peterson) secures probation for Connie after a newsboy reveals that Connie was pushed into the getaway car. Back in Irvingdale, Connie gets a job with Neil, who's now an assistant district attorney and apparently no longer an item with Gloria. Who should appear but Hilda, intent on blackmailing Connie. Connie reveals all to Neil, who doesn't care about this blemish. Tony, meanwhile, busts out of the pen but is gunned down at Hilda's apartment. She, too, is mortally wounded, but clears Connie with her dying breath.

The New York Times said, "As entertainment, it is slow, obvious and deficient in even the slight caloric content which sometimes makes a bald-faced melodrama bearable."[26]

Although she's ninth-billed, Hayward has lines to say and acts the catalyst. Thus *Girls on Probation* is generally considered her true film debut. In her two scenes she makes an impression and looks great in her own dancehall dress. The basic plot (attractive young woman erroneously convicted) was gussied up—or down—for Linda Blair's 1983 women-in-prison exploitation film, *Chained Heat*.

Publicity portrait ca. 1938.

Paramount

Hayward's Warner Bros. days were short-lived, but Paramount picked her up. A Press Release described her as "a former New York model, native of Brooklyn, out of work in a strange land. She had no friends within the closely guarded gates of the studios, no motion picture experience, and just the sketchiest sort of stage record." More apocrypha: She walked into the office of Paramount's talent department head Arthur Jacobson, asked for a job and was given a long-term contract, with her first assignment a small but significant part. "Miss Hayward, a slender blonde whose rich speaking voice is not the least of her bountiful physical endowments, will portray Isobel in the Wellman version of P. C. Wren's great novel."[27]

It's more likely that her agent Ben Medford took her to Paramount.[28] Hayward already knew Jacobson from her Selznick days.[29]

1939

Beau Geste (Paramount, 1939)

The story: Arriving at Fort Zinderneuf with his relief column, Major de Beaujolais (James Stephenson) finds its garrison dead. But from whence did the lone gunshot come? A bugler sent into the fort does not return and de Beaujolais enters again. On the body of a dead sergeant is a note saying he stole "the Blue Water," a precious gem. More shots cause the relief column to retire to an oasis. An explosion rocks the fort. Flashback to the young Geste brothers Beau (Donald O'Connor), John (Billy Cook), and Digby (Martin Spellman), creating a Viking funeral for a toy soldier. Beau has his brothers promise him a like funeral when he dies. The boys and Isobel (Ann Gillis) are wards of Lady Brandon (Heather Thatcher), who secretly sells the sapphire "The Blue Water" for funds to educate them. Beau sees her replace the family heirloom with an imitation. Years pass and Lord Brandon (G. P. Huntley) intends selling what he thinks is the real sapphire. Beau (Gary Cooper) steals it and joins the French Foreign Legion. Digby (Robert Preston) and John (Ray Milland) join him, although John must leave Isobel (Hayward). Training in the Legion is harsh, especially under the rules of Sergeant Markov (Brian Donlevy): "I make soldiers out of scum like you, and I don't do it gently. You're the sloppiest looking lot I've ever seen. It's up to me to prevent you from becoming a disgrace to the regiment. And I will prevent that, if I have to kill half of you with work. But the half that lives will be soldiers. I promise you!" During training, Rasinoff (J. Carrol Naish) informs Markov that there is a jewel in the brothers' possession. Markov sends Digby to Fort Tokotu while Beau and John join his detachment at Fort Zinderneuf. After the lieutenant in command dies, Markov takes charge. The men mutiny under his harsh rule, but not the Geste brothers, whom he orders to shoot the mutiny leaders. They refuse and he threatens them with death. A desert tribe attacks and most of the garrison is killed. John finds Markov

Publicity portrait ca. 1939.

searching Beau's body and bayonets him after the mortally wounded Beau grabs Markov's feet. The dying Beau gives John a note to place in Markov's hand saying he stole the gem and a letter to Lady Brandon explaining his own actions. John places Markov's body at Beau's feet and sets the fort ablaze. He leaves the fort and is found by Digby, the bugler, who is later killed by nomads. John makes his way back to England and Isobel's arms.

Recalling the 1926 silent version, the *New York Times* found the sound remake was "still good cinema—that the absurd nobility, brotherly devotion and self-sacrifice of the Geste tribe are still unflagging ingredients for action melodrama…. On the whole, it is perhaps an unfortunate thing for Beau Geste the Second that Beau Geste the First was so distinguished, for Mr. Wellman's film seems dominated by the tremendous shadow of its predecessor."[30] *Newsweek* found that "the story of P. C. Wren's best seller is still a reliable springboard for colorful screen melodrama. More demanding in activity than acting, the film receives competent performances from a hard-working cast that includes Heather Thatcher, Susan Hayward, James Stephenson, and J. Carrol Naish."[31]

Percival Christopher Wren's novel became *the* classic French Foreign Legion opus, and this version was one of the plethora of outstanding films in many genres that gave 1939 the well-deserved reputation of the greatest year in Hollywood history. *Beau Geste* became Hayward's "official" debut, her screen time occurring near the beginning and at the end. She is bright and chipper in her few scenes.

Ronald Colman had starred in the silent version. Coincidentally, Hayward had been studying Colman's speech patterns in *The Prisoner of Zenda* (1937) to improve her diction and delivery.[32] *Beau Geste* received an Academy Award nomination for Art and Set Decoration. Brian Donlevy received a Best Supporting Actor nomination. He'd play Hayward's on-screen flame seven years later.

Back to B Programming

As successful as *Beau Geste* was, it did not lead to stardom for Hayward, and she was saddled with lesser films, if not less screen time. There are three explanations. First, she had the chutzpah to request better roles. Perhaps *demand* is a better word. Second, her looks intimidated other leading ladies who wouldn't want the competition.[33] Third, she was aloof.[34]

Our Leading Citizen (Paramount, 1939)

The story: Lawyer Lem Schofield (Bob Burns) makes young Clay Clinton (Joseph Allen, Jr.) his partner. Clay loves Lem's daughter Judith (Hayward). But Clay aspires to fame and fortune and is swayed by the blandishments of industrialist J. T. Tapley (Gene Lockhart). When Tapley imposes a wage cut, the employees strike and a labor war is unleashed. Lem withdraws as Tapley's attorney. Oblivious to Tapley's robber baron mentality, Clay remains with him. Tapley uses Shep Muir's (Charles Bickford) strikebreakers while union leader Jim Hanna (Clarence Kolb) tries

Beau Geste (Paramount, 1939), left to right: Robert Preston, Ray Milland, Hayward, Hether Thatcher, G.P. Huntley, Jr., Gary Cooper.

to find a peaceful solution. Communist agitator Jerry Peters (Paul Guilfoyle) arrives and advocates violence. Riots occur. The mill is bombed and one man killed. Lem forces Tapley to agree he won't nominate Clay to the Senate by threatening to reveal that Tapley once filched valuable property from Aunt Tillie Clark (Elizabeth Patterson). Tapley signs an agreement to pay her. Lem helps to arrest Peters and Muir and create a labor settlement. Clay nominates Lem for U.S. Senator. Clay and Judith are reunited.

Even though Hayward is the female lead, she gets no mention in the *New York Times* review, which called the movie "an affront to intelligence and good taste. For nothing so synthetic, so confused and so full of balderdash has come this way in months...."[35] The working title was *Us Americans*. Rumors have it that Martha Raye was to have starred. There's a 1922 silent version whose characters have different names.

$1,000 a Touchdown (Paramount, 1939)

The story: Martha Madison (Martha Raye) inherits a school, and with the help of actor Marlowe Mansfield Booth (Joe E. Brown), turns it into a dramatic school after securing a loan from Fishbeck (George McKay). When no students enroll, Martha takes her ex-butler's (Eric Blore) advice and forms a football team. That and the romance course taught by Betty McGlen (Hayward) attract students from other schools, including Bill Anders (John Hartey). Bill has eyes for Betty, and the other players attract coeds. A problem arises when the team can't get other schools to play them. Martha hires a pro team for an exhibition, and during the game wages Fishbeck that the school team can score a touchdown. She also promises to pay the pro team's captain $1,000 for every TD *her* team scores. Fishbeck pays up but eventually quits, at which point the pros begin to score again. Marlowe, who'd used a book to coach the team, now enters the game himself and leads the school team to victory.

The *New York Times* called it a "painfully witless football farce of almost fantastic unoriginality."[36]

Although Martha Raye and Joe E. Brown had followings of sorts, this film was roundly trounced by reviewers. Hayward wasn't mentioned at all, which some argue was a plus for her career.[37]

The Redheaded League

The Titianettes, a national organization of redheads, elected Hayward their 1939 queen. "Still unattached, Miss Hayward is considered one of Hollywood's loveliest and most eligible young ladies."[38]

1940

Mentor

Providentially, Susan had made the acquaintance of influential Hollywood gossip columnist Louella Parsons, who took her on her nationwide tour. "Louella Parsons Presents Her Galaxy of 'Hollywood Stars on Parade' with her Stars of 1940," read an ad for the RKO Golden Gate theater. The fledgling stars performed live, singing, dancing and clowning around. Besides Hayward (pictured third below Parsons and noted as "Paramount Pictures Star"), the actors included Arleen Whelan, Ronald Reagan, Joy Hodges, Jane Wyman, and June Preisser. Those who stayed after the live show at this theater were treated to the Jean Hersholt film *Meet Doctor Christian* and a Donald Duck cartoon.

Hayward (left) publicity photo with Virginia Dale (Paramount, 1940).

1941

Adam Had Four Sons (Columbia, 1941)

The story: At the turn of the century, Adam Stoddard (Warner Baxter), his wife Molly (Fay Wray), and their four sons welcome Emilie Gallatin (Ingrid Bergman) to America as their governess. Emilie fits right in, and when Molly dies Emilie has the unexpected opportunity to fulfill her promise to oversee the children as long as she's needed. Adam's financial business goes bust in a stock market crash and he sells their Connecticut home and moves to a New York apartment with his youngest son. Cousin Phillippa pays for the private schooling of the older three. Reluctantly, Emilie returns to Europe. Stoddard's fortunes revive when economic activity increases as the U.S. enters World War I. He buys back his old home and sends for Emilie. She relishes the opportunity to keep her promise to Molly. As the war progresses, each of the sons enlists. David (Johnny Downs) comes home on leave with a wife, Hester (Hayward). Emilie's suspicions about Hester's character prove well founded when she discovers Hester trying to seduce Jack (Richard Denning) while Tom is in Europe. To protect the family when Adam comes to believe that Jack and Hester are involved, Emilie allows Adam to think that she and Jack are attracted to each other. Nevertheless, on his first night home after the war, David realizes that Hester is a cheater. He tries to commit suicide in a plane. Emilie tries to make Hester leave the home. Hester turns the tables until Jack arrives and sets things straight about Hester's true nature. Adam goes to Emilie and explains, and they realize they are meant for each other.

The *New York Times* found it "heavily charged with sentiment" and noted, "Susan Hayward so coyly overacts the romantically unlicensed mischief-maker that often she is plain ridiculous."[39] A fan magazine was more positive about Hayward: "The unquenchable Menace that almost burned up the film?"[40]

Warner Baxter had been a Best Actor Academy Award winner for his role as the Cisco Kid in *In Old Arizona* (1929) but has been more often seen through the years as the definitive theatrical director who sends Ruby Keeler out to become a star in *42nd Street* (1933). It was the second U.S. film for Ingrid Bergman, who was on the cusp of her sterling international career. The sentiment decried by the *New York Times* may be more palatable today, or maybe it seems an excellent film because it has a story. It's a taste of things to come for Hayward, who in this loanout for Columbia gets third billing, acts tipsy and lets down her hair into what would become a trademark coiffure. Hayward made a friend of director Gregory Ratoff and would later name one of her twins after him.

In 1946 Hayward called the role of Hester her favorite. She said she'd needed a bad girl role:

Hester fascinated me and, as it was my first really dramatic role, also frightened me. However, Gregory's kidding and clowning soon had me relaxed. He was fun, even when he got mad. I liked him so much that even when

***Adam Had Four Sons* (Columbia, 1941), with Warner Baxter.**

he would roar in desperation, "Susan, you are the most steenking actress I've ever seen!" I'd collapse in laughter and not be hurt.[41]

Hayward got on well with Ingrid Bergman and said, "Some actors and actresses are like blank walls, so unresponsive you can't do your best. Ingrid is just the opposite—she worked as hard for my close-ups as her own."[42] Hayward was never so responsive to her own supporting actors.

Promotion

Louella Parsons' junkets were not the only live publicity Hayward received. Paramount sent her and other starlets to exhibitors meetings to promote the studio's product. At a Paramount sales convention Hayward took the bull by the horns and told Paramount's Y. Frank Freeman, "Mr. Freeman, the exhibitors today have been asking me why I haven't made any pictures this year. They want to know and, frankly, I want to know too. You are paying me a very nice salary, and I am doing nothing to earn it. It isn't fair to the stockholders."[43] Actress Patricia Morrison's recollection is similar: "I'm Susan Hayward and if you want me you better tell Paramount to give me good scripts."[44]

Sis Hopkins (Republic, 1941)

The story: Thinking her Uncle Horace Hopkins (Charles Butterworth) is in financial straits, Sis Hopkins (Judy Canova) invites him and his family to live on her farm. But Sis' farm has burned down and Uncle Horace has to take in Sis. Sis' cousin, Carol Hopkins (Hayward), is not pleased to host this hayseed, who is sent to her college and who gets the role in the play Carol was to have had. Carol has more grounds for indignation when her boyfriend Jeff Farnsworth (Bob Crosby) compliments Sis. Carol fools Sis into thinking that a burlesque show is part of a sorority initiation, and when the police raid the club, Sis' dress is rigged to fall off. Sis is expelled. Carol has misgivings and tells her father Horace what she's done. Horace talks to the dean and has Sis reinstated. The show goes on and Sis is a smash.

The *New York Times* called it a "silly farce.... Through it all blows the flavor of ripening corn."[45]

This had been a Broadway play and a Mabel Normand 1919 silent film. Again Hayward is a schemer—at least initially. And once more she's a catalyst with significant screen time, but it's Canova's film. A veteran of vaudeville and Broadway, Canova's film debut had been in 1935's *In Calinte*. She was known for a trademark yodel and playing unsophisticated hillbillies in such films as *Joan of Ozark* (1942), *The WAC from Walla Walla* (1952) and *Carolina Cannonball* (1955).

Among the Living (Paramount, 1941)

The story: Returning to his hometown for his father's funeral, John Raden (Albert Dekker) is astonished when Doc Saunders (Harry Carey) reveals that Paul, John's twin brother thought dead for the past twenty-five years, has been living at Raden House. If "living" is the proper term—when coming to his mother's aid, Paul was thrown across the room by his father and became a "hopeless maniac." As John wrestles with the unexpected news, Paul becomes agitated about the fact that his father has been buried next to his beloved mother. He kills old servant Pompey (Ernest Whitman) and escapes. Making his way to Doc's house, Paul flees when Doc tries to sedate him with a hypodermic injection. Wandering the town, Paul takes a room at a boarding house and becomes friends with the proprietress' fetching daughter Millie (Hayward). Learning that John is at the Raden Hotel,

Sis Hopkins **(Republic, 1941). Hayward is fourth from left.**

Paul goes there and confronts John's wife Elaine (Frances Farmer) before John appears. In a pushing contest, John is knocked out and Paul takes a powder. In a cafe he meets blonde Peggy Nolan (Jean Phillips), whom he later strangles in an alley. Millie shows Paul the new dress purchased with money he'd given her and takes him out to spruce him up. With a $5,000 reward for the capture of Peggy Nolan's murderer as bait, the unemployed mill workers become a mob, searching the town and environs. Even Millie lusts after the reward, responding to Paul's question about fear by saying, "For five thousand bucks I'm not afraid of anything—even death!"

Millie gives Paul her father's old .38 and they go to Raden House, where Millie believes the murderer is hiding. Her old boyfriend Bill (Gordon Jones) and a friend follow them none too soon, because Paul loses control in his mother's old room. Millie is saved when Paul is shot and wounded. Rushing from the room, Paul knocks down his brother John. Mistaken for Paul, John is hauled before a lynch mob. While Elaine and Doc try to quell them, John leaps through a window. Pursued into the cemetery, he trips over the body of his dead brother, thus ending a nightmarish incident in the mill town.

The *New York Times* reviewer could hardly realize that this and the same year's *The Maltese Falcon* were harbingers of what would become film noir,[46] and didn't like it. His criticism is actually approbation when we consider what noir is. He said it "has a good chance of being the dreariest film of the year, [with] somber photography [and] at least one outstandingly bad performance by Albert Dekker ... Susan Hayward, Frances Farmer and Harry Carey all look about equally unhappy in it." [47] Yet a retrospective analysis detects and applauds the noirish elements. "What makes *Among the Living* more than a curio, however, is the near brilliant photography of Theodor Sparkuhl, who worked on a number of classic German films in the 1920s and was [Jean] Renoir's photographer for *La Chienne*. Sparkuhl's work is one indication of the American noir film's debt to German Expressionism and French poetic realism. The jazz sequence in a bar and the shot of Paul killing the B-girl in the alley (an extreme example of depth staging), are particularly important and set a stylistic precedent for expressing confusion and violence."[48]

This is one of those B-films so very much more satisfying than many high-class productions. Like a few other short feature films, e.g., *House of Dracula* (1945), it is amazing how much is packed into it. Hayward makes the most of her role. Billed behind Dekker and ahead of Carey and Farmer, she's saucy and perky and aggressive and lends a hand in the rousing fight scene in the Raden House bedroom. One school of thought has it that *Among the Living* should have made Hayward a star, but (again) that the attractive newcomer posed a menace to other Paramount actresses who wouldn't have her in their films for fear she'd steal the movie.[49] By decade's end, director Heisler would guide Hayward to her first Academy Award nomination in *Smash-Up* (1947).

Albert Dekker had another eye-catching role prior to this: as the bald scientist who created miniature people in one of the very few pre-war American science fiction films, *Dr. Cyclops* (1940). Dekker, whose violent death in 1968 remains an unsolved mystery, became a great character actor over the ensuing decades in such films as *The Killers* (1946), *East of Eden* (1955) and *The Wild Bunch* (1969). Frances Farmer, whose mental problems and or addictions compromised her long-term career, hasn't much to do but is key in a couple scenes. Made today, filmmakers would milk her character for all she's worth by lengthening the time she fails to realize she's in the company of her brother-in-law, not her husband.

1942

Reap the Wild Wind (Paramount, 1942)

The story: Assisted by crusty old Captain Phillip Philpott (Lynne Overman), salvage-schooner operator Loxie Claiborne (Paulette Goddard) sails to a ship wrecked off the Florida Keys and finds its captain, Jack Stuart (John Wayne), incapacitated and the nefarious team of King Cutler (Raymond Massey) and Dan Cutler (Robert Preston) already in the process of salvage. Loxie tends to Stuart, and before long they fall in love. In order to help Stuart take command of the new steamship *Southern Cross*, Loxie goes to Charleston to convince the ship owners that pirates caused Stuart's misfortune. Attending her is her cousin Drusilla Alston (Hayward), clandestine lover of Dan Cutler. Loxie meets the Devereaux Line lawyer, Stephen Tolliver (Ray Milland), who returns with her to Florida to confirm the facts and give Stuart his commission for *Southern Cross*. King Cutler sends his cutthroats to shanghai both Tolliver and Stuart, but the pair fends them off. Mistakenly thinking that Tolliver is trying to steal Loxie away, Stuart makes a deal with Cutler to sink the steamship. When the ship does go down off Key West, it takes Drusilla to the bottom. She'd asked Stuart for passage but he'd refused, and she hid in a large basket until the ship was underway. Tolliver suspects foul play, and Stuart is put on trial. During the proceedings it is learned that Drusilla was hiding on the *Southern Cross*. Donning diving suits, both Stuart and Tolliver descend into the depths to learn if Drusilla was indeed aboard. They find her scarf—and a giant squid, which kills Stuart after he rescues Tolliver from its clutches. Upon surfacing, Tolliver produces the scarf. After accusing his brother of piracy, Dan is shot by King, who is then killed by Tolliver. Loxie comforts the dying Dan Cutler.

The *New York Times* said, "It is the master [DeMille] turned loose, with no holds barred.... Lynne Overman, Susan Hayward and Robert Preston handle lesser roles in true romantic style."[50] *Newsweek* found that it had "all the elements that De Mille exploited so successfully in the past, including robust action, a colorful period, and a sweeping canvas brilliantly filled in with Technicolor.... Susan Hayward, Lynne Overman, and Robert Preston mark time in lesser roles."[51]

Reap the Wild Wind was an epic from the form's master, director Cecil B. DeMille. As one writer said, the craftsmanship involved in making an outdoor adventure on indoor sets can actually be more praiseworthy than filming on location.[52] There were Academy Award nominations for Art and Set Direction and Cinematography, and a win for Special Effects. It was the second of three films featuring Preston and Hayward. (Preston had also been comforted by Goddard in the 1940 DeMille epic *Northwest Mounted Police*.) Although her part was relatively small in proportion to the roles of the others, Hayward's character again is of paramount importance, her presumed drowned body indirectly becoming the reason for Wayne's death—and in a swift flow of events, the demise of the Cutler brothers. After *Reap the Wild Wind*, Hayward changed agents from Ben Medford to the better connected Ned Marin.[53]

Principal cast members of *Reap the Wild Wind* (Paramount, 1942), left to right: Ray Milland, Paulette Goddard, John Wayne, Hayward.

The Forest Rangers (Paramount, 1942)

The story: District forest ranger Don Stuart (Fred MacMurray) searches for an arsonist in the nearby burg of Hallis but finds the ravishing Celia Huston (Paulette Goddard) instead. Before they know what hit them they are married. Nobody at the ranger station thinks Don made a wise decision, especially Tana Mason (Hayward) of the Mason Lumber Company. When Don takes Celia along on a trip to investigate the possible culpability in arson of Twig Dawson (Albert Dekker), Tana rides along to make life difficult for the city-bred Celia. Twig is murdered and a fire is started. Smoke jumpers parachute into the forest to control the blaze, assisted by an observation plane piloted by Frank Hatfield (Regis Toomey). Celia helps the firefighters by driving a truck with food and drink, but she and Tana are cut off by the inferno. Don learns of their predicament via radio, and Frank flies him to the area. On the way, Don learns that Frank is the firebug. Frank clobbers Don and parachutes from the plane, but descends into the heart of the fire. Coming to, Don saves himself via parachute. Locating the women, he is astonished to find Tana cowering in fear while Celia fights the flames with a pump in a stream. Obviously Celia can take a licking and come up kicking.

The *New York Times* said, "A good deal of film goes over the sprockets while Miss Hayward subjects Miss Goddard to the vicissitudes of frontier life—log jumping and sleeping al fresco with one blanket for three.... If this sounds like synthetic nonsense, it is. It is also popular entertainment at par."[54] As for *Time*, "Miss Goddard, a tenderfoot, acts cute and brattish. Jealous, woods-wise Miss Hayward makes life in the tall timber as unpleasant for her as possible."[55]

For all the inherent drama and adventure of smoke-jumping into the wilderness to combat fire, this, *Red Skies of Montana* (1952) and *Always* (1989) seem to be the only major Hollywood films tackling the subject. And typical of "Hollywood," even back in the 1940s, *The Forest Rangers* writers can't resist souping up the action with criminality in the form of an arsonist. So there are three plot threads: fighting fires, fighting a firebug, and fighting females. The filming was not without hazard. Hayward lost her balance spinning a log and skinned her legs. But she was back on the set the next day.[56] As one biographer noted, the ending of the film is nonsense, with Hayward's character—previously totally woods-savvy—so uncharacteristically losing her wits.[57] At least in Goddard and Hayward the film possessed two vivacious, equally attractive actresses. How often has that happened? Maybe Goddard was not a leading lady who felt threatened by Hayward.

Although Hayward wasn't the prime star of these films, some people were taking more notice. *Screen Album* (1942): "With those two major roles behind her she should be all set.... Plenty of brass, straight-from-the-shoulder and down-to-earth honesty have caused Sue to arrive. Red's always got what she set out to get, although she's had to blast her way through a few mountains to do it."[58]

I Married a Witch (United Artists/Masterpiece Productions, 1942)

The story: New England Puritans burn a presumed—and, in fact, actual—witch at the stake. As revealed by Jonathan Wooley (Fredric March), who was obviously enamored of her, witch Jennifer put a curse on his descendants, namely making the males unlucky in love. And so it is—in 1770, 1861, 1904, and now, at mid–20th century. Released from the bonds of the oak tree placed over their graves, Jennifer (Veronica Lake) and her sorcerer father Daniel (Cecil Kellaway) observe Wallace Wooley (March), gubernatorial candidate and fiancé of the harridan-like Estelle Masterson (Hayward). Given human form once more in the Hotel Pilgrim fire, Jennifer is rescued by Wallace. At first pleased to see her fiancé in heroic form, Estelle can't be convinced at the hospital that Wally never laid eyes on the blonde before. Even Dr. Dudley White's (Robert Benchley) conclusion that Jennifer is unbalanced doesn't convince Estelle, and she storms out ahead of Wally. Estelle drives Wally home, where he is amazed to find Jennifer ensconced in his easy chair. He ships her off in a taxi but it's not long before she reappears. Nevertheless, she can't make Wally love her. Daniel appears in the fireplace and they agree that a potion is needed. But when Jennifer is knocked out by a falling picture, Wally gives her the potion he thinks is water. Now *she* loves *him*. Daniel finally makes his presence known in fleshly form on Wally's wedding day. When he learns that Jennifer drank the potion instead of Wally, he and she head for Estelle's. In the presence of Jennifer, Wally and Dr. White, Daniel has himself shot and presumably killed. This is one of the events drawing Wally back and forth between the wedding ceremony and the upstairs room. Resurrecting himself but become tipsy from imbibing while out of his body, Daniel falls from the balcony and is hauled off to jail. Estelle calls off the wedding when she finds Wally kissing Jennifer, who took her own life—sort of. Estelle's father (Robert Warwick) vows to ruin Wally's election chance, but Wally has become convinced of Jennifer's love and doesn't care. They drive out of state and are married by a justice of the peace at a rather magically appearing hostel. Jennifer uses her powers to give Wally the election in a landslide, over two million to zero. Daniel would have liked to have meddled but his imbibing had muddled his brain and impaired his ability to cast spells. When he is released from jail he warns Jennifer that she'll lose her powers should she reveal her real persona to Wally—if he believes her, which he finally does. Daniel really wants Jennifer to come with him back to the peace beneath the tree and masquerades as a cabby to take her and Wally there. But after becoming mist, Jennifer convinces her father to go back and see what's going on at Wally's. He's hovering over the "dead" body of Jennifer. The witch Jennifer resurrects the body, opens the window, and caps the bottle into which Daniel had settled. That bottle is kept under lock and key on the mantle of the happy home of her and Wally. But they might have trouble with one of their children: young Jennifer likes to run around the house on a broom.

Time said, "The comedy is either barn-broad or razor-sharp and the cast who serve this cider-&-absinthe cocktail make it more than easy to take."[59] The *New York Times* called it "quaint and agreeable nonsense."[60]

It's cute and Hayward is suitably bitchy. A major European expatriate director, two-time Best Actor Academy Award winner March, wit Robert Benchley, and a hot property in Veronica Lake equaled a step up for Hayward. It was made for Paramount, which sold it to United Artists.[61] It's not much of an imaginative stretch to say this film inspired the hit 1960s TV series *Bewitched* with Elizabeth Montgomery.

Star Spangled Rhythm (Paramount, 1942)

The story: On-leave sailors follow one of their number, Johnny Webster (Eddie Bracken), to Paramount Studios wherein his father (Victor Moore) is supposedly a top executive. In reality, the one-time "Bronco Billy" western star is a mere gate guard. But with the often unwanted assistance of Johnny's fiancée Polly (Betty Hutton), Johnny passes himself off as Mr. De Soto and gives the gobs a studio tour. They witness the filming of a musical number, wave as Paulette Goddard drives through the gate, meet director Preston Sturges, and are keen on an all-star review to be given (they think) at the naval auditorium. Although the real Mr. De Soto (Walter Abel) tries to figure out what's going on, he's unsuccessful, and the musical comedy review takes place before a packed house.

The *New York Times* said, "That quaint old Paramount custom of producing an annual all-star variety show ... has been hopefully revived with new vigor and a few new faces, too ... it's ups and downs and spread all over the place."[62] Conversely, *The New Republic* found that it "blatantly misuses more talents than any other picture in recent history.... It has some good laughs ... this movie would scare Dracula."[63]

Hayward's only scene is a tableau in which she lounges in a negligee on a fancy bed to welcome sugar daddy Ernest Truex. But in standard Hayward fashion, the welcome is obviously fraught with danger. One does not toy with this lady. The film itself is a World War II propaganda pastiche with one standard, "That Old Black Magic." The puttin'-on-a-play-for-the-boys finale is purest Hollywood, but not as well done as, say, Warner Bros.' *Thank Your Lucky Stars* (1943). Did audiences so suspend disbelief that they bought such a lavish production created in an afternoon with bathtubs onstage, full-blown comedy skits and large-scale musical numbers presented without rehearsal? As the baffled studio exec, probably based (in name, at least) on Paramount production chief Buddy De Sylva, character actor Walter Abel has the most amusing scenes and lines.

1943

Short Subjects

For the war effort, Hayward made two propagandistic short films. *A Letter from Bataan* was a 14-minute Paramount short released in September 1942.[64] *Skirmish on the Home Front* was a 13-minute 1944 Paramount short with Alan Ladd, Betty Hutton, William Bendix and Hayward.[65]

Paramount Pictures publicity photo, 1942.

Radio Gigs

Hayward got lots of vocal experience on radio between 1941 and 1953. Her speech and diction model, Ronald Colman, even appeared on one program with her: "The Petrified Forest" on Lux Radio Theatre in 1945.[66]

Hollywood Canteen

During World War II, Bette Davis was responsible for opening the

Hollywood Canteen, where stars and budding stars hobnobbed with servicemen to build morale. Susan attended and was photographed with sailors in the December 1943 issue of *Movie Life*. She was more approachable than most.

> For Susan, the Canteen was more than an obligation—it was a haven from the phony Hollywood social scene where she knew she would never fit. The servicemen she met were her kind of people, and unlike many of the glacial glamour queens named Dietrich, Crawford, Stanwyck and Fontaine, Hayward had a robust, all-woman approachability that made her a star attraction where stars were in plentiful supply.[67]

Susan met her future husband at the Canteen. Jess Barker was an actor and Canteen emcee.[68] To great response, Hayward would spout her standard question, "Anyone here from Brooklyn?"[69]

Young and Willing (United Artists, 1943)

The story: Secretly married, Tony Dennison (James Brown) and Marge Benson (Barbara Britton) repair to the apartment they share with other prospective actors: Norman Reese (William Holden), George Bodell (Eddie Bracken), Kate Benson (Hayward), and Dottie Coburn (Martha O'Driscoll). Although Norman is angry that he flunked an audition for a juvenile role, he is energized upon learning that landlady Mrs. Garnet (Mabel Paige) is preparing producer Arthur Kenny's (Robert Benchley) apartment for his return. However, Kenny's goal is to remain incognito. "I'd adore spitting on a producer," says Kate, who is sent down to Kenny's apartment. Kenny pretends to be a cook. Kate strikes Kenny for tossing out food. Meanwhile, the imminent arrival of Dottie's dad makes Norman and George pack up and hide. Mr. Coburn arrives with Muriel (Florence MacMichael), who'd informed him that men were living in the apartment. Unaware of what's going on, Tony appears in his skivvies. Norman and George enter and pretend that "Stanislavsky" (Tony) is insane and they're there to take him away. Arriving in chef attire, Kenny seems to Mr. Coburn to be yet another lunatic. Mr. Coburn tells Dottie he'll be back Monday. Marge confesses to Tony she's with child. George inadvertently reveals that Tony's joined the Army. Dottie and Kate visit Kenny and ask him to read their play. He gets the idea that they are acting out *his* play, *Mostly Murder*. Kenny goes to the girls' apartment with a dictaphone, and Norman and company begin the play, which begins as Kate voices the somber tones of a medium and Muriel plays a corpse. Mrs. Garnet barges in and Kenny accuses her of giving the kids his play. The actors start again but the police show up, convinced foul play has taken place. Eventually they discover that Muriel is not a casualty. The next day the girls pack while the guys wonder what Kenny thought of their performances. Dottie's father arrives and drags Dottie away. She professes her love for Norman as she leaves. Having requested the presence of the acting troop, Kenny approves of the way—as he sees it—they made his play a burlesque, and he's starting rehearsals. Mrs. Garnet informs Norman a young lady downstairs requests his presence. It's Dottie, who flings herself on Norman.

Unheeded at the time, *Young and Willing* found a later reviewer (Leonard Maltin) who decided that the "Perennial summer-stock comedy *Out of the Frying Pan* becomes naive but zany comedy of show biz hopefuls trying to make good."[70]

With a spare set and only mildly amusing screenplay, this is of historic interest only. We get to see the apprenticeships of major stars Hayward and Holden, and the versatility of long-lived Bracken, who would shortly star in Preston Sturges' comic classics *The Miracle of Morgan's Creek* (1943) and *Hail the Conquering Hero* (1944). This was Hayward's second film with Bracken. Robert Benchley (d. 1945), grandfather of novelist Peter, was a well-regarded humorist, writer and actor whose acting credits included *China Seas* (1935), *Foreign Correspondent* (1940), *The Major and the Minor* (1942) and that other 1942 Hayward film, *I Married a Witch*. James Brown achieved more visibility in the 1950s TV series *Rin Tin Tin*. Barbara Britton was Joel McCrea's leading lady in the remake of *The Virginian* (1946) and the first commercial 3-D feature, *Bwana Devil* (1953). This was to be future superstar Holden's last film before entering the Army Air Force, and his next film wouldn't be until 1947's *Blaze of Noon*. His official debut had been in 1939's *Golden Boy*, and in 1940 he'd starred in *Our Town*. Hayward's last theatrical film, *The Revengers* (1972), would find her his co-star once more. In *Young and Willing* one watches Hayward wondering what she's thinking as she sits there in her gypsy outfit. She seems as amused as the theater audience—moderately.

Hit Parade of 1943 (Republic, 1943)

The story: Songwriter Rick Farrell (John Carroll) "borrows" lyrics from other lyricists, including newcomer Jill Wright (Hayward). Upon hearing her song in a new guise at Club Rio, Jill confronts Rick and slaps him hard. Nevertheless, Rick convinces her to become his collaborator, or "accomplice," as she puts it. Despite her cousin's (Eve Arden) warning that Rick can smell a double cross, Jill plans to feed Rick some of her copyrighted songs so someday she can expose him. He shows her his lyric master—a wall-sized contraption he uses to write and title songs. Needing a tune for Bradley Cole's nightclub, Jill and Rick find inspiration in the melodies of the night cleaning man and produce "The Harlem Sandman." Jill becomes smitten with Rick. Coming up with another winning tune, Rick knows that if he can get on the radio hit parade, he's really made it. Rick's sometimes girlfriend, singer Toni Jarrett (Gail Patrick), throws a monkey wrench into the proceedings by leading Jill to believe "A Change of Heart" was written for her. Seeing Toni with Rick, Jill is once more determined to ruin his career. In order to make sure his song gets on the hit parade, Rick makes a $10,000 pledge to the "Bonds for Victory" campaign. He plans to sing the song and then explain how he'd taken credit for others' work. Meanwhile, his partner Mac (Walter Catlett) reveals to Jill and Belinda that Toni was trying to break up Jill's relationship with Rick, and that Rick is going to confess his shortcomings over the radio. Jill takes a taxi to the station in time to accompany Rick on the piano and rip up his confession.

The *New York Times* called it "a pleasant and unpretentious entertainment.... [It's] a bit surprising to learn that Susan Hayward and Gail Patrick can include singing among their accomplishments."[71]

Hit Parade of 1943 (aka *Change of Heart*) was released in March 1943. This time Hayward had been loaned to Republic. Except for addicts of big bands, a typically gutsy Hayward or the inimitable Eve Arden, the film is something of a trial to sit through. When singing, Carroll's voice is very obviously not his own.

1944

Jack London (United Artists, 1944)

The story: Observing a female jute mill co-worker being taken to a hospital after her hand was smashed, Jack London (Michael O'Shea) quits and tells Mammy Jenny (Louise Beavers) he can no longer stand the noise, the pay and the hours. He must have time, time to think and to learn. She loans him money to buy a boat which he and Mamie (Virginia Mayo) use to become "oyster pirates." During a shootout that leaves his friend Nelson (Regis Toomey) dead, Jack quits both the boat and Mamie. He signs on with seal-hunters heading for the Bering Sea, a copy of Darwin's *Origin of Species* in his luggage. On board, Jack gets background for his future novel *The Sea Wolf*. Using his wages to enroll at the University of California, Jack finds that Professor Hilliard (Harry Davenport) has concerns

CHANGE OF HEART—1

Hit Parade of 1943 (Republic, 1943) publicity photo, with John Carroll.

over his brutal writing. Jack explains that he's seen such things. In the Yukon goldfields he becomes friends with dancehall singer Freda (Osa Massen) but moves on into the back country. Snowed in with a dog in an isolated cabin, Jack begins *Call of the Wild*. Back in the lower 48, Jack meets with Mr. Brett (Ralph Morgan), a publisher who will do *Call of the Wild*. When he is introduced to Charmian Kittredge (Hayward) on the street, Jack is shocked when Mr. Brett's reader flees back to the office. He follows and learns that she'd asked Mr. Brett to never introduce her to Mr. London, else she'd be lost as Brett's favorite reader. A romance develops, though Jack tells Charmian about "traps" such as poverty, money and even words. She assures him she won't be a snare. At a New Year's Eve party Jack tells guests that despite technology, greed and selfishness rule. *The Globe* assigns Jack to cover the Boer War. Charmian tells him to go, but he only gets as far as Plymouth, England, before the war is over. But before long a new war breaks out in the Far East between Russia and Japan. Jack finds himself among experienced correspondents, but he alone manages to leave Japan in disguise and find his way to the Korean front. There he meets Captain Tanaka (Leonard Strong), who reveals Japan's plans for an inexorable march toward world conquest. Jailed as a Russian spy, Jack is released when President Theodore Roosevelt tells the Japanese Ambassador in Washington to have London returned. Back in the U.S., Jack and Charmian approach Mr. Maxwell with his warning, but the *Globe* publisher won't publish Jack's account, telling Jack that the Japanese are America's friends.

The *New York Times* found it "an uneven narrative, filled with colorful incident but lacking in dramatic point," but noted that, "Susan Hayward plays his sweetheart with charm and vivacity."[72]

Made in November 1943 and released in 1944, *Jack London* was another loan-out, this time for United Artists. For a rather low-budgeted film with a short running time, there's plenty of London's life packed into it. How much is true is debatable. The later reels are propaganda filled. It is implied that London was aware decades in advance that the Japanese would attack the United States via a "sneak punch." The destruction of the Russian Fleet is presented as one of these dastardly attacks. London's discovery that cannon used by the Japanese are made by Germany's Krupp is specious. And the scene where grinning, howling Japanese soldiers machine-gun Russian POWs rushing for water is absurdly propagandistic. These sections probably were designed to make our World War II Soviet allies look good and make them appreciate the gesture. The film opens with the launch of a World War II Liberty Ship, *Jack London*. London is described as "a real American." "He lived and wrote that others might be free—free to read the truth, free to right a wrong, free to raise their voices on behalf of the welfare of their fellow man."

Hayward doesn't appear until the film is virtually half over, but she makes her time count. She's as captivating as ever one of her characters was. There's a charming scene when Jack pursues Charmian to her office, introduces himself and attempts to discover why she fled after meeting him outside.

> CHARMIAN: I'm afraid I was a little abrupt on the street just now.
> JACK: Abrupt?
> CHARMIAN: I'm glad you didn't notice it. [*turns toward desk*] Why, I have to get back to work, but I'm happy you gave me the chance to explain that I didn't snub you purposely.
> JACK: Of course you didn't. [*shakes hands, then draws Charmian in before she can put her desk between them*] Why did you snub me? Purposely.
> CHARMIAN: But I assure you, I didn't.
> JACK: You snubbed me. Purposely.
> CHARMIAN: Believe me, Mr. London, I didn't.
> JACK: Purposely.

Jack London (United Artists, 1944) wih Ralph Morgan (left) and Michael O'Shea.

> CHARMIAN: But everyone says you're going to be a gold mine for this firm. I wouldn't dare snub you. Why, what would Mr. Brett say?
>
> JACK: Purposely.
>
> CHARMIAN: Mr. London, if you're not going to believe me.... [*interrupted by secretary*]

The Fighting Seabees (Republic, 1944)

The story: After some of his unarmed civilian construction crew are killed by Japanese on a South Pacific island, Wedge Donovan (John Wayne) confronts Lt. Commander Bob Yarrow (Dennis O'Keefe) and learns that Yarrow too would like to fix the situation. But red tape deters Wedge and he takes his untrained civilian crew back to the Pacific to build an airfield. Accompanying the men are war correspondents, including Constance Chesley (Hayward). A romantic triangle develops between Wedge, Connie and her presumed flame, Bob. During a battle with the Japanese,

Connie is wounded. Before falling unconscious, she indicates to Wedge that she loves him. Wedge later tells Bob he only told Connie he loved her to comfort her. Despite that, and the fact that Wedge and his men have breached orders and gotten themselves shot up, Bob still believes that he can work with them. Wedge and his men join the Navy and undergo training. A recovered Connie must choose between Wedge and Bob, and though she intimates that she loves both men, she chooses the former. Only he doesn't know it. After returning to the Pacific, the "Seabees" are faced with a Japanese landing force. Bob is wounded. Wedge uses a bulldozer and explosives to thwart the enemy but is shot and dies in the explosion. His action turns back the Japanese, who are virtually annihilated by the other Americans. Back in the States, Bob learns that Connie really loves him.

Newsweek termed it a "tough, exciting, and reasonably factual story … and if the girl journalist has a way of popping up unexpectedly on an atoll and jaywalking in a cross fire of shot and shell, at least Miss Hayward always manages to look attractive in the shade of the shell-shocked palms."[73] The *New York Times* found it a "pretty lively melodrama, of the familiar bravura type, once it gets going…. The Messrs. Wayne and O'Keefe and Miss Hayward fit their respective roles snugly…."[74]

This time the loan-out was Republic. It was the second Hayward film in a row to grind an axe against the Japanese. *The Fighting Seabees* is a patriotic, flag-waving action movie. At one point Wayne spouts, "I have a contract here for an airfield on Island X214. I'm goin' there personally and take my best crew, and if Tojo and his bug-eyed monkeys get in our way, you and the Navy may find out you have a construction unit *and* a combat unit rolled into one!" Hayward gets a fair amount of screen time. During filming, Hayward autographed items for real Seabees at Camp Rousseau, Port Hueneme, California. Hayward, Wayne and O'Keefe were pictured on the cover of the sheet music for "The Song of the Seabees."

Note: If one were to shut one's eyes, the gunshot sounds would convince one this was a Paramount western. (Each major studio had its own distinctive sound effects for guns).

Wake Up Call

In the January 30, 1944, issue of the *Los Angeles Times*, Philip K. Scheuer bemoaned Susan's status, claiming that "One of these days some producer will really wake up to the possibilities of this vixen with velvet claws, and then movie history will be made." Paramount was said to be paying her $1,000 or less a week in the sixth year of her contract. "One more year—providing they take up my last option—and I'll be free!" "Known (in polite terminology) to be 'temperamental,' Miss Hayward is simply a smart young woman who places her career above everything else." Susan told Scheuer, "If I play a meanie once, I want to be likable the next time." "Looking at her in the tight black evening gown, shoulder-less and sleeveless, that must have been held up only by capillary attraction or some other phenomenon of a bountiful nature, I could only shake my head. Either she was dissembling, or she doesn't know her own strength—which I certainly doubt." Scheuer told her she should have gotten a role in *The Guest in the House*. She replied that Hunt Stromberg told her she was too sexy.[75]

The Hairy Ape (United Artists, 1944)

The story: In Lisbon, ship stoker gang leader Hank Smith (William Bendix) tells Paddy (Roman Bohnen), Long (Tom Fadden), and anyone else who will listen that he and the stokers make the ship go, not the engineers or officers. During the course of an evening at the local nightspot, Hank opines that dames don't amount to nothin' and flips a coin into the cleavage of the waitress. A brawl ensues with another stoker gang leader when he christens Hank's ship a mere "tub." The police stop the melee, and Second Engineer Tony Lazar (John Loder) ushers his men back to the ship. Hank discovers that passengers will be aboard on this passage to New York. They include Tony's old friend Helen Parker (Dorothy Comingore) and refugees she's helping leave war-torn Europe. At a swank ball where Helen's old schoolmate Mildred Douglas (Hayward) dances and flirts with Baron Aldo (Raphael Storm), Helen informs her they're leaving that night. The baron is perturbed and asks, "You always tease the animals but never feed them?" Mildred promptly tosses a drink in his face. On the ship Tony meets with Chief Engineer MacDougald (Alan Napier) to discuss keeping up with the convoy. Down in the boiler room, Hank urges on his stokers with "Feed 'em!" On deck, refugees thank Helen for helping them journey to America. Mildred, who's managed to exchange her "primitive" accommodations for Tony's cabin, receives a tour. In the boiler room she is mesmerized, as is Hank by this vision. But Mildred retreats after shouting, "Get away from me. Don't touch me, you ape. You hairy ape!" Later Hank proclaims, "No white-faced dame can call me an ape!" He attempts to see Mildred but Tony pushes him back down the ladder and tells his team to take him below. Hank is not his old self in the stoker room but musters enough to start a fight with the rival team leader.

In spite of losing speed and thus the convoy, the ship reaches New

York safely. In her stylish apartment, Mildred pays off her housekeeper, who complains of shabby treatment. Helen arrives and says she's returning to Lisbon. Mildred bathes while Helen tells her she's finally realized what a nasty person she is. Mildred doesn't care. Hank arrives but Mildred tells the doorman not to send him up. Hank makes a ruckus and is jailed. Paddy and Long vouch for him and get him out. Hanks observes an ad for the gorilla Goliath and wonders how he's going to get out of *his* cage. He'll smash that woman so she can't smash him.

Tony visits Mildred, who says he's never been important to her. After Tony leaves, Hank barges in. Mildred swoons as Hank approaches. He carries her to the sofa. She wakes up and he strokes her head. She smiles, sits up and attempts to run for it. Hanks catches and shakes her, and thrusts her to the sofa. About to leave, he turns back and flips a coin into Mildred's décolletage. In a bar Hank says he's seen how the other half lives and it ain't no different. Hank hoists up a drunken Tony and takes him back to the ship.

Time called it a "rudderless melodrama…. William Bendix is a likable and sincere actor, but his natural good temper shines fatally through his industrious soot-and-greasepaint toughness. Susan Hayward, as the girl who drives him crazy, is much tougher—too coarsely so for the size of the girl's penthouse or the height of her social standing—but she is more convincing."[76] The *New York Times* said it "rises to some pretty impressive heights but in the main it runs along the level of a fair-to-good production.William Bendix, the ubiquitous character actor, also had some starring roles, notably this and as the title character in *The Babe Ruth Story* (1948). Dorothy Comingore was the second Mrs. Kane in *Citizen Kane* (1941); like her character here, she had contact with Hayward before, in *Campus Cinderella* and *Comet Over Broadway.* Her character is very likable, noble, and attractive. Hayward's role in this United Artists loan-out is, by contrast, a rich snob who uses people. Even in dimly-lit, fog-enshrouded confines of the ship, Hayward is radiant. One might object that Comingore took too long to see through her or that Loder's Tony had been too long out of Comingore's life to make a difference when he reappears.

Goliath, the "gorilla," is a man in an ape suit, apparently the same kind of hideously ugly simian suit everybody wore at that time.

And Now Tomorrow (Paramount, 1944)

The story: An attack of meningitis has left Emily Blair (Loretta Young) deaf. In this condition she does not want to marry fiancé Jeff (Barry Sullivan) and travels from one specialist to another. After fruitless months, she returns to Blairstown. During her absence her sister Janice (Hayward) and Jeff fall in love. Janice is all for telling Emily, but Jeff feels an obligation. Emily follows general practitioner Dr. Weeks' (Cecil Kellaway) suggestion to allow young Dr. Mark Vance (Alan Ladd) to work on her. Back in Pittsburgh, Dr. Vance had cured some people—mostly the poor—of deafness. He's not thrilled with Emily, whom he views as a stuck-up rich girl. He begins to change his mind when she helps him operate on a young boy from the opposite side of the tracks. Vance's traditional treatments on Emily have no effect, but one day he reluctantly agrees to give her his experimental serum. She collapses and is briefly comatose. Vance leaves town. When Emily awakes, she can hear. Knowing this, Janice tricks Jeff into admitting he wouldn't marry Emily if she weren't deaf—as Emily now hears. Emily demonstrates to Jeff that she heard and wishes him and Janice well. She goes to Pittsburgh to show Vance that his cure worked.

The *New York Times* said that "Susan Hayward and Barry Sullivan are a couple who mix up the plot in a thoroughly conventional fashion. As you may guess, this is a very stupid film."[78]

The real stars were Loretta Young and a new discovery back from a brief military tour. Alan Ladd had made such an impression as the killer Raven in *This Gun for Hire* that he'd rocketed to the top.

To promote the film, Susan modeled Deltah Pearls in magazine ads.

Marriage

Louella Parsons reported on July 19, 1944, that Susan Hayward would marry actor Jess Barker. "This news was whispered to me yesterday and Susan, who is one of the girls who went on a personal appearance tour with me several years ago, confirmed the story." Susan had met Jess while both worked at the Hollywood Canteen entertaining World War II servicemen.[79]

The wedding took place at 4:30 p.m. on July 23, 1944, at St. Thomas [Episcopal] Church in Hollywood.[80] It was a double-ring ceremony, with the Reverend Walter M. Howard officiating.[81] Susan and Jess had signed a precedent-setting pre-nuptial agreement.[82] The 10-year marriage that ensued would be rocky, but its stumbling blocks were generally hidden from the public.[83]

Rebel on Horseback

That September Susan was profiled in *Motion Picture Magazine*, accompanied by a photo of her in a rather belligerent pose. In the article Hay-

With first husband Jess Barker at New York's Stork Club, ca. 1945.

ward was painted as a rebel whose obvious talent, looks and no-nonsense work ethic had kept her in the business despite the pugnaciousness witnessed by Paramount three years before when she complained that she hadn't done any work in eighteen months. She was termed unorthodox and said to possess "a cloud of dark-red hair, a pair of enormous topaz eyes flecked with yellow, camelia-like skin and a five-foot-three figure." Her horseback riding is discussed. She rode out of a San Fernando Valley stable. (This reveals why she looked secure while mounted on horseback in such future films as *Canyon Passage, Untamed* and *Garden of Evil*.) The article must have been written well in advance of her marriage because Jess Barker is merely noted as an escort, much like actor John Carroll. Hayward's evening habits were said to be donning her four-year-old pink pajamas and reading best sellers, sketching or painting, playing the organ or eating.[84]

Although she'd kept working, Hayward's reputation apparently did prevent her from getting the lead in a major 1944 movie: *Dark Waters*. Established star Merle Oberon (*Wuthering Heights*) got the part in a movie now largely forgotten. Hayward complained to Paramount production chief Buddy De Sylva, who told her she was being taught a lesson for her lack of cooperation on previous sets.[85]

Chapter 3

Star Billing and Recognition

"Miss Susan Hayward never talked to her co-workers when waiting for a take. She took no interest in the rest of us. It was extremely strange, as if we did not exist."

—Marsha Hunt[1]

On February 19, 1945, Susan gave birth to twin sons Timothy and Gregory in Santa Monica's St. John's Hospital. Gregory was named after Gregory Ratoff, Susan's director on *Adam Had Four Sons*.[2] Child-rearing would engage enough of Hayward's time to keep her absent from the screen until 1946.

1946

Deadline at Dawn (RKO, 1946)

The story: Hoping to recover $1,400 from his ex-wife Edna Bartelli (Lola Lane), blind piano player Sleepy Carson (Marvin Miller) merely elicits the reaction, "Aren't you dead yet?" The following day sailor Alex (Bill Williams) ponders the $1,400 in his possession. With seven hours until his bus leaves for Norfolk, he visits a dancehall and ingratiates himself with foot-weary hostess June (Hayward). Despite reservations, June takes him to her apartment for sandwiches. Alex tells her he lacks confidence and that people tell him he's too slow. When June learns he's headed for her hometown she asks him to look up her mom and tell her she's a successful singer and dancer. Alex tries to give her his wad of money, but she tells him to give it back to the woman whose radio he'd fixed. Together they take a taxi to the woman's apartment. The woman is Edna Bartelli and she's been strangled. Scanning the room, June finds lipstick she says fits a blonde. Edna was a brunette. Alex theorizes that only a man would strangle a woman. It's definitely not a robbery: Edna still has her jewelry. Outside in the shadows a man observes Alex and June. June goes downtown to check out a lead from the refreshment stand operator. Alex's mission is to find a "nervous man." A building superintendent directs June to the apartment of a Mrs. Robinson (Osa Massen). Listening at the partially open door, June overhears a husband-and-wife spat. When Mrs. Robinson comes out, June tells her she left her lipstick in a murdered woman's apartment. Mrs. Robinson says she was at a party and she doesn't wear lipstick. She returns to her husband and asks him his whereabouts when Edna was killed. When Alex and June rendezvous at Edna's apartment, they are joined by Alex's taxi driver, Gus (Paul Lukas). After hearing their story, Gus responds, "The Divine Being made many loathsome creatures, but none so low as a woman with a cold heart." New suspects include Lester Brady (Jerome Cowan), who had left a check for Edna, and Mrs. Raymond (Constance Worth), who enters Edna's apartment looking for personal letters. She pulls a gun and escapes. A new plan is hatched. Alex calls Brady and is told to bring the check. Brady phones Edna's brother Val. Taxi follows taxi, but the man in the shadows (Steven Geray) turns out to be a desperate but harmless dance partner of June's. Meanwhile, Val (Joseph Calleia), Brady and Mrs. Raymond parley about the need to retrieve the letters. Suspecting Alex of killing his sister, Val knocks Alex out and pummels him a few more times after dragging him to Edna's. Arriving with June, Gus gets the drop on Val and Brady, and proposes a deal to clear Alex. They leave for the club where Sleepy plays piano. After they go, a drunken suitor of Edna's (Joseph Sawyer) finds her body and calls the police. Ironically, the police chief is being toasted at Sleepy's club. June puts on Edna's perfume and stands beside him. He seems to recognize the scent but remains mum. "Edna's dead and you killed her," says June. Followed by Val and Gus, Sleepy retires to the lounge and collapses of heart failure. A policeman arrives and asks, "Which one of you spoiled the captain's party?" At the police station Alex is grilled until a phone rings and everyone learns that someone else has confessed. Going to another precinct, they find that Mrs. Robinson's husband has owned up to the deed. But it's not over. Gus reveals that Mrs. Robinson is his daughter and that *he* killed Edna because she refused to break off her affair with his daughter's husband. Before being booked, Gus urges June to move back to Norfolk to be closer to Alex. Outside, Alex knocks Val silly before a police car takes him and June to the bus station.

The New York Times said, "Clifford Odets has assembled a great deal of vivid incident from a novel by William Irish and has blessed it with some bristling dialogue ... the performances are thoroughly engaging. Bill Williams is winning as the gob, Susan Hayward is spirited as a night-moth who assists him, and Paul Lukas plays a taxi driver well." Later evaluation continued the praise, though broaching some concern for the language: "By virtue of *mise-en-scène*, *Deadline at Dawn* captures a major ingredient of [novelist] Woolrich's ethos: the quiet despair of the nighttime people of New York City.... Ironically, the dialogue of Clifford Odets, a writer of much greater reputation than Woolrich, is the one incongruous element in the film. Odets' patronizing concern for the common people and, even worse, his pseudopoetic, elliptical dialogue are out of place in the lower-class locales of the film."[4]

Although the story pivots around the Williams character, this RKO loan-out gave star billing to Hayward. Williams was a newcomer. But Hayward also outranked veteran Paul Lukas, the Hungarian-born actor who had won the Best Actor Academy Award in the Academy Award–winning Best Picture *Watch on the Rhine* (1943). Producers probably viewed Lukas strictly as a character actor by this time.

Maybe Lukas' character *is* a mite too literate, but it's a minor point in a very engaging movie. The shadows, the urban milieu, the subject matter, the characters who seem to have no prospects (Hayward's character has just about been beaten into the city's cold pavement) evince the hallmarks of film noir. But this time the protagonists find redemption without death.

Walter Wanger

Good fortune came Susan's way when producer Walter Wanger spotted her potential. Wanger (born Walter Feuchtwanger, July 11, 1894) had been a producer for various studios and had overseen such classics as the Marx Bros.' first film *The Cocoanuts* (1929), *Stagecoach* (1939), *Foreign Correspondent* (1940), and *Scarlet Street* (1945). In his future would be B-movie classics *Riot in Cell Block 11* (1954) and *Invasion of the Body Snatchers* (1956), along with several for Susan, including *I Want to Live!* (1958). Susan signed a seven-year deal with Wanger at $100,000 per year.[5]

Deadline at Dawn (RKO, 1946), with Paul Lukas and Bill Williams.

Canyon Passage (Universal, 1946)

The story: In pre–Civil War Oregon, Logan Stewart (Dana Andrews) aims to expand his mule transport service. He leaves Portland with cash and Lucy Overmire (Hayward), bound for the wilderness community of Jacksonville. His departure is briefly delayed when a large man enters his hotel room and attempts to steal his money—or kill him. Logan beats the man off. He knows it's Honey Bragg (Ward Bond) and explains to Lucy that he'd seen Bragg leaving the scene of a lynching but can't prove his culpability. On the way to Jacksonville the duo stop at the Dance cabin, where Caroline (Patricia Roc), who'd come from Britain, seems to have eyes for Logan. In Jacksonville, Lucy reunites with her fiancé, banker George Camrose (Brian Donlevy). Honey Bragg confronts Logan at his hardware store but backs off. Camrose, meanwhile, though he warmly welcomes Lucy, seems more attracted to saloon owner Lestrade's (Onslow Stevens) wife, Marta (Rose Hobart). Nor does Lucy know that gambling is Camrose's bane, or that he uses miners' gold to bankroll him in games he invariably loses. Logan finally realizes the town wants him to fight Bragg. Logan wins. Camrose kills MacIvar (Wallace Scott), the miner about to discover his gold dust had been used for Camrose's gambling. Asking Lucy to marry him soon, Camrose spurs her to accompany Logan to San Francisco for a dress. On the way Lucy and Logan kiss. They never make it to Frisco. Bragg ambushes them and kills their horses. Returning on foot to Jacksonville, Logan finds Camrose on trial for murder and helps him escape. True to his nature, Bragg had gotten himself into more trouble: killing an Indian woman after stumbling on several bathing. The tribe goes on the warpath. Bragg is turned back by Logan and the townsfolk, and killed. While they are out rescuing Caroline, the townsfolk leave Jacksonville defenseless and it's burned to the grown. Logan is broke. Johnny tells Logan one of his men found and killed Camrose. It's time to start over. Logan, Lucy and Hy Linnet (Hoagy Carmichael) head for San Francisco. Logan will rustle up some credit.

Despite it being directed by Jacques Tourneur,[6] contemporary reaction to *Canyon Passage* was standard for westerns. *Time* said, "Feeling harried? Overworked? Jittery about the Bomb or the price of butter? Try *Canyon Passage* for quick temporary relief. Unlike bridge, alcohol, the ponies and other popular forms of escape, this brilliantly engineered movie is non-habit-forming and has no nagging after-effects ... better-than-average dialogue and competent players (Dana Andrews, Susan Hayward, Brian Donlevy, Britain's Patricia Roc) ... slick, colorful, romantic movie."[7] The *New York Times* said, "Almost every type of familiar character one might expect to encounter in a sagebrush melodrama is on hand ... and there is Susan Hayward and Patricia Roc to remind the boys—and the audiences, too—that love is a wonderful thing.... Good acting by all concerned, a smooth-flowing script and generally well-paced direction are definite assets. Still there is not quite as much drive to the story as one could wish."[8]

Reappraisal stressed the atypical nature of *Canyon Passage*: "A richly assorted cast of characters inhabits a complicated and romantically realistic plot.... The ensemble turns in an exquisite gathering of performances.... The only flaw, and it is a slight one, is the casting of Susan Hayward; she is far too strong a personality to be altogether believable as the vacillating heroine torn between Andrews and Donlevy."[9] In truth, the story moves so fast between a plethora of characters and situations that there's little time for the viewer to even think that Hayward's character is vacillating. Others found Hayward refreshing:

> It is fascinating to see Susan in this film today because she is so natural and unstudied in it and shows none of the mannerisms that were soon to become her trademark. Her walk is not peculiar, she doesn't use her hands much and her voice is normal: she is like a hundred other actresses, as Jacques Tourneur directed her. We have in *Canyon Passage* a rare and unforgettable

view of the young Susan Hayward without those oddities of personality which would eventually elevate her to great celebrity. Underneath Hollywood's most remarkable façade, she was spirited and competent.[10]

The house-raising scene in *Canyon Passage* is in some degree a forerunner of the front-yard stump-clearing episode in 1953's *Shane*. There's an uncompromising look at the terror of a lone farmhouse. Once again, and contrary to perceived wisdom about how Hollywood treated Native Americans, they are presented as victims. Ben Dance (Andy Devine) states that it's the Indians' land, they've got reasons for anger. The reason is a brutish white man, Honey Bragg. There are complicated relationships: Logan and Caroline, Logan and Lucy, Lucy and Camrose, Camrose and Marta. Unless it is as John Wayne's nemesis in *Tall in the Saddle*, the always busy and usually likable Ward Bond has the most despicable part of his career as Bragg. By contrast, that other screen villain, Brian Donlevy (Sergeant Markov of *Beau Geste*), is hardly a rat. In fact, the viewer empathizes with his dilemma without excusing his actions.

Canyon Passage was Hayward's first pairing with 20th Century–Fox star Dana Andrews. In a few years she'd become very familiar with this studio. She and Andrews would make another memorable duo in *My Foolish Heart*.[11]

As part of the promotion for *Canyon Passage*, Hayward plugged Royal Crown Cola in magazine ads.

Postwar Housing Problems

In 1946 Hayward and her husband had housing problems exacerbated by postwar needs of returning servicemen and women. Facing eviction, they moved from 1712 Chevy Chase Drive in Beverly Hills into the Miramar Hotel in Santa Monica. They complained that any house they'd looked at came with a phony deal to buy the furniture at outrageous prices.[12] "We'd rather live on a studio lot than be a party to such jet black dealings."[13] Another house they looked at had a "no-children" restriction. "I could have cried," said Susan.[14]

1947

Smash-Up: The Story of a Woman (Universal-International, 1947)

The story: At White Memorial Hospital a heavily-bandaged woman gasps, "I need a drink" and flashes back to the Elbow Room nightclub.

Angelica Evans (Hayward) takes a snort before going on stage to sing "I Miss That Feeling." Under the tutelage of agent Mike Dawson (Charles D. Brown), Angelica headlines such larger venues as Chez Giono and Club Biarritz. She gladly gives it all up, however, to become Mrs. Ken Conway, wife of a small-time singer-songwriter (Lee Bowman). After Ken takes a radio job as the singing cowboy, he and Steve (Eddie Albert) write "Life Can Be Beautiful," and Ken sings his new song over the radio as Angie is in the hospital having a daughter. The song is such a smash that Ken and Steve get a 6 p.m. slot. Rising rapidly in popularity, Ken is told by radio manager Fred Elliott (Carleton Young) that he must be constantly available for promotion and exploitation. Ken and Angie move back into town from their wonderful country house. Ratings skyrocket for Ken's new show, "An American Sings." In order to handle the parties and fame accruing to her husband, Angie hits the bottle hard. She has nightmares. Ken has little time to be alone with her or their child. Compounding Angie's fears is Ken's indispensable secretary, Martha (Marsha Hunt). With nothing to do but worry, Angie continues to imbibe. Dr. Lorenz (Carl Esmond) tries to make Ken realize that Angie's enforced idleness is causing her alcoholism. He argues that she must give up alcohol entirely and tells Angie only she can help herself. Steve convinces Ken to let Angie plan and host a party. But Angie lets visions of Martha and Ken distress her. Loaded again, Angie pursues Martha into the ladies room and says, "Oh, I'd love to see you all mussed up. I can't think of anything that would give me a bigger kick." She attacks Martha. After the party, Angie asks for help, but Ken says there's a limit to everything. They argue and the next morning Angie wakes up alone. Staring into the mirror, she berates her weak, pitiful self. Meanwhile, Steve reminds Ken that Dr. Lorenz was right: Angie has a disease. Ken replies that he's told his lawyer Angie can have everything except the baby. Steve helps Angie find a new apartment. Angie uses Mike to audition for a dinner theater, where she'll be Angelica Evans, not Mrs. Ken Conway. Meanwhile, Martha admits that she does love Ken but understands her role as a good Joe. Instead of going to her singing engagement, Angie visits some bars. At the Raven Club a singer presents "Life Can Be Beautiful." A new father (Robert Shayne) tells Angie not to let anybody take her baby away. Angie winds up drunk on a stoop and awakes in an unfamiliar apartment, with a strange man in the next room. The man's wife appears and says her husband took pity on Angie. Angie finds Angel at the zoo and takes her to their country house. Leaving a lit cigarette in Angel's room, Angie sits on the couch downstairs and recalls both good and bad times. Roused from her stupor by Angel's screams, Angie rescues her from a raging inferno. Flash forward to the present and the hospital where the bandaged Angie screams for her baby. Dr. Lorenz talks to Ken about how he's excluded Angie from his life, and later tells Ken and Angie that Angie's scars will disappear. Angie tells Ken she had to hit rock bottom before she could be cured. Now they'll have a wonderful life.

Theatre Arts thought it had "excellent intentions, nice beginnings and clarity of purpose even after the accomplishment has ceased to equal the aim.... That it has not achieved total success is due to the fact that the excellent young player, Susan Hayward, has not been sufficiently tutored in the progressive stages of drunkenness. Each successive event is merely a repetition of an advance along the inevitable path."[15] The *New York Times* compared it unfavorably with 1945's *The Lost Weekend*, complaining that "the current booze drama ... is soggy and full of (figurative) corn.... Susan Hayward performs the boozy heroine with a solemn fastidiousness which turns most of her scenes of drunken fumbling and heebie-jeebies into off-key burlesque. And it is notable that her appearance is never unflatteringly disarrayed."[16] One biographer makes a good case for Susan's character as needful and shy, despite her showbiz job.[17]

Director Stuart Heisler found that Hayward had to work herself up for particular scenes, and created hand and head movements to signal when she was ready. "What an ordeal that picture was.... I was a rag every night."[18]

Smash-Up received two Academy Award nominations: Hayward for Best Actress and Dorothy Parker and Cavett for Original Story. Loretta Young won for *The Farmer's Daughter*. Dorothy McGuire (*Gentleman's Agreement*), Joan Crawford (*Possessed*), and Rosalind Russell (*Mourning Becomes Electra*) were the other nominees. *Smash-Up*'s song "Life Can Be Beautiful" wasn't nominated, though it really sticks in the mind. "Zip-a-Dee-Doo-Dah" from Walt Disney's live-action and animated film *Song of the South* won. The other song nominees were "A Gal in Calico" from *The Time, the Place and the Girl*, "I Wish I Didn't Love You So" from *The Perils of Pauline*, "Pass That Peace Pipe" from *Good News*, and "You Do" from *Mother Wore Tights*. Susan was dubbed by Peg LaCentra.[19]

If an Academy Award nomination is what counts, in *Smash-Up: The Story of a Woman*, Hayward had her first major success. The movie would be the female version of *The Lost Weekend* (1945), which had garnered Ray Milland an Academy Award as Best Actor. Producer Walter Wanger tailored *Smash-Up* for Susan. It is said to be loosely based on the life of crooner and movie star Bing Crosby and his wife Dixie Lee, who gave up acting to bear his children. In the film Crosby is referenced as someone who rose to fame from poor circumstances like the lead character Ken. Perhaps this was inserted to stave off possible litigation.

Contrary to the *Theatre Arts* caveat that she hadn't much experience

Smash-Up: The Story of a Woman (**Universal-International, 1947**).

with alcohol, Susan and husband Jess were said to have visited high and low class bars where Hayward got tipsy in order to bring realism to the part. She told an interviewer,

> One of the reasons that I jumped at the chance to play the part of the young wife in *Smash-Up* ... is that the movie deals with a serious social problem. More and more women are working and seeking careers, and the truth is that they can do almost anything as good as a man. But when these girls marry, some husbands treat them like they were something that came with the apartment. They shut the wives out of their own lives just like Lee Bowman does to me in the movie. Then they get enraged if the wife feels so insecure that she drinks. I've seen it happen to my own friends.[20]

It should probably be taken with a grain of salt that Hayward told the interviewer that her father had been a frustrated actor who once made her drink a bottle of whisky to prove how sick it would make her.[21]

True to form, Hayward was all business on the set. Co-star Marsha Hunt said, "I had a big fight onscreen with Susan Hayward in a powder room and we went right at it. No retakes. The bruises were showing. It was a hard movie to make."[22]

Hayward's standoffish reputation would dog, if that's the proper term (Susan didn't care what people thought), her throughout her career. More recent generations might label it tunnel-vision. "Some people add that Susan, for all her talent and shrewd use of emotion on the screen, is an inhibited woman—one of those who find it impossible to achieve warm, easy human relationships in their personal lives."[23] "Some people in Hollywood call Susan snooty and stand-offish. She isn't really. It all stems from the fact that she is extremely nearsighted and refuses to wear glasses in public."[24]

They Won't Believe Me (RKO, 1947)

The story: Larry Ballantine (Robert Young) is on trial for the murder of his wife Greta (Rita Johnson). Ballantine was a financier, a broker of sorts, who didn't really need the income because Greta was independently wealthy. With time on his hands, his roving eye focused on Janice (Jane Greer). He told her his marriage was a sham and he'd divorce Greta and go off with her. But Greta found out and provided a tender ultimatum: money. She and Larry moved west and Larry became a partner in Trenton and Ballantine. After secretary Verna Carlson (Hayward) did him a favor, Larry took up with her. She didn't deny the term "golddigger." Greta found out about this affair, too, with "a little tramp," but said she couldn't walk out of the marriage—he'd have to. But Larry couldn't and, jobless, accompanied Greta to their secluded ranch. There wasn't even a phone. Finally Larry got to the hardware store and called Verna, setting up a rendezvous in L.A. They hatched a scheme to get $25,000 out of Greta before heading to Reno for a divorce and marriage. Along the way both decided not to take the money. An oncoming truck blew a tire and caused an accident in which Verna was killed. While recovering from his injuries, Larry decided to pretend Verna's body was Greta's. He returned to the ranch with ideas of shooting Greta and hiding the body. He found the note he'd left about leaving with Verna. When he found Greta, she was already dead—from a fall or as a suicide near a hidden canyon and waterfall. He tossed the body into the swirling pool. Only Greta's palomino was a witness. Single at last, Larry traveled to South America, then Jamaica where he ran into Janice. They renewed their affair. Back in Los Angeles, Larry overheard Janice speaking with his old partner Trenton. It appeared that Janice had been sent to find him and Verna. Trenton thought Verna was killed for blackmail. And two women were missing. The police took Larry to his old ranch where a patrolman spotted the palomino by the pool. They found Greta's body. Back in the courthouse, during a recess

Janice tells Larry she believes his story. He's not convinced the jury will, and back in the courtroom makes a break for the window. Shot and killed, Larry will never know that "Not guilty" was the verdict.

The *New York Times* found it "a minor but impressive nugget out of the film Gold Coast ... an adult yarn, adroitly spun.... Susan Hayward, no stranger to this sort of assignment, is first-rate as the hard, scheming and ill-fated siren."[25] *Theatre Arts* discovered "many things to recommend it: a well-devised script by Jonathan Latimer; creditable performances by Robert Young as the murderer, and Susan Hayward, Rita Johnson and a handsome newcomer, Jane Greer, as the women who find his attractions more or less fatal."[26]

In *Film Noir*, Bob Porfirio opined "*They Won't Believe Me* is an atypical film for director Irving Pichel, but not for producer Joan Harrison, who has been primarily associated with such sardonic directors as Hitchcock and Siodmak. Additionally, the post–*Murder, My Sweet* expressionistic photography of Harry Wild and the cunning reverse casting of Robert Young in the role of the cad makes this a very unusual and underrated film noir."[27]

Film noir indeed—one ubiquitous element of *noir* is the hero (or antihero) and his problems with the opposite sex, the femme fatale. Yet there's a slightly softer edge to this *noir*. In reality, no character is wholly bad or unsympathetic. In fact, no character does anything overtly criminal. But that, too, can be noir. Hayward's character may be a golddigger in theory, but in practice she declines to do bad.

A sign of Hayward's status is that she receives top billing, despite Robert Young's protagonist and her character's relatively late appearance and early demise. It is a generally well-regarded film, though after Young's success in TV's *Father Knows Best*, it's often recalled as something Young should not have done. Some deride the change of hearts the Young and Hayward characters have, i.e., deciding to relinquish his wife's money and "elope."

Marital Problems Come to a Head

In the autumn Hayward made the newspapers, but not for her film roles. On September 30, 1947, she filed for divorce, charging her husband with "grievous mental anguish." She sought custody of the twins and requested support from Barker. It was revealed that the couple had a brief separation less than two months after their 1944 marriage.[28] Reconciliation took place.[29] Hayward had withdrawn the action on November 26 when, after seeing a marriage counselor, Barker had promised to try harder at making their marriage work.[30]

Hayward's last cheesecake publicity poses were for *They Won't Believe Me* (RKO, 1947).

The Lost Moment (Universal-International, 1947)

The story: Intent on securing the lost letters of the late poet Jeffrey Ashton from Ashton's still living lover, Juliana Bordereau (Agnes Moorehead), Lewis Venable (Robert Cummings) comes to Venice in the

guise of American writer William Burton. He wants to publish the letters so that the world may know more of beauty. Although Charles Russell (John Archer) made the arrangements for his stay, Juliana increases
the price for rooming in her manse. Lewis, aka William, agrees. He
makes friends with the maid Amelia (Joan Lorring). Not so friendly is
Juliana's imperious "niece" Tina (Hayward), whom Amelia says is usually "wicked." William speaks with Father Rinaldo (Eduardo Ciannelli),
who suspects that the young man will set in motion events of disastrous
consequences. William wonders why the rental contract signed in his
presence by Tina shows two distinct signatures: her own is markedly
different from the one she uses for Juliana, who at age 105 is apparently
incapable of holding a pen. Six weeks into his residence, William hears
haunting music and prowls the house, encountering Juliana, who asks
William if he would care to purchase the small painting of Jeffrey done
by her father—for one thousand English pounds. William agrees.
Juliana tells him not to tell Tina of the transaction. In the hall, William
again hears music and tracks it to an upper room in which the now
transformed Tina—in sparkling gown and her hair flowing about her
shoulders—speaks to herself of her lover, Jeffrey. She perceives William
as Jeffrey, and he does not dissuade her.

  In passing, William's gondolier and gardener says that one patch of
earth seems sterile. Charles makes an unwelcome appearance and says
William is likely to make a million from the published letters. Angered,
William sends him on his way. During tea in Juliana's room, William is
asked to return the ring he assuredly took from Tina when they were
together the previous night. William puts it back on Juliana's finger.
Juliana reveals that Ashton's letters to her are ensconced in a box in the
music room, and that Tina now considers them hers. Repairing to the
music room, William is distracted by a bird which flies into a wall and is
killed, and cannot secure the letters before Tina, as Juliana, enters and
leaves with the box. He follows her to the garden where they hear a scream,
followed by the sight of a man swinging down from the apartments via a
tree limb. William is unsuccessful in catching the presumed thief. Father
Rinaldo, who's sure William was not the intruder and who now realizes
it's not been healthy for Tina to live in the past, asks William to take Tina
to dinner. Registering shock, Tina nevertheless agrees. At the elegant
restaurant, the now limping Charles fails to slip Tina a note revealing
William Burton as Lewis Venable.

  With the unsolicited help of Amelia, William finally obtains and reads
the letters. Later he hears an altercation in Juliana's room and discovers Tina
demanding the letters from Juliana, whom she perceives as a former housekeeper. Juliana tries to make Tina realize who she is, and says that Jeffrey is

gone and that, she, Juliana, killed him and buried him in the garden. William offers Tina the letters. When Tina collapses, William carries her outside.

Juliana falls from the chair as she attempts to retrieve the scattered letters and dislodges a candle, setting the draperies ablaze. From the garden Lewis sees the flames, rushes back upstairs and carries the dying Juliana outside, where Tina places Juliana's ring in her hand. The letters are lost, except for a scorched one in Juliana's hand. It bears the closing, "Forever, Jeffrey."

The *New York Times* called it "little more than average 'horror' and Susan Hayward and Robert Cummings are weak in the department of romance. Miss Hayward performs as the daft niece with a rigidity that is almost ludicrous...."[31] *Newsweek* was kinder: "Obviously, Henry James wouldn't have loved everything that went into *The Lost Moment*.... But he would have appreciated the tiptoeing respect and the meticulously somber mood contributed by both the adapter Leonardo Bercovici and the director Martin Gabel ... Susan Hayward, in a baffling role, is better than the producers had a right to expect."[32]

The Lost Moment was based on Henry James' 1888 novelette *The Aspern Papers*, which was inspired by possible lost letters of the poet Byron. It is not a tale of supernatural horror, but some cinema audiences probably expected a ghost or mummy to emerge from one of the dim recesses of the Venetian manse. Certainly the twisting staircases, alcoves, and enclosed walkways give it an air of intense creepiness. Set and art directors did themselves proud. Agnes Moorehead, unrecognizable as the centenarian Juliana, enters the ranks of memorable crones inhabiting forbidding residences, much like Martita Hunt's Miss Havesham from *Great Expectations* (1946), her Baroness Meinster in *The Brides of Dracula* (1960), Mrs. Bates in *Psycho* (1969), the Davis-Crawford sisters in *What Ever Happened to Baby Jane?* (1962), and, though not so cronish, Geraldine Page's mistress of the Civil War–era southern girls school in *The Beguiled* (1971). Consider the possible psychological trauma experienced by the Robert Cummings character. He masquerades as a young writer and is taken for a dead poet. When falling into the role of Juliana, Hayward's character wears a stunning white dress touched with sparkling jewels. Although Hayward's character may be "baffling," she does demonstrate two distinct personalities: sane and mad, or at least disturbed.

The film did not please Hayward, who had a difficult time with director Martin Gabel. "I played a schizophrenic, and the director went around telling everybody not to talk to me. Yes, even warned the crew not to speak to me because he said I had to maintain a mood for the part. At one point, I lost my temper and crashed a lamp over his head, and to this day, I've never felt sorry."[33]

1948

Tap Roots (Universal-International, 1948)

The story: Big Sam Dabney (Russell Simpson) carved a home from the Mississippi wilderness in 1815. Now, in 1860, he lives with his son Hoab (Ward Bond) and his family, including the beautiful Morna (Hayward), who plans a house and a marriage to Clay (Whitfield Connor). The latter is hesitant to wed until the outcome of the national election of 1860 is known. If Abraham Lincoln is elected, secession may occur. Then he'll have to be away fighting for the South. After Big Sam dies, his alter ego, the Choctaw Indian Tishomingo (Boris Karloff), learns from Morna that her brother Bruce (Richard Long) is riding to Jackson to challenge Keith Alexander (Van Heflin) over what Bruce considers a scurrilous obituary in his newspaper, *The Mississippi Whig*. Tishomingo accompanies Bruce and they learn that Keith actually admired Big Sam. Keith invites himself to the Dabneys, where he becomes enamored of Morna and finds her beau insufferable, telling Clay, "Frankly, Captain, I don't give a picayune what you resent." Clay leaves when the town bells signal Lincoln's election. Keith stays on and the next day encounters Morna riding in the woods. When he kisses her, she insults his birth, and he slaps her. But he says he'll keep making love to her whether or not she marries Clay. Hoab asks Keith to use his newspaper to issue a call to those who want no part in secession. Keith considers Hoab's scheme to keep the Lebanon Valley neutral mad, but agrees to help. When Morna's riderless horse gallops up, the men realize something's amiss. Tishomingo reverse tracks the horse to the river, where they find Morna. She was riding to Clay but fell and injured her back. Ignoring the doctor's diagnosis that she may never walk again, Keith agrees with Tishomingo that constant massage may be the answer. Knowing she needs a reason to live and to walk, Keith uses his influence in Washington to have Clay furloughed. When Clay arrives and learns of the accident, his first response is, "Is she scarred?" Yet he tells Morna he's in the relationship till death do them part. His newspaper office attacked by a mob, Keith leaves Jackson for Lebanon, and as he approaches the Dabneys he witnesses a liaison between Clay and Aven (Julie London). He realizes he can't kill Clay until Morna is over him. "Mississippi Quits United States" blazes forth from a newspaper. Keith's makeshift press prints flyers to attract those not wanting to secede. After heated words between Hoab and Clay, the latter leaves—with Aven. When Morna feels sorry for herself, Keith taunts her so much she *stands* to accost him. Later, after a therapeutic swim in the river, she tells Keith, "And if I couldn't have walked to you I'd have crawled." Keith shoots the ring-leader of citizens disgruntled about being blockaded in the valley. When the rains come, Keith leads 300 men to the cache of rifles. But Hoab learns that Clay intends to attack from a different direction. Morna overhears, and to gain time for the men to return, rides off to keep Clay busy—by seduction. Tishomingo tries to head her off but is killed by a Confederate sentry. Clay falls asleep during a conversation, and Morna thinks she's accomplished her mission. However, Clay had divined her intent and cancelled the attack for fear of falling into an ambush. Now he'll use cannons. During the bombardment Hoab loses his senses. Keith rallies the valley men, conducting an orderly, fighting retreat into the swamps. But Bruce gets carried away and leads a counter-attack, thus dooming the valley forces. Nevertheless, Keith gets a shot at Clay and causes his death as his horse goes down and several of his own men ride over him. Keith drags the wounded Hoab to safety. Morna arrives and Hoab rants that she caused the destruction. Keith retorts that it was Hoab's arrogance that led him to think he could hold the valley; Morna was the brave one. Hoab collapses. Keith follows Morna and tells her the valley still has soil and timber and they'll rebuild. Even the severed tree before the old house has a tap root and will grow again.

Newsweek said, "The battle in which the Confederate Army finally overcomes the intrepid warriors of Lebanon is depicted in luridly realistic Technicolor. But the film owes its effectiveness mostly to the unobtrusive accuracy of its background and the expert performances of Bond, Karloff, Heflin, and especially Miss Hayward, who should more than compensate the bedraggled warrior who ultimately finds himself in her arms for the tactical loss of even so pleasant a valley as Lebanon."[34] The *New York Times* said, "The script is a conglomeration of clichés, oral and visual, and none of the characters possess individuality or substance…. Susan Hayward, generously endowed by nature and further enhanced by Technicolor, is, however, defeated at almost every turn by the script."[35]

For Hayward, this was a distinctly Scarlett O'Hara–type role, with incidents and characters so very reminiscent of *Gone with the Wind*. Like Gable's Rhett Butler in *GWTW*, Van Heflin's Keith Alexander is the world-weary character who knows he's involved in a lost cause while Hayward is the willful, headstrong Morna, who even gets corseted-up à la Scarlett. Then there's the family patriarch—Thomas Mitchell in *GWTW*, Bond here. (Bond played a Union officer in *GWTW*. The late Philadelphia radio DJ Ken Garland once suggested that if one is at a loss in a trivia contest about what character actor was prominent in an old movie, answer "Ward Bond.") *Tap Roots* even features an important tree, much like that of Tara.

The film itself is quite entertaining, a semi-epic. The 1965 James Stewart film *Shenandoah* has a somewhat similar plot.

The Saxon Charm (Universal-International, 1948)

The story: Novelist Eric Busch (John Payne) finds theatrical producer Matt Saxon (Robert Montgomery) interested in his first play, *The Comic Spirit: A Tragedy*, which is about Molière. Eric agrees to modify it. After all, Saxon is well versed in stagecraft and story. At a dinner, Eric's wife Janet (Hayward) meets Saxon and his girlfriend, Alma Wragge (Audrey Totter). Alma reveals that she loves Saxon, but tells Janet that Saxon has a certain contempt for people and advises her to get her husband away from him. On the way home Janet asks Eric to ask for a release. Having witnessed the boorish behavior of Saxon in the restaurant, Eric agrees. But while he agonizes over the letter, Saxon arrives and convinces him to work with him. Janet overhears and later tells Eric she understands. Saxon entices Eric to the Fuss 'n' Feathers nightclub to talk over the play while Alma auditions for a singing spot. Janet attends, and while she and Eric walk home, says, "Don't let anything change you, Eric. Please don't." When Eric finds re-writing for Saxon confusing, Janet convinces him to take a break at their island house. Saxon intrudes—sailing up in a yacht. When Hermie (Henry Morgan) arrives and tells Saxon his latest production has been labeled "Stinko" by the press, Saxon says they'll put Eric's play into production. Saxon hates the third act, however, and urges "action, supercharged with emotion." Flying to Mexico to meet Saxon, Eric meets Saxon's ex-wife Vivian (Heather Angel), whom Saxon is hitting up for money. Disappointingly, a call from Hermie reveals that Vivian is broke. Returning to New York, Saxon gets money from Eric so he can travel to Hollywood to hire an actor for the play. Arriving at his apartment, Eric is followed by a drunken Janet and some of her friends from St. Louis. After a confrontation, she packs. Saxon meanwhile squashes Alma's Hollywood contract by insinuating that she's a drunk. Peter Stanhope (John Baragrey) and director Abel Richman (Addison Richards) ask Eric for his original draft. They'd turned down Saxon on the rewrite. Alma leaves Saxon. When Saxon calls Eric, the latter finally insists that Saxon come to *him* if he wants to talk. Saxon wants more money. He says it's good riddance to Janet. Later Saxon goes to his office, where Hermie wonders where his boss got the black eye. Hermie tells Saxon he's finished on Broadway because he doesn't consider people people. A Western Union telegram arrives revealing that Vivian is dead. Saxon rifles through his desk for a copy of the manuscript for *Scarlet Miracle* and phones its author to set up a meeting at the Fuss 'n' Feathers. Janet, now living with Alma, arrives at the club where the latter is singing. Eric is there. They reconcile and head for their island.

Newsweek said, "But for all its somber possibilities the story deftly avoids being tragic.... Montgomery succeeds in making Saxon more of a 'man who came to dinner' than a 42nd Street Citizen Kane.... And Payne, Miss Hayward, and Audrey Totter ... nicely offset his sophisticated comedy by playing their roles straight and looking very much like genuine human beings."[36] The *New York Times* said, "John Payne is convincing as the author and Susan Hayward is nicely subdued and appealing as his wife."[37]

It's consistently interesting. Although Hayward had a number of key scenes, the relationship between Montgomery and Payne is the crux of the situation. The father of actress Elizabeth Montgomery, Robert Montgomery is an unjustly neglected actor today. In the 1930s and early 1940s he was a handsome and charming matinee idol, well suited to light comedy and later, like Dick Powell, hard-nosed film noir. He directed and starred (as Philip Marlowe) in *Lady in the Lake* (1947), also with Audrey Totter, and *Ride the Pink Horse* (1947). Many will know him as the lead in *Here Comes Mr. Jordan* (1941).

Like Montgomery, Payne is hardly thought of today, despite a decent movie career and successful TV series. He'd grown from the second lead in *The Razor's Edge* (1946) to tortured protagonist in such noir films as *Kansas City Confidential* (1952), *99 River Street* (1953) and *Slightly Scarlet* (1956).

Chapter 4

Star and Superstar

Susan Hayward is spoiled and headstrong or bitchy...
—Hortense Powdermaker on the
Hayward movie persona, Hollywood:
The Dream Factory *(1950)*[1]

Befitting her growing status, Hayward regularly graced the cover of such fan magazines as *Movie Album* and *Movie Fan.* Sometimes her expression was seductive, sometimes winsome. Convening in San Francisco in 1949, the American Beauticians' Congress designated Susan Hayward "the most beautiful girl in the world" because of "the piquant beauty of her face, which combines personality with classic features." Plus, she had "the perfect figure."[2]

1949

Under Walter Wanger's wing again, Hayward obtained a leading role in a large-scale production, at least for Eagle-Lion. Once again she was teamed with Robert Preston, with whom she'd appeared in *Beau Geste* and *Reap the Wild Wind.*

Tulsa (Eagle-Lion, 1949)

The story: In the 1920s, Oklahomans must juxtapose the needs of cattlemen with a new breed: oilmen. When her father is crushed to death by derrick debris, Cherokee Lansing (Hayward) blames the Tanner Petroleum Corporation. In Tulsa she petitions Bruce Tanner (Lloyd Gough) for $20,000 to replace the cattle killed by polluted streams. Failing in her mission, she complains to cousin Pinky (Chill Wills), "It must be wonderful to be rich and powerful enough to step on people and be respected for it." Coming into possession of crude oil leases from Johnny Brady (Ed Begley), a man she'd befriended, Cherokee finds Bruce Tanner offering her $20,000 for them. But Cherokee's Native American neighbor and friend Jim Redbird (Pedro Armendariz) provides monetary assistance, and Cherokee Lansing Oil is formed. When Johnny Brady dies his Princeton-educated geologist son Brad (Robert Preston) appears with a scheme to use concrete casing to improve drilling. A well finally spouts a gusher that makes them $1,000 per hour. Brad says oil and cattle can coexist with one well per ten acres. Years pass and the ambitions of Cherokee and various native tribes increase. "What are you, a Boy Scout, or a man?" Cherokee asks Brad when the latter disputes her goals. Cherokee merges her company with Tanner's. Despite her willingness to marry him, Brad is heavily into conservation and demurs. Jim threatens those who would mar his land with more wells, and an injunction is issued to stop him. Having second thoughts about her mission, Cherokee tells Tanner she's *not* going to put more wells on Jim's land. It's too late because a mentally distraught Jim finds sick and dying steers at the creek. Striking a match, he watches the oil in the water flame up and spread. A nearby derrick explodes. Brad, Cherokee, Pinky and Tanner try to halt the fire by shutting off valves and dynamiting to create fire breaks. Brad uses tractors to pull over derricks. Cherokee runs to an injured Jim and is trapped by a falling derrick. With water hoses trained on his back, Brad maneuvers a steam shovel into the holocaust to rescue his friends. Jim's homestead is also saved by the judicious use of dynamite. Brad says Tanner should be glad this happened because it proves that conservation is necessary.

Newsweek said, "Aside from a commendable obeisance in the direction of such worthy causes as the preservation of grazing lands and the conservation of our oil resources, *Tulsa* is an uninhibited, simon-simple melodrama of the great open spaces ... an ambiguous love affair with Brady that is almost as trying on the audience as it appears to be on the patient geologist."[3] The *New York Times* complained of the film's "cliché-filled script."[4]

As well as playing Cherokee's cousin, Chill Wills is the narrator (Wills would have a similar role in George Stevens' 1956 epic of Texas—and oil and cows—*Giant*), opening the story with reminiscences about Oklahoma's past inhabitants, including various Native American tribes. *Tulsa* may be the first major film with an environmental conscience. And again, *Tulsa*, as with almost all Grade-A Hollywood westerns, presents Native Americans in a positive light: free-ranging nomads whose warpaths are the result of white eyes' perfidy. Here the Native American Jim (Armendariz) never varies in his wish to protect the land.

Hayward's character was again in a fire, as she had been in *The Forest Rangers* and *Smash-Up* (not to mention the one she'd watched close up in *I Married a Witch*). Was any other leading lady at the time suitable for the role of Cherokee? One who looked good covered in oil or soaked in water? One who could believably stand up to the robber baron characters?

Hayward used the film to explain to an interviewer that "Emotions of natural redheads are close to the surface.... Film acting requires a girl to produce any one of a dozen emotions before the cameras without preliminary build-up, so the redhead has an immediate advantage." As for her mentor Walter Wanger: "It means ... that I can concentrate all my arguments on one man instead of the corps of executives you find at any major studio." She concluded the interview by saying that "I have often said that one day, when I have enough money, I'll walk away from the camera and stay away. But then again I wonder ... can it be done?"[5] There's a germ of truth here. Years later Susan *would* walk away—but return. Creative artists, whether painters, musicians, writers or actors, usually die with their boots on. Cary Grant and Doris Day may be the only major stars to retire of their own accord.

The Fox Contract

Tulsa would be Hayward's last picture for Walter Wanger for almost a decade. Wanger sold her contract to Darryl F. Zanuck at 20th Century–Fox for a reputed $200,000.[6] Why? He'd sunk so much of his own money into *Joan of Arc* (1948). Despite the presence of Ingrid Bergman in the title role, the movie was a financial failure.

Incredibly, although Hayward would become Fox's top female attraction over the next several years, books about legendary studio chief Darryl F. Zanuck are strangely silent about her impact.[7] There *are* Zanuck comments reported elsewhere. "Susan is a rare combination of two elements.... She's beautiful. And she can act."[8]

Just before Hayward's first Fox production, *House of Strangers*, was released in July 1949, nationally-syndicated columnist Hedda Hopper interviewed her. Perhaps because Hopper's rival, Louella Parsons, had been a Hayward supporter, the interview is refreshingly prickly. Hayward tells Hopper she's acting like the district attorney. Hopper responds, "Now

Susan, you don't want to be pictured as a sweet, innocent, and rather dull and colorless little character, do you?" Hayward says no, but husband Jess doesn't want her to talk about their fights. She says hubby doesn't run her career but only advises her. They'd agreed that the script for *Uncle Wiggily in Connecticut* (release title: *My Foolish Heart*) would be right for her. Hopper wondered if Hayward's twins are "showoffs and spoiled." As for friends, Hayward says Jess has a legion but that her own best chum is Martha Little, whose sister Sarah went to Girls Commercial High School with her. Hopper sums up the interview by telling the reader that Susan is rare—an actress who works hard and thinks hard about her roles and gets better all the time.[9]

House of Strangers (20th Century–Fox, 1949)

The story: Italian immigrant Gino Monetti (Edward G. Robinson) became a success by creating a bank and dealing fairly with the residents of New York's East Side. But he keeps many of the figures in his head, and in 1932, because of new banking laws, finds himself in hot water. The youngest of his four sons, Max (Richard Conte), a lawyer, defends him in court, but Gino is headstrong, admits to no wrongdoing and antagonizes witnesses and attorneys alike. Feeling his father has little chance of staying out of jail, Max attempts to bribe a woman juror. She turns him down, and he's arrested as he leaves the building. Watching from their car is Irene Bennett (Hayward), his current paramour. Although he'd been engaged to Maria (Debra Paget), Max had found the strong-willed Irene more his type. Theirs had been a volatile relationship. Convicted of bribery, Max spends the next seven years in jail. His dad got off during a second trial but no longer has a bank. His other sons had their mother sign it over to them. Joe (Luther Adler) tells Gino he's an old man who should go to the park and feed the pigeons. Instead, Gino convinces Max to plan their revenge. During Max's internment, Irene goes to Gino and tells him to stop writing Max letters about the other sons. It'll just ruin Max's life. Irene tells Gino she knows he realizes he should be the one in prison, not Max. Max unexpectedly gets a twelve-hour pass. It's to go home and attend his father's funeral. When released years later, Max plans to accede to his dad's wishes. But that afternoon, staring at Gino's portrait, he realizes he could ruin the lives of each brother. He has a change of heart, calls Irene and tells her to pick him up. His brothers arrive before she does. Joe doesn't believe Max will leave them alone and has Pietro (Paul Valentine) beat Max up and carry him upstairs. Pietro is not keen on throwing Max from the balcony as Joe demands, and when Joe calls him "Dumbhead," Pietro drops Max to the floor and starts choking Joe. Max struggles to his feet and intervenes, shouting that if Pietro kills Joe it would be what their father wanted. Pietro relents and Max wobbles into the hall. He hears a car horn and smiles. Outside he stops a moment, then quickly takes the last steps and jumps into Irene's car. They leave the "house of strangers" for a new life.

The *New York Times* said the film "has its decidedly entertaining points.... At one point she [Hayward] is a hedonist, at another she is a virginal type, and always she is, like a chameleon, adapted to the coloration of this plot. As played by Susan Hayward, she is nifty to look at—and that's all."[10] More recently it has received more in-depth analysis: "Paradoxically, while the other sons have bitter dreams of freedom from their father's rule, Max is both the most independent and the most loyal. As a result, the relationship between Max and Irene, a conventional romance, acquires a distinctive tension by virtue of her existence as an outsider relative to his family's cultural preference."[11] The *Manchester Guardian* said Hayward's "love duet with Richard Conte has at least the distinction of being one of the most acid tongued to be heard in an American film."[12]

Her first Fox film gave Hayward second billing behind veteran Edward G. Robinson and ahead of the story's real star, Richard Conte. Robinson's Gino is not entirely nasty. The audience can empathize with some of his views and actions while deploring what he becomes. Robinson is one of those actors about whom it can be said he never gave a bad performance. Richard Conte may be most remembered by modern generations as Marlon Brando's enemy, Barzini, in *The Godfather*. Before *House of Strangers* he'd toiled for years as a recognizable but supporting actor. His redemption on the steps of the house at the end, as the music swells, is moving. Luther Adler is appropriately villainous as the eldest son. Hayward is worldly-wise but has a soft spot. She has good lines, whether berating Robinson or goading Conte.

According to a 20th Century–Fox Press Release, Mushy Callahan trained Hayward in fisticuffs for the picture. "Mushy, who has trained most of the stars for their film bouts, told her to practice at home nights on her husband, Jess Barker." Susan said she certainly didn't do that. Instead, she got a studio dummy for practice.[13]

Director Joseph L. Mankiewicz was in the midst of his golden age. He would win back-to-back Academy Awards for Direction and Screenplay on both *A Letter to Three Wives* (1949) and *All About Eve* (1950).

In 1954 Fox remade *House of Strangers* as the fine western, *Broken Lance*, with Spencer Tracy in the Robinson role, Robert Wagner in Conte's, Jean Peters in Hayward's, and Richard Widmark in Adler's.

At Home

Sidney Skolsky, noted columnist, gave a picture of Hayward's life that June as she'd finished *House of Strangers*. She and hubby Jess and the twins were residing in an English-cottage style house in the San Fernando Valley. The living room was still unfurnished. Hayward was described as a light eater, casual dresser and financially frugal.

> She is not the jovial sort on the set, but is very pleasant. While making *House of Strangers*, she stayed by herself most of the time. She is now making *My Foolish Heart*, and between shots she usually goes immediately to her dressing room and reads books or magazines. She doesn't have very many Hollywood friends.... She is nearsighted and for that reason is sometimes accused of snubbing people she actually doesn't recognize.[14]

My Foolish Heart (RKO, 1949)

The story: When her husband Lew (Kent Smith) threatens to take their daughter Ramona (Gigi Perreau) and leave a wife who's become a lush, Eloise (Hayward) alludes to a counter-threat that her friend Mary Jane (Lois Wheeler) knows will further rock the marriage. Eloise begins to remember her past as Eloise Winters, a Connecticut coed fresh from Boise. Attending a swank party, she finds she'd made a faux pas by wearing a dress less than chic. But party-crasher Walt Dreiser (Dana Andrews) comforts her. Some time later Walt phones and arranges a dinner date. Afterward, Eloise reluctantly goes to his efficiency apartment but successfully wards off his advances. Still, she has second thoughts. But Walt realizes he shouldn't take advantage of the "nice girl" with the aristocratic ears. He takes her back to school. They continue a long-distance romance when Walt is drafted. Trouble arises when the school principal finds them in a clinch in the elevator. Eloise is expelled, and her mother (Jessie Royce Landis) and father (Robert Keith) come to New York to take her home. Eloise introduces Walt to her dad, who believes Walt has not compromised his daughter's virtue. On the train to Boise, Eloise complains to her dad how miserable she'll be in Boise, thousands of miles from Walt. Dad drops her off at the next station and she returns to New York, getting a job and seeing Walt on his rare leaves. While attending a football game one afternoon they learn that Pearl Harbor has been attacked. Walt must report to his base. Walt finally says it: he loves Eloise. Eloise becomes pregnant but can't tell Walt, who thinks he may never return from the war, or her father, who has a heart condition. At his airbase, Walt begins a letter a friend takes when the plane leaves for maneuvers. The plane crashes after

With twins Gregory and Timothy, ca. 1950.

takeoff. Arriving at the base, Eloise learns that Walt did not survive. Back in New York, she is comforted by Mary Jane. At the site of the party where she first met Walt, she allows Lew to take her for a ride. Stopping by the river, Lew admits that he never got over her. Eloise hints at similar feelings and asks if she can think of Lew as her guy when he's overseas. Back in the present, Eloise, having had time to consider her threat, decides that for the sake of Ramona the girl should live with Lew. Before leaving, she stops by Ramona's room and comforts her after a bad dream. Mary Jane and Lew observe this concern and determine that it is they who should leave. Ramona belongs with her mother.

Variety was impressed with the film, saying it "ranks among the better romantic films ... loaded with dialog that is alive.... Hayward's performance is a gem, displaying a positive talent for capturing reality."[15] Nevertheless, some major contemporary critics were downbeat, including *The New Yorker*, which found it "full of soap-opera clichés, and it's hard to believe that it was wrung out of a short story by J.D. Salinger that appeared in this austere magazine a couple of years ago."[16] Acknowledging its professionalism—as befit a Goldwyn film—The *New York Times* was nevertheless unimpressed with the story and labeled it a mere tearjerker.[17]

But *Newsweek* liked it, however, finding that, "the skillful handling of the romantic drama makes it a superior film of general adult appeal.... This is very much Susan Hayward's picture, and she makes the most of her first chance at an honest, demanding characterization by realizing it with an admirable sincerity and understanding."[18]

The movie has resonated down the years. In 1991 critic Andrew Sarris analyzed its appeal. He noted that the *New York Times* neither discerned "the strikingly noirish look and mood of the film" nor gave credit to "legendary cinematographer Lee Garmes and melodious composer Victor Young."[19] Sarris also quotes from A. Scott Berg's *Goldwyn: A Biography*. Berg said that J.D. Salinger, whose short story in *The New Yorker*, "Uncle Wiggily in Connecticut," was the movie's basis, was so disappointed with the film version he would never again allow Hollywood to film his works. As Sarris said, "What a burden for a mere movie to bear! Think of it: If the Epstein twins had not persuaded Goldwyn to purchase a short story from which about ten lines of dialogue could be salvaged for the screen, a legendary author might have been saved from self-imposed exile."[20]

As for Sarris, he liked *My Foolish Heart* when he and his brother first saw it in the year of its release.

> What impressed me most was Susan Hayward's blistering toughness in every crisis, as if she were a Brooklyn-born Scarlett O'Hara, a part for which she had once auditioned. Neither of us was yet culturally brave enough to admit that Victor Young's score really got to us, particularly in the car scene near the end of the flashback when she decides to grab the life-preserver of a loveless marriage. In this and every other big moment, Hayward displayed the distinctively American brand of gallows-humor spunk Murray Kempton would admire a decade later in her death-house scenes in *I Want to Live*.[21]

The audience *can* see Hayward's character considering her options in the car scene by the river. For anyone who's lost a loved one, her return to the site of the party where she met Walt is emotional. Lois Wheeler is the kind of friend anyone should be proud to have. Character actor Robert Keith is, as always, very special.

My Foolish Heart re-teamed Hayward with *Canyon Passage* co-star Dana Andrews. Its general release was 1950, but Samuel Goldwyn gave it a one-week New York run in December 1949 so that it would qualify for Academy Award nominations. *My Foolish Heart* received two: song and Hayward for Best Actress. The song became at least as much of a standard as the winner: "Baby, It's Cold Outside" from the Esther Williams film *Neptune's Daughter*. Olivia de Havilland won Best Actress for *The Heiress*.

Part of this film's promotion involved Susan plugging Jergens Lotion in magazine ads featuring scenes from the film.

Glamour Queen, and a Missed Opportunity

The Hollywood Motion Picture Photographers' Association declared Hayward its third "Queen of Glamour." The runners-up included Elizabeth Taylor, Lana Turner, Betty Grable and Rita Hayworth. The first two winners had been Ava Gardner and Jane Greer.[22]

If writer-director Joseph L. Mankiewicz, who'd used Hayward in *House of Strangers*, had had his way, she would have been the lead in *All About Eve*.[23] Zanuck wanted Claudette Colbert, but a back injury precluded that and, as all know, Bette Davis got the plum part of Margo Channing. Jeanne Crain was to have been Eve but became pregnant. Another Crain pregnancy would give Hayward her role in *I'd Climb the Highest Mountain*.

1951

In 1951 four Hayward movies would be released—a western, a rural contemporary drama, an urban drama, and a historical pageant—demonstrating her versatility.

Rawhide (20th Century–Fox, 1951)

The story: Rawhide is a relay stop for "The Jackass Mail" stage transporting passengers (for $200) between St. Louis and California. The line's

20th Century–Fox publicity still, ca. 1951.

owner has detailed his son Tom Owens (Tyrone Power) to apprentice there and learn from the school of hard knocks under gruff Sam Todd (Edgar Buchanan). Tom can't wait to leave, and despite the harsh environment keeps himself clean-shaven and neat. One day an eastbound stage arrives with Vinnie Holt (Hayward) and young niece Callie in tow. Following on their heels is a cavalry detachment warning that the murdering bandit Zimmerman has broken out of jail and ambushed another wagon. When she hears that company rules forbid the carrying of children in such an eventuality, Vinnie puts up a spirited fight and must be dragged from the coach. A stranger arrives, presenting himself as Sheriff Miles (Hugh Marlowe) from Huntsville. When Sam and Tom's backs are turned, he pulls his pistol and reveals himself as Zimmerman. Joined by the rag-tag gang of Tevis (Jack Elam), Gratz (George Tobias) and Yancy (Dean Jagger), Zimmerman lays out his scheme for robbing the next eastbound stage. Sam makes a break for the corral and a rifle, but is shot down by Tevis. Mistakenly thought to be her husband, Tom is locked in with Vinnie. Tom makes a case that they should continue the ruse because he's indispensable until the stage arrives. The westbound stage shows up first. Sam's absence is excused on the grounds that he went to a dentist. "Sheriff Miles" is quizzed about Zimmerman, and it's learned that the outlaw had been in the calaboose for killing his Creole woman and her lover. After the stage departs, Zimmerman has trouble with Tevis due to the latter's roving eye for Miss Holt. Tom hides a knife with which he and Vinnie begin digging a hole through the adobe. The next day Tom is enlisted to ready the mules for the pending stage. Unseen by Vinnie, Callie crawls through the hole. Seeing her outside by the horses, Vinnie becomes hysterical. Tevis lets her out to shut her up, but she makes a break for it. He grabs her by the throat until she's unconscious. Returning to the ruckus, Zimmerman is told by Tevis that he just had to subdue the wild woman. His back turned, Zimmerman is shot dead by his erstwhile companion. During the melee inside, Tom had attacked Zimmerman but been knocked senseless by a well-placed pistol butt. Rising, he makes it to a gun Vinnie had secreted behind the water trough. Tevis comes outside, shoots Gratz off the water tower, and is unhappily surprised to be wounded by a shot from Tom. The two wage a duel until Tevis sees Callie and starts putting bullets into the ground around her. Forcing Tom to come out, Tevis is about to plug him when Vinnie pulls the rifle from beneath Gratz and ends Tevis' rotten life. The stage arrives and the drivers ask Tom what's been going on. He says he's just been learning the business.

The *New York Times* said, "With only one set and a screenplay by Ludley [sic] Nichols which covers a fitfully dramatic situation, Director Henry Hathaway has turned out a surprisingly good entertainment.... Miss Hayward, who has more opportunity to express her indignation and gnawing terror in warding off the advances of a leering member of the gang, does well by her role."[24] Years later, Brian Garfield commended its photography, extolled Hugh Marlowe's performance, and said, "The suspense builds thrillingly and Hayward is very good as the tough lady protecting her infant."[25]

Rawhide was the first of two films Hayward co-starred in with Tyrone Power, who'd been a Fox matinee idol since the 1930s. At this point in his career Power shared top leading man spot at Fox with Gregory Peck, whose film career had begun in 1944. Studio head Darryl Zanuck gave Peck most of the prestigious acting tasks (*Gentleman's Agreement, Twelve O'Clock High, The Gunfighter*), though critics often enough complained that Peck was "wooden." Power, the epitome of the tall, dark and handsome leading man, demonstrated acting talent when the occasion demanded it, especially in *The Razor's Edge* (1946) and *Nightmare Alley* (1947).

Except for shots of the stage crossing deserts and snowy passes, *Rawhide* is essentially a one-set western, like *Rio Bravo* (1959). Yet it does not feel claustrophobic or anti-western. Attribute that to Henry Hathaway and Robert Simpson, who combined on a directorial/editorial tour de force. Close-ups are employed judiciously. Note, in particular, those of Power and Hayward digging a hole in the adobe wall while lying on their stomachs beneath the bunk, or Jack Elam's magnificently ugly leer as he waits for Power and Buchanan to try something so he can plug them. It is also one of the rare films in which a major plot element—the escape hole—is never used by the protagonists.

The film's quality is also due to the mix of major stars (Power, Hayward) with excellent supporting players (Marlowe, Jagger) and character actors (Buchanan, Elam, Tobias, James Millican, Louis Jean Heydt, Jeff Corey). It's amazing how good Hayward looks simply attired: white blouse, scarf, skirt. Tobias is cast against type but very well as the illiterate Gratz. Normally Tobias was lovable, as in *Air Force* (1943) or *Objective, Burma!* (1945), or later on TV's *Bewitched*. Jagger is one of those actors who moved betwixt and between character and major supporting roles. In 1949 he'd won the Best Supporting Actor Academy Award for *Twelve O'Clock High*. (Who will forget his character's penchant here for bean sandwiches?) The movie has some incredibly violent scenes: Marlowe beating up Buchanan; Elam back-shooting Buchanan, then walking up close to finish the job; Marlowe slugging Power for attempting to steal a gun; Elam grabbing Hayward by the hair and virtually strangling her to keep her quiet. With his one good eye, his magnificently ugly/scruffy countenance, and the barely controlled tremor when insulted by Marlowe, Elam was made for this psychopathic role. (Apparently Everett Sloane [*Citizen Kane, Prince of Foxes, Lady from Shanghai*] was to have played Tevis but knocked Hayward down so hard in one scene that she had him replaced with Jack Elam.[26]) The theme music had been used in 1948's *Yellow Sky*. On its first TV telecast in the 1960s, *Rawhide's* title was changed to *Desperate Siege* so as not to confuse viewers with the Eric Fleming–Clint Eastwood television series *Rawhide*.

Susan Hayward as she appeared in *Rawhide* (20th Century–Fox, 1952).

I Can Get It for You Wholesale (20th Century–Fox, 1951)

The story: Fashion model Harriet Boyd (Hayward) convinces designer Sam Cooper (Sam Jaffe) and salesman Teddy (Dan Dailey) that if they pool their resources her designs will lead them to success. "I know plenty and I've learned it the hard way," she tells Teddy while he admires her sketches. Successfully scheming to add her sister's money to their bankroll, Harriet raises enough cash to form Sherboyco. Angry when a client fawns over Harriet after hours, Teddy proposes marriage but is turned down. At the Annual Buyers Ball, Harriet wonders how she can meet guest speaker J. F. Noble (George Sanders). Before Teddy can grant her wish, Harriet is seen dancing with the great Noble. Later Harriet has a drink in Noble's apartment. In due course Noble makes Harriet a proposition, namely that she join his firm and produce her own line, Harriet of Nobles. She's willing but says she's got an ironclad contract with her partners. Noble knows he—and she—can get her out of it. As part of her ploy, Harriet rants at Sam that nobody is doing justice to her work. Teddy reads her the riot act, and Harriet tells him she's just overworked. After Teddy again suggests marriage, Harriet says she needs to be alone to think things out. Teddy and Sam agree they should send Harriet to Paris. Teddy goes to tell her but finds she's out—but not at the hospital where her sister has her baby. Instead, she's at Noble's apartment. Unknown to Teddy, she's actually declining Noble's offer in favor of the satisfaction she believes she can get out of her own business. Teddy arrives and misunderstands. After he leaves, Harriet tells Noble to pry her out of her contract. Traveling through Texas and the south, Teddy gets many orders that Sam worries can't be filled. Meanwhile, Harriet is signing on with Noble, who says Teddy has no choice but to get rich under Noble's banner. Harriet packs for a trip to Paris on the S.S. *Queen Anne*. Teddy arrives back in New York, calms himself when he finds out the lay of the land, then tells Harriet he and Sam have agreed to close down Sherboyco and thus ruin Harriet. Sam tells Harriet he and Teddy still love her. Harriet boards the *Queen Anne* and asks Noble to postpone the trip. He counters that Harriet must choose between Teddy and himself. He wants her to stay only if she wants to stay. Otherwise it might do her good to crawl back to Teddy. He had to crawl once, only it was too late. Harriet disembarks, returns to the office and finds Sam and Teddy going over the accounts. Sam makes her and Teddy see reason.

The *New York Times* decided to "give Susan Hayward some quick recognition for bringing to life a hard-shelled dame, who travels just as fast and loose as the screenplay written by Abraham Polonsky permits her to…. Stories about such chameleon-like characters as Miss Hayward plays … are difficult to put over with complete success and that is why this film falters as a character study, though Miss Hayward does nobly."[27]

Library Journal found it

> An adult treatment, making few concessions and pulling no punches, of Jerome Weidman's glimpse into the jungle of the New York garment industry and fashion designing. Susan Hayward is entirely convincing as the lovely and hard-boiled model, Harriet Boyd, who stops at nothing on her upward climb until she runs into the immovable fact that people eventually refuse to be pushed around. Dan Dailey plays her blunt and no-nonsense lover as though he enjoyed discarding his dancing shoes for awhile; Sam Jaffe as their elderly partner who helps tame the shrew is as good as always. Scenes of the New York garment district and attractive shots in Central Park give the film extra authenticity.[28]

Here was the "Hayward you love to semihate."[29] In many ways this is a definitive Hayward character, both reel and real: getting her own taxis, offering to light the man's cigarette. Her pre–Hollywood modeling days in New York gave Hayward some definite connections with this subject. It moves at a nice clip. When initially aired on TV, this was titled *Only the Best*.

I'd Climb the Highest Mountain (20th Century–Fox, 1951)

The story: Early in the twentieth century, city-bred Mary Thompson (Hayward) and her new husband William Thompson (William Lundigan) take up residence outside rural Tallulah Falls in north Georgia. Will is a preacher for the locals, who include bad boy Jack Stark (Rory Calhoun), general store owner Mr. Brock (Gene Lockhart), and the atheistic Salter (Alexander Knox). The pair deal with a flu epidemic, the drowning of young George Salter, Mary's premature baby, the flirtatious Mrs. Billy-wirth (Lynn Bari), and the conflict between Jack Stark and Mr. Brock, whose daughter Jenny (Barbara Bates) is in love with Jack. After three years, Will is assigned another district, Atlanta. The community gathers to see them off, even Mr. Salter, who though still a heathen thinks some benefit of religion might be had by his wife and other children.

Library Journal thought it a "delightful photoplay in Technicolor.... Susan Hayward in the role of the city-bred young wife and William Lundigan as the minister husband are well cast. There are scenes of comedy and tragedy in this simple story of the young preacher and his flock."[30] The *New York Times* said it "is not what you'd call a picture with a strong dramatic plot, rising to peaks of high excitement or theatrical suspense.... But it is done with such winning affection and it is so agreeably played by William Lundigan as the parson that it carries a warm and cheering glow.... Miss Hayward is a bit on the unbelievable side as the parson's wife, running too often to artifice and attitudes...."[31]

In retrospect, *I'd Climb the Highest Mountain* seems an odd vehicle for Hayward. She was on the verge of genuine superstardom, yet in this film her co-star was William Lundigan. Lundigan would continue in B movies, and in a few short years would have the opportunity to contribute a great line in 1954's *The White Orchid*: "This is what I came to see, all the barbaric splendor of an ancient culture." Actually, Susan was filling in for Jeanne Crain, who'd had to opt out due to one of her many pregnancies.[32] Girl-next-door Crain would have been perfect in the role. The movie is episodic in the extreme, but not to its detriment.

Said Hayward of the her part, "I'm nice but not naive. When Lynn Bari makes passes at the parson I dispose of her in a sharp-tongued manner that only a hep gal would know about."[33]

The film was set in Georgia, where Hayward narrowly escaped injury and death. Her chauffeur William Gray caught her as she was photographing the 729-foot Amicalola Falls in Dawsonville, north Georgia.[34]

A few years later Hayward said,

We were working deep in the heart of the backwoods country ... among the friendliest, kindest people I'd ever met. They were like kin to me, because some of my own family had come from that part of the South. The townspeople, most of whom were appearing in the picture, had gone out of their way to be nice to me. I counted many of them among my warmest friends.[35]

Susan's husband Jess snapped many photos during the shoot. Eleven were printed in the February 1951 issue of *Movies*.

Award

Hayward received a "Youth Career" award from the New York Supreme Court Justice George J. Beldock, President of "Youth United," which combated juvenile delinquency. She was to fly east after completing *David and Bathsheba* to accept the award. Hayward responded that her own inspiration was another Brooklyn-born actress, Barbara Stanwyck, and met her for the first time at the Waldorf dinner.[36]

I'd Climb the Highest Mountain (**20th Century–Fox, 1951**).

David and Bathsheba (20th Century–Fox, 1951)

The story: While investigating the Ammonite stronghold Rabbah, the Israelite general Joab (Dennis Hoey) is exasperated when he discovers that King David (Gregory Peck) has joined a scouting party and suffered a wounded arm. No matter, says David, who, with the help of Uriah the Hittite (Kieron Moore), had survived an ambush. Returning to Jerusalem, David accepts a ceremonial dagger from the Egyptian ambassador (George Zucco) and tells the prophet Nathan (Raymond Massey) to locate the Ark of the Covenant in a propitious locale. In his chambers David comes upon Michal (Jayne Meadows), one of his wives and the late King Saul's daughter. After an argument over love and royalty, David repairs to the palace ramparts and observes a beautiful woman at her bath on a nearby rooftop. He learns from Abishai (James Robertson Justice) that the woman is Uriah's wife Bathsheba (Hayward). David explains that it was in his mind to reward Uriah for his brave efforts. He will give that reward to the wife. During the private dinner, David learns that Uriah has spent very little time with his wife. Moreover, she did not even know him till the day of their marriage. After giving her a jeweled necklace, David tells Bathsheba, "This Uriah is a fool! When I looked on you from my terrace tonight, I knew that every future moment spent away from you would be a moment lost. Yet he's found only six days for you in seven months. The perfume of his beloved is the stink of war! Does he think that a man was made only for the agony of battle? Does he call that manhood? Has he no blood, no heart? Now go. Be thankful that I am not Pharaoh. At least I can console myself with the thought that your modesty matches your beauty." Bathsheba confesses that she knew David walked upon the terrace and would spy her. She wants him as much as he desires her, but she has conditions, namely that if they break one of Moses' Commandments, she become a proper consort never to be discarded. During a countryside tryst, Bathsheba elicits recollections of David's childhood. Later, while helping a crippled shepherd free a sheep from a thicket, David learns that the one-armed man lost his limb in a battle serving King Saul. The man still thinks of Saul as the true king and his dead son Jonathan as true successor. David gives him some coins and after dark trudges up to the site of the battlefield. He pictures it in his mind as Bathsheba discreetly observes from a distance. The next day they return to Jerusalem and find Nathan leading a caravan transporting the Ark of the Covenant. Before sending Bathsheba on to her abode, they observe a woman being stoned to death for infidelity. David greets Nathan and leans close to touch the Ark, but Nathan cries out to stop, he is not consecrated. When a guard pushes the Ark back onto its pedestal he suffers a fatal attack. This convinces Nathan that a temple must be built outside of the city. Bathsheba reveals to David that she is with child. After soul-searching, and in order to gain time, David calls Uriah back from Rabbah in hopes that he will spend a night with Bathsheba. But Uriah does not go to his wife. Irritated with the man's sense of honor that precludes any other human feeling, David sends him back to Joab with secret orders to send Uriah into the front lines, withdraw and let him be killed. Ira (John Sutton) returns to tell the King of the battle and deaths. Uriah has indeed been killed. Drought that had been brewing overcomes the land. Nathan declares it the result of sin. After a month of mourning, Bathsheba and David are wed. But as the drought deepens and the Egyptians turn down David's request for grain, Nathan confronts David with his sin. The only real accuser is Michal. David goes to Bathsheba, who is resigned to her fate. But David sees a way out. Praying before the Ark, he remembers when, as a youth (Leon Pessin), he was anointed the chosen one by Samuel (Paul Newlan), and of how he'd defeated Goliath (Walter Talun) as King Saul (Francis X. Bushman) looked on. Rising, he touches the Ark and is not killed. David passes Nathan and returns to Bathsheba. Their sin has been forgiven.

The Saturday Review was unimpressed, calling it "a misguided effort to beat Cecil B. DeMille at his own game. Of course, it can't be done.... Gregory Peck lends dignity and his virile good looks to the role of David; but Susan Hayward as Bathsheba appears still to be playing a scheming little dress designer from Seventh Avenue [reference to *I Can Get It for You Wholesale*], while Raymond Massey is a plum-colored grotesque as the fire-breathing prophet Nathan."[37] The DeMille analogy was perceptive. As someone once said, DeMille's historical epics might be corny and simplistic, but they were heaps of fun.

Variety was more positive: "This is a big picture in every respect.... Expert casting throughout focuses on each characterization.... Peck is a commanding personality as the youth destined to rule Israel. He shades his character expertly. His emotional reflexes are not as static as the sultry Hayward in the femme lead.... Massey ... is a dominant personality throughout."[38]

The New York Times labeled the film "a reverential and sometimes majestic treatment of chronicles that have lived three millennia," but was unimpressed by Hayward, calling her "a Titian-tressed charmer who seems closer to Hollywood than to the arid Jerusalem of the Bible."[39] According to *Christian Century*, "Peck creates a believable portrait of king, other characterizations approach stereotypes."[40]

Location work, including a mock Jerusalem, took place near Nogales, Arizona. The perils of location filming once again came to the fore. An airplane carrying a freelance photographer stampeded a herd of camels and forced cast and crew to take evasive action.[41]

Hayward's bath scene was hyped—or, perhaps, exploited. According to a columnist, Hayward said,

> I ran to the Bible to find out what kind of a gal this Bathsheba was because all I could remember was that she took a bath that somehow had rocked a kingdom. I found that Samuel dismissed her in three or four lines.... I discovered that Philip Dunne, the writer, had figured Bathsheba out this way: She had to possess great physical charms to interest David in the first place, and then she had to have intelligence and understanding to hold him.... So I reasoned Bathsheba was the kind who had taken that bath on the rooftop deliberately to catch the eye of David. She was a siren, all right, and not unlike some girls I've known in Brooklyn—and in Hollywood—and once I got acquainted with her I felt better.[42]

In a press release, she said,

> When I approached the role I had pretty well formulated in my mind the woman I would portray, and her behavior under the circumstances which would befall her. But it wasn't until we actually began playing the scenes

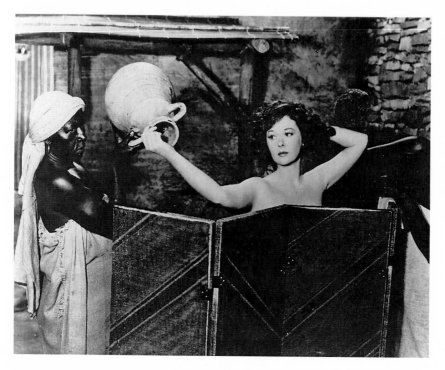

David and Bathsheba (20th Century–Fox 1951).

that Bathsheba came alive for me. This was due, I was quick to discover, to the fact that Mr. Peck *was* David for every second that the cameras turned. He was no longer the actor: he was the character.[43]

Hayward concluded with the old John Wayne summary: "An actor doesn't act—he re-acts."[44]

It is fully Peck's film, with Hayward on standby for several key scenes. She hardly has time to be the schemer Arthur Knight condemned in the *Saturday Review*. She underplays and does a commendable job during her initial "interview" with Peck's David, convincing us that she's modest and shy. Thus, we, as well as David, are surprised when she admits to having created the scenario whereby he would notice her.

Hayward was being recognized. One writer commented that past neglect had led to a sulky disposition, but because of four big pictures in a row and fights by producers for her services her outlook had mellowed. "She is far more outgoing, talkative, peppery…. She's found her tongue— and it quite often bears a resemblance to a whiplash. People don't mind. It goes better with her flaming red hair than her former gloom."[45]

The film itself is very talky and could have benefited from more action. The confrontation between David and Goliath is subdued, to say the least. Fox boss Darryl Zanuck belatedly realized it:

> I have been bombarded by letters from our people all over the world who have learned that we are going to make *The Robe*. They are delighted, but they take this opportunity to beg me not to make the same mistake I made in *David and Bathsheba*. They send me letters from exhibitors telling of their efforts to cut some of the "talk" out of *David and Bathsheba*, so as to make it more entertaining and interesting for their foreign audiences. They tell of the disappointment their patrons have experienced on sitting through a picture where there was talk, talk, talk through some of the biggest scenes of the picture. I'm sure you can understand the disappointment of people who have to depend on titles to tell them what's happening in the climax of a picture.[46]

More Recognition

Prior to *David and Bathsheba*'s August 30, 1951, West Coast premiere at Grauman's Chinese Theater, Susan Hayward put her hand and footprints into cement. Gold flakes were sprinkled over the prints. The teenage Ed Colbert was on the spot:

> She was making a movie—came over on her lunch hour. Drove herself and I believe it was her mother (an older lady) with her in her Cadillac—parked in the parking lot next door—came in the side way to the forecourt. I remember she had cotton at the bridge of her nose because she was wearing glasses (which she did) and she had her studio makeup on. So the cotton protected the studio makeup. We got her autograph and she was nice as usual. (It was part of the business with her.) There were some professional photographers there—fan mags in those days had their own photographers—not like today. NO PAPARAZZI! Everything was simple—no fuss. I was in high school then. Things were so much simpler and easier and civil before the rock star mess. Stars were nice and drove themselves (rock stars really started the limos in the '60s).[47]

Negative reviews had no impact on U.S. business. Depending on the source, *David and Bathsheba* was number four for the year at $4,720,000[48] or made $7,000,000 domestically to top all other films.[49] In one survey *Quo Vadis?* was number one for 1951 at $11,901,662[50]; in another, *David and Bathsheba* was number one for 1951 at that $7,000,000 figure.[51]

David and Bathsheba was Hayward's fourth 1951 release. After the premiere she took a needed vacation on the Campbell River, British Columbia.[52]

Ralph Hathaway (standing) helps Hayward put her hand- and footprints in cement outside Grauman's Chinese Theater, August 10, 1951. (Photograph courtesy of Eduardo Moreno.)

The Korean "police action" pitting United Nations forces against the North Koreans was under way, and Hayward was chosen "Communications Queen" by the 452nd Communications Squadron of the U.S. Air Force. They thought of Susan as the "girl we'd most like to keep communicating with" and considered her the girl "whose beauty, talent and heart give us our biggest lift."[53]

1952

With a Song in My Heart (20th Century–Fox, 1952)

The story: During the annual New York newspapermen's ball, the award for most courageous entertainer of the year is given to singer Jane Froman (Hayward). Sitting in the audience, John Bern (Rory Calhoun) recalls why. Flashback to a young girl singer rushing into WCKX Radio in Cincinnati. Unknowingly auditioning for Don Ross (David Wayne), who himself was auditioning as a singer-songwriter, she finds his moxie helps her secure a day job singing for peanut commercials. At night she gets to do real songs. Soon she's on stage in Chicago and New York, warbling such hits as "Blue Moon." Then she's voted Number One Girl Singer on the Air. Don finally succeeds in getting Jane to say yes, she'll marry him. They honeymoon in Hollywood. Back in New York, Jane produces records and continues singing on radio and in nightclubs while Don is rather unsuccessful at composing songs. Marital arguments ensue. But personal problems are pushed aside as the Japanese attack Pearl Harbor on December 7, 1941. Unknown to her, John Bern is in the audience at the Roxy when she sings such songs as "With a Song in My Heart." Coincidentally, he is part of the plane crew that is taking her via Bermuda and Lisbon to London, where she plans to entertain troops. The plane crashes into the water upon approaching Lisbon. In the hospital, Jane meets nurse Clancy (Thelma Ritter), who cheers her up despite the possibility that Jane will lose her right leg below the knee. Fifteen survived the crash, but not the woman in the seat behind Jane—the seat she originally had. Clancy tags along when Don arrives to take Jane home. Doctors prescribe a "bone graft operation"— one of many. When John arrives and expresses his love for her, Jane tells Clancy she doesn't know what to do because she also has feelings for John. More operations are necessary and Jane returns to showbiz in *Artists & Models*, where she's propped up and attached to supports. The show is a success but she needs yet more surgery. At the Riviera club she sings to a young paratrooper (Robert Wagner). That soldier she meets again when, crutches in tow, she finally gets to Europe. He's now shellshocked, but she elicits some conversation. At her farewell performance she sings songs of the U.S.A. Back home, Don calls John and says he's splitting and that John should meet Jane when she returns. Flashback to the present as John and Clancy watch Jane singing at the ball.

The public liked it. Critical opinion was lukewarm. *The New York Times* said, "We wish we could say that the picture ... was as genuinely affecting as the true-life story it endeavors to extol, for the gallantry of Miss Froman merits sincere regard. But we have to report that Lamar Trotti, who wrote and produced the film; Walter Lang, who directed, and Susan Hayward, who plays the leading role—that of the popular singer— have combined to do a job that is just about as grandiose and mawkish as Hollywood homage can be.... One would not call [Miss Hayward's] performance either subtle or restrained."[54]

Variety said, "While not entirely at home in the dancing accompaniment to some of the production numbers, Susan Hayward punches over the straight vocal-simulation and deftly handles the dramatic phases."[55]

But *Theatre Arts* found it a step up from most biopics. "As a biography *Song in My Heart* seems a bit truer to life than most of its ilk. Its characters are less goody-good, more human"[56]

Look, which featured Hayward on its April 8 cover and numerous photos inside, said, "All in all, Susan Hayward, with the warmth and range of the artist she has become, makes the Froman story a convincing experience."[57] In the same article the film's subject, Jane Froman, said of Susan, "She *looks* like a singer. Every singer knows that when you breathe—it shows. Susan breathes. She understands how to stand, to move, and that gestures must mean something. She didn't copy me slavishly, either. She had tricks of her own up her sleeve."[58]

Years later, critic Molly Haskell pinpointed one reason *With a Song in My Heart* worked: "There's something in her [Hayward] that's kind of spiky and tough that keeps it from becoming completely sappy."[59]

This was one of Hayward's best remembered and best loved roles. Hayward actually let her hair be cut for the part.[60] Around this time she started secretly dying her hair to keep it as red as it had been.[61] *With a Song in My Heart* would give Hayward her third Academy Award nomination. Although he'd appeared the previous year in *Halls of Montezuma*, Robert Wagner is often cited as debuting in this film and is often said to have appreciated Hayward's support.

Although Hayward was allowed to get soaked in a 70 by 70 foot back lot tank doubling for the Tagus River,[62] realism did not extend to using her own voice. Jane Froman herself did the songs. Hayward said, "I'm trying to recreate the essence of Jane's warmth and beauty rather than imitate

As Jane Froman in *With a Song in My Heart* (20th Century–Fox, 1952).

her."[63] She dubbed the songs very well, however, and the music department named her "Sync Queen."[64] Years later, Hayward told Joey Bishop about meeting Jane Froman. "Jane was on the set throughout the shooting of that picture and I mean she really held my hand. You know, Jane's voice was in that picture and I just dubbed to the soundtrack. Every once in a while the boys would cut the soundtrack, and I'd hear myself and I'd think, 'Quick, soundtrack back on.' I couldn't stand myself singing."[65]

Although she didn't sing, Hayward did dance. Dance director Billy Daniel gave her lessons.[66]

According to another press release, after being told to provide luke-warm applause for the "Right Kind of Man" number, the extra said, "Can you beat that—Hayward does a number so hot it makes Hayworth's *Gilda*[67] look ice-cooled—and they want us to be tepid about it! Oh, well, they pay us, but you really work when you have to look bored at that kind of a num-ber. Real groovy how she shakes those hips—and hey, she's got nice steps, hasn't she? Never saw her in tights before. She oughtta show 'em oftener!"[68]

Co-star Rory Calhoun always commented about Hayward's profes-sionalism.[69] Leonard Doss, Fox's ubiquitous Technicolor or Color by DeLuxe color consultant, was one of many behind-the-scenes people who found Hayward prompt and patient and knowledgeable about what was right for her.[70]

With a Song in My Heart won an Academy Award for Best Scoring of a Musical Picture. In addition to Hayward's nomination as Best Actress, nominations came for Best Supporting Actress (Thelma Ritter), Color Costume Design, and Sound.

Said Hayward, "Sure … playing Jane Froman was a rich experience. But let's not kid ourselves. What would *Song in My Heart* have been with-out Jane's voice on the soundtrack? The only good female dramatic chance at Fox [Susan's home studio] since the war was the title role in *My Cousin Rachel*. They told me I wasn't suited for it. It wasn't my type."[71]

With a Song in My Heart was in a sense all surface: glamour and songs. But it's affecting, especially the scenes with the soldiers and when the dis-abled Froman returns to the stage and the audience rises to its feet. Hay-ward is especially entrancing in her "Hallelujah!" red dress and glovelets. Like all studios, 20th Century–Fox made its own share of musicals. Its most successful were the '40s entries with Betty Grable. But it could never com-pete artistically with Warner Bros. (Busby Berkeley) or RKO (Astaire and Rogers) in the 1930s; and in the '40s and '50s MGM was at the top. The actual musical talent that Fox had was often wasted. Like Hayward in *With a Song in My Heart*, Mitzi Gaynor starred in such (smaller in scale) biopics as *The I Don't Care Girl* (1952) and *Golden Girl* (1951). Invariably, Fox did what MGM eschewed: settling its musicals in the theatrical world. Thus all the songs came from performers on stage rather than sung spontaneously wherever the character happened to be. The latter is the art of the cinema musical. Only later, with the Rodgers and Hammerstein epic musicals (such as *Oklahoma!* and *Carousel* and *The Sound of Music*) would Fox convert.

Again, film promotion involved Hayward's portrait in magazine ads. She promoted Tru-Glo Liquid Make-Up from Westmore Hollywood Cos-metics.

Susan Hayward, ca. 1952.

Hayward's personal beauty tips were said to hinge on pure castile soap, two showers per day, and a tub bath followed by rubbing the body with bath oil. During filmmaking, however, she showered in the morning and tubbed at night to soak off the make-up.[72] She wore a pure silk pajama top in winter, slept "raw" between silk sheets in summer. She favored pure silk lingerie.[73]

A handwritten note on the last page of a 1951 Fox press release:

"Johnny. This can be brought up to date. Figured out $14,500,000 studio invested in Susan since 1949–51 making her most valuable player on lot. *Rawhide* with Ty Power, *I'd Climb the Highest Mountain*, *I Can Get It for You Wholesale*, *David and Bathsheba*, *With a Song in My Heart*."[74]

In February 1952, *People Today* said Susan's four 1951 films had taken in $12,500,000, even while a San Francisco film critic voted her "Worst Actress of 1951."[75]

In the Press

Although Louella Parsons was still Hayward's chief champion among the gossip columnists, Hedda Hopper had come around: "When high frequency sex is needed in a starring role, Susan Hayward is the girl who can deliver it. This red head, whose perfect profile runs clear to the ankles, epitomizes everything men look for in a woman."[76] Hayward told Hopper that her favorite actresses were Barbara Stanwyck, Olivia de Havilland and Shelley Winters. Of the actors, Gregory Peck and Dana Andrews.[77]

On March 12, 1952, Hayward visited her old Brooklyn school, which had become Prospect Heights High School. It was "Susan Hayward Day," and 4,500 girl students were in attendance. Hayward visited her favorite English teacher, Florence O'Grady, and told the students, "Keep a strong heart, and don't be afraid to hope and work for whatever you want—as a direct result of working in high school, the doors of Hollywood opened to me."[78]

On October 26, 1952, a taped interview Hayward had granted ABC Hollywood commentator Bill Tusher was broadcast. She said that actors should stay out of politics. "I have an intense interest in my country and in politics but I will not put my views on other people. As just a plain, ordinary citizen I can argue with my friends and the man in the street. But I don't think it's right for me to stand up and give speeches."[79]

Photoplay ran a feature article extolling Hayward's relationship with her sons and husband. They were reported to use the station wagon for fishing. Television? She was said to be lukewarm, preferring a good movie or a play. Dinner parties were small. Cleo was the staff.[80] She liked swimming, seafood and cakes from Ebinger's bakery in Brooklyn. "An instinctive reserve discourages the over-familiar. People like her at Fox but they're not free-and-easy with her. Her faith is simple. She believes God put her into the world for a purpose, and feels a deep responsibility in fulfilling that purpose."[81]

Susan Hayward, ca. 1952.

The Snows of Kilimanjaro (20th Century–Fox, 1952)

The story: His leg infected and possibly gangrenous, writer Harry Street (Gregory Peck) lies depressed and entertaining morbid thoughts as vultures alight in trees near his African camp. When not verbally abusing his wife Helen (Hayward), Harry recalls various episodes in his life, beginning with his adolescence and the rifle his uncle (Leo G. Carroll) gave him to take his mind off losing a girl. Uncle Bill suggested that to be a writer Harry must not be tied down. Grown and gone to Paris to soak up life experiences and write, Harry meets Cynthia (Ava Gardner). She's a sometimes model—sometimes in the all-together—who's made Paris her home after coming over to bring back her father's body. He'd been killed in the Argonne during World War I. Harry and Cynthia take an apartment and Harry writes a book. The advance check allows him to fulfill his dream of traveling to Africa. Learning that she's pregnant, Cynthia becomes distraught when Harry plans a trip and wants to put off having children. Intentionally falling down the steps and losing the child, Cynthia also loses Harry. Harry becomes so successful he can relax on the Mediterranean, where he meets and becomes engaged to the Countess (Hildegarde Neff). Yet he yearns for Cynthia and breaks his engagement. Seeking Cynthia in Madrid, he finds himself involved in the Spanish Civil War. On a battlefield he discovers Cynthia—fatally injured beneath her ambulance. Surviving the war, Harry returns to Paris and meets Helen, who from a distance resembles Cynthia. His reveries over, Harry finds that Helen has tended him back to unexpected health and the vultures are gone. An airplane that can take him to hospital finally arrives. They look toward a better future.

Reviews were lukewarm. *The New Yorker* said, "Occasionally in the course of the picture, we get a glimpse of Hemingway, but to compensate for these lapses Mr. Zanuck and Mr. Robinson have contrived to have the rich lady with whom the hero is sharing a tent on Kilimanjaro display all the nobility of Florence Nightingale and save the boy when the chips are down."[82]

The *New York Times* found it a "handsome and generally absorbing film ... constantly fascinates the eye and stimulates the emotions in small, isolated ways.... Susan Hayward is cool and gentle as his [Peck's] virtually undefined wife...."[83]

Newsweek said, it "represents a considerable perversion of Hemingway's famous tale.... The movie has Gregory Peck and Susan Hayward as the writer and his wife, and their relationship somewhat suggests the original Hemingway. But the flashbacks are mainly new and garishly romantic inventions."[84]

Variety said, "A big, broad screen treatment ... broadens the 1927 short story considerably without losing the Hemingway penchant for the mysticism behind his virile characters and lusty situations. Ava Gardner makes the part of Cynthia a warm, appealing, alluring standout. Gregory Peck delivers with gusto.... Susan Hayward is splendid, particularly in the dramatic closing sequence, in the less colorful role of Peck's wife."[85]

Today *Snows* is less a compelling film than a piece of film history. It was the second pairing of Peck and Hayward, following the previous year's *David and Bathsheba*. It's a movie intended to take advantage of CinemaScope and Technicolor and rouse interest because of exotic African locales. No one would make this today, what with our modern sensibilities about saving rather than shooting African wildlife. In some ways, the movie may be most notable for having been scored by Bernard Herrmann.

Even those with a grasp of the timeline of real history will occasionally think this is set in the time it was released. The only clues to dates are "Argonne" (World War I), a Mideast conflict between French and Syrians, and the war in Spain (Spanish Civil War, 1936–39). More so than even *David and Bathsheba*, it's Peck's picture. Although she receives second billing, Hayward is only around at the beginning and end, and during brief flashbacks. But she gets to voice her trademark scream when a hyena appears at the tent, and then act tough: "I'm not afraid of you. I never was."

Hayward composed her own press release for this film, at least according to 20th Century–Fox. She called attention to the story's breadth and the on-location filming in Africa. She focused on the dangers encountered by location cinematographer Charles Clarke. (Leon Shamroy was principal cinematographer.) She wrote that Hildegarde Neff came down with influenza [not in Africa] and Gregory Peck wrenched his knee, which postponed shooting for 10 days. She spoke of a Masai tribal curse on white men.[86]

Incredible as it now seems, *The Snows of Kilimanjaro* (1952) was a big grosser. One source indicates that it was number four at $6,500,000 with *The Greatest Show on Earth* ($12,000,000), *Quo Vadis?* ($10,500,000), and *Ivanhoe* ($7,000,000) ahead of it.[87] (It seems that 1951's *Quo Vadis?* was still making money and was the ultimate number one at $12,500,000 in North American receipts.[88]) Attribute the grosses to the power-house cast: Gregory Peck, Susan Hayward and Ava Gardner. A few years hence Ava Gardner would return to France and Spain to make another Hemmingway story, *The Sun Also Rises*.

The Lusty Men (RKO, 1952)

The story: After the bull Razor gives him yet another injury, rodeo cowboy Jeff McCloud (Robert Mitchum) hitches a ride to his boyhood home, now the rundown residence of ol' Jeremiah Watrus (Burt Mustin). A jeep pulls up with Wes Merritt (Arthur Kennedy) and his wife Louise (Hayward). They periodically inspect the place, which they intend buying after they save Jeremiah's $5,000 asking price. Recognizing McCloud as the world's saddle bronc champ, Wes invites him home and secures him a job on the ranch where he cow punches. Louise looks askance at Jeff, perceiving him as a threat to her and Wes' goals. Jeff tries to explain the buzz he gets from rodeo. He's done it for eighteen years and has only quit because of busted ribs. Wes enlists Jeff's help in preparing for the San Angelo Rodeo and wins over $400. Louise tries to dissuade Jeff from becoming Wes' handler, and Jeff wonders about her background. "They tell me anything's better than working in a tamale joint—even marriage," he says. She tells him she's a migrant fruit picker's daughter who's never had a home, which she aims to get. When she leaves, Jeff expostulates, "Redheads. What gives a guy the idea that redheads are any different? All they got is bad temper." In the trailer park at the Tucson Rodeo, Jeff renews his acquaintance with Booker Davis (Arthur Hunnicutt) and Rusty (Carol Nugent). Louise meets Grace Burgess (Lorna Thayer), who says her husband Buster is scared and warns Louise to keep her husband away from bull riding. More cheerful is trick rider Rosemary Maddox (Maria Hart), who invites Louise for coffee and a shower in her trailer. At the rodeo, Louise sits with the wives and watches Wes successfully ride the bronc Yo-Yo. Afterward, Wes picks up a cool $879.14, but Louise gives a swift kick in the butt to the floozy making a pass at him. Grace appears. "You call this a *sport*?" Her husband has been killed by a bull. Wes buys Grace's trailer and the trio hit rodeos in Phoenix, Salinas, and Gallup. Wes is a roaring success but Louise can't watch any longer. In Pendleton, Booker tells Jeff he knows the only thing that keeps Jeff in one place is a crap game—or a woman. Louise shows Jeff a telegram from Jeremiah that indicates he'll accept $4,100 for the ranch. Wes, however, ain't havin' none of that. He's rarin' to continue rodeo. What's more, he's sick of Jeff freeloading. Louise is fed up, too. Jeff asks her if she could fall in love with somebody else. Her demeanor suggests a negative, but she dresses to the nines to accompany Jeff to the post-contest party. The floozy (Eleanor Todd) has planted lipstick on Wes' face, and Louise knocks her over. In the hall, Louise asks Jeff to get Wes out of rodeo. He admits that he'd only hung around this long because of her. Wes appears. Jeff tells Louise he'd like a kiss before leaving and she grants his request. When Wes tells Jeff he's yellow, Jeff knocks him into the wall. At the Pendleton Roundup the next day, Jeff enters all contests. Even Wes says "Good luck" to Jeff when he mounts a bronc. Caught in the stirrup, Jeff is severely injured, a busted rib having punctured his lung. Louise comforts him as he passes away. When Wes learns of Jeff's death and then hears his name called for the next event, he calls out, "Pass Wes Merritt." Louise removes his contestant number and, with Booker and Rusty in tow, leaves the world of rodeo.

The *New York Times* said, "With a literal and candid use of camera that would stand out in the documentary field, Director Nicholas Ray has really captured the muscle and thump of rodeos.... And indeed, insofar as a direct and uncomplicated plot demands, Robert Mitchum, Susan Hayward and Arthur Kennedy do creditable jobs in the leading roles." [89] Retrospectively, western historian Brian Garfield said, "Of the three stars two are notably miscast: New Yorkers Hayward and Kennedy are not believable as Westerners," but found that it "has justly become the classic rodeo movie, the one against which all others must be measured."[90]

As denigrated a subgenera as rodeo movies are, there are a number of very good ones. *The Lusty Men* is possibly the best.[91]

The working title was *This Man Is Mine*. It was another loanout for Hayward, this time to RKO. She's first billed. As in *My Foolish Heart*, her character's face shows the thinking going on. As for the miscasting of New Yorkers Kennedy and Hayward about which Garfield complains, both have solid western credits—and believability, especially with Kennedy in *The Man from Laramie* (1955). Hayward, of course, had creditably ridden the range already in *Canyon Passage*, *Tulsa*, and *Rawhide*. Highly evocative are those scenes underscored by Roy Webb's understated music when Mitchum returns to his boyhood home. Rarely has the pathos of the drifter come across so well.

1953

The President's Lady (20th Century–Fox)

The story: A stranger in buckskin rides into a stockaded fort outside Nashville, Tennessee, and spies a young lady trying to nail a picture to the wall. Embarrassed at allowing the man to see her petticoats, Rachel Donaldson Robards (Hayward) demands to know what he wants. Andrew Jackson (Charlton Heston) introduces himself as the district's attorney general in need of lodging. Rachel's mother grants his request. At a dance, Rachel's husband Lewis (Whitfield Connor) comes for her, but upon returning to his home she overhears his conversation with a new young slave girl and confronts him over his infidelity. Jackson shows up some days later at Rachel's request and, after thumping Lewis, takes her back to her mother. Rachel's husband, who rode through the night, vows to come back with his relatives and reclaim her. She secures passage on a riverboat upon which, unbeknownst to her, Jackson is also traveling. Indians attack the boat, but a narrow escape is affected. Rachel and Andrew visit

The Lusty Men (RKO, 1952), with Robert Mitchum.

her relatives in Natchez. A letter arrives indicating that Rachel's husband
received a divorce—on the grounds of adultery. Andrew and Rachel marry.
Two years later they learn that there was no divorce, merely a petition for
one. They are remarried. But the affair leaves its mark, and Andrew has
to fight Rachel's ex-husband's brother, as well as lead the militia against
the Creek Indians, while Rachel tends the farm. Upon his return he builds
the Hermitage and is elected to Congress. Despite Andrew's status, Rachel
is shunned by the Nashville culture club. Their child dies. After winning
a horse race, Andrew is wounded in a duel with the opponent who slurred
Rachel's name. Years pass and he runs for president of the United States.

During a stump speech in Nashville, Rachel, who had been ill, has an attack. Andrew is elected president but Rachel dies. On the steps of the capitol, Andrew remembers his life with the love of his life.

The *New York Times* found it a "reverent and highly sentimental tribute to Andrew and Rachel Jackson…. In this spaciously picturesque offering the equally picturesque Susan Hayward and Charlton Heston are allowed an emotional gamut perfectly befitting one of the most compelling and poignant romances of the early American scene…. The stars make sincere and energetic but hardly memorable protagonists."[92] *Variety* called it "a particularly moving narrative…. Through it all, Charlton Heston supplies the kind of ammunition to this film that is as loaded as any carbine slung across his broad shoulders. It is a forthright steely-eyed portrayal. Susan Hayward gives the pic a simple, sustained performance in addition to physical beauty."[93]

Hayward's co-star, Charlton Heston, yet to play Moses, Ben-Hur or El Cid but rising in the ranks, got on well with her. "If there was an actress who could keep the audience interested in the Jacksons' domestic affairs, it was Susan Hayward. As Rachel, she gave us the tough frontier girl, the passionate wife, and the doughty companion."[94] Heston added that in an early scene Hayward "was really cooking."[95]

Jackson's recollection scene of his life with Rachel is moving. Heston would play Andrew Jackson once again in *The Buccaneer* (1958).

Honors

In 1953, *Photoplay* announced that Hayward and Gary Cooper were the winners of its Audience Research, Inc.–conducted poll. Hayward would receive her gold medal for *With a Song in My Heart,* and Cooper for his performance in *High Noon.*[96] Cooper couldn't make the ceremonies at the Beverly Hills Hotel on February 9, but Hayward was on hand to accept her award.[97]

The Foreign Press Association of Hollywood presented gold statuettes to Susan and John Wayne at the World Film Festival held at the Club Del Mar in Santa Monica on February 14. They were voted most popular motion picture stars internationally. Vincent Price was master of ceremonies. William Holden and Greer Garson presented the awards. Robert Wagner was one of the new stars given recognition.[98] Accepting the award from William Holden, Susan said, "Thank you very much, ladies and gentlemen. I'm very happy to receive such an honor and I accept it with great humility, knowing full well that a performer is only the result of many people working very hard together. Thank you."

Wardrobe test for *The President's Lady* (20th Century–Fox, 1953).

Susan appeared on the cover of the March 1953 issue of *Filmland*.

Also in 1953, Hayward took another much-needed rest. She and husband Jess spent several months traveling around Europe, stopping in Paris, Madrid, Rome, Biarritz, and Valencia.[99]

White Witch Doctor (20th Century–Fox, 1953)

The story: Ostensibly guiding nurse Ellen Burton (Hayward) to a remote African village via canoe, Lonnie Douglas (Robert Mitchum) and Huysman (Walter Slezak) are determined to venture into the Bakuba country in hopes of finding gold. On the way, Ellen cures a chief's wife (Dorothy Harris), but in so doing threatens the witchdoctor's prestige. He unsuccessfully looses a tarantula upon her. After saving a boy injured by a lion, Lonnie discovers that the boy is the Bakuba chief's son and is wearing a golden necklace. After the boy returns home, the chief sends for Ellen. Ellen explains to Lonnie that she'd come to Africa to do penance for a wrong she perpetrated upon her late husband. In the Bakuba chief's camp, Lonnie and Ellen are accused of having guided Huysman and his henchmen to the vicinity. Lonnie owns up to Ellen but petitions the chief to let him convince Huysman to leave the territory. Huysman naturally doesn't believe there's no gold in the area. Wrestling for a gun, Huysman is killed. Lonnie returns to the village, finds the chief's son fully recovered, and learns he and Ellen are free to leave. But they decide to stay and do what service they can for the tribe.

The *New York Times* found it an "amazingly unsurprising romantic adventure moving methodically along well-beaten film paths.... Susan Hayward is fetching even in the apparel of the safari."[100]

Whereas Hayward had been loaned to RKO to co-star with Mitchum in 1952's *The Lusty Men*, now it was Mitchum's turn to be loaned to Fox for this distinctly old-fashioned and merely adequate jungle adventure not much filmed in a real jungle.

Travel Experiences

Upon her return from Europe to film *Demetrius and the Gladiators*, Hayward wrote a guest column for Dorothy Kilgallen. She compared the Continental with the American way of life, and extolled the pleasures of touring by car. "This way you really see the countryside, you really meet the people, since no city gives you anything but a one-sided conception of how people really live. Primarily, I was interested in the life of the everyday woman in Europe." They did get to the cities, though, and in

Paris ran into Gregory Peck, who gave them tips. She spoke of the Marshall Plan, and said she loved Spain. As for the ordinary European, "They find it difficult to believe, for instance, that motion picture stars have been first gas station attendants, ditch diggers, elevator girls. This, to them, symbolizes America—this is democracy—where class distinctions don't stand in the way of the individual's progress. I agree with them one hundred percent. Amen."[101]

1954

Demetrius and the Gladiators (20th Century–Fox, 1954)

The story: After sending the tribune Marcellus and the patrician Diana to their deaths, the Roman Emperor Caligula (Jay Robinson) becomes agitated during a thunderstorm. Entering the apartments of his uncle Claudius (Barry Evans), he passes through the bedchamber of Claudius' wife Messalina (Hayward). The three confer on the supposed supernatural power inherent in the robe of a crucified Eastern messiah named Jesus. Messalina says it was given to a slave. That slave is Demetrius (Victor Mature), who hides it from the legionnaires searching for it amongst the Christian community. After Demetrius attacks a legionnaire accosting his friend Lucia (Debra Paget), he is overpowered and sentenced to a gladiator school. Learning that he is a Christian who will not take another's life, Messalina schemes to make him fight. Befriended by Glycon (William Marshall), Demetrius pretends to fight, but the crowd and Emperor sense that the men are perpetrating a sham. Glycon warns Demetrius that he must try to kill him, but he falls and Demetrius has the upper hand. He asks the Emperor to spare Glycon. Caligula does so, but only to release three tigers upon Demetrius. Nevertheless, Demetrius is triumphant. Under the care of Messalina, Demetrius recovers. Claudius questions him about Jesus' robe and expresses admiration for the young man, who seems the bearer of virtue the Romans once possessed. Claudius urges Messalina not to harm him, but she begins a seduction of the new palace guard. Caligula accuses Messalina of trying to assassinate him, but she employs her wits, telling him that as Priestess of Isis she has been informed that Caligula is indeed a god. Retiring to her villa, Messalina is unsuccessful in seducing Demetrius and sends him back to the gladiator school. Ordered to have him fight, Strabo (Ernest Borgnine) assigns him to the next day's contest. That evening the designated gladiators are free to frolic with wine and women. Learning of Demetrius' whereabouts from

Paula (Anne Bancroft), Lucia inserts herself into the crowd of women. Watching from a hidden alcove, Messalina realizes that Lucia knows Demetrius. She tells Strabo to remove Demetrius from the next day's contests. Demetrius is forcibly removed but watches the evening's proceedings from behind an iron grate. Dardanius (Richard Egan) and others grab up Lucia. Demetrius calls on his god to protect her but she collapses, seemingly dead. The harassing gladiators look on Demetrius with much trepidation. The next day Demetrius grabs a sword and rushes into the arena and overcomes trident and net man Dardanius. After Glycon uses a flaming rod to urge Dardanius' cohorts into the arena, Demetrius dispatches them all. Praetorian Prefect Cassius Charea (Charles Evans) asks the Emperor to grant Demetrius his freedom and induct him into the Praetorian Guard. Messalina asks Caligula to put the question to Demetrius, who responds that there is no god but Caligula, "in this world or any other." Members of the Guard raise him on his shield. Attending Messalina in the Temple of Isis, Demetrius tells her that he didn't denounce his god to accept this obscenity. There's only this world, him and her. While they revel at her villa, Caligula taunts Claudius about Messalina's trysts. During one, Peter (Michael Rennie) arrives. Messalina tosses wine in his face before Demetrius appears. In a heated discussion, Demetrius tells Peter he will no longer listen to him. After Peter leaves, Demetrius learns that Glycon had asked Peter if a man such as himself who'd killed thirty men in the arena could ever sleep at night. Messalina tells Caligula that the Fisherman (Peter) is back in Rome, whereupon Caligula orders the Guard to capture the holy man. Demetrius goes to his former Christian friends and finds Peter, and, more importantly, Lucia— still alive but in a catatonic state, and gripping the robe. Kneeling beside her palette, he remembers that day on Calvary. Then he feels Lucia's hand on his head. She's awake. Peter gives Demetrius the robe to take to the Emperor. Bearing the robe, Caligula retires to a dungeon and has Macro (Karl Davis) kill a prisoner. But calling on the power of the robe to resurrect the man does not work. It's a fraud, he tells Demetrius, who advances in a rage and must be restrained. Caligula orders him into the arena to fight Macro. Messalina pleads with Demetrius to put up a fight but he drops his sword. Macro knocks him to the earth but the Guard expresses its disapproval and Cassius Charea demands life. Caligula rejects the overtures, only to witness the spearing of Macro and then his own impalement. Claudius is made Emperor on the spot. Taking his position in the throne room, Claudius tells Demetrius to tell the Christians that as long as they commit no acts of disloyalty they are free to practice their religion. Messalina addresses the crowd: "It's no secret from any of you that I've mocked my marriage vows, that I've openly disgraced my husband and myself. That too is ended. I am Caesar's wife and I will act the part." She wishes Demetrius well. Demetrius and Glycon exit, meeting Peter on the Augustan steps.

Taking it literally, *The Times* of London was harsh:

> So far as Cinemascope is concerned there are no grounds of complaint, but there is something repugnant about a formula which shows itself determined to exploit sensationalism under the cloak of religiosity. This convenient formula allows the utmost license when it comes to the killing of men and animals in the arena and revels in the wickedness of Messalina, and then thinks it can put itself right by references to the robe Christ wore, by perfunctory introductions of St. Peter (Mr. Michael Rennie) and by a flashback to the foot of the Cross. Nor is it the real corruption, the reeking madness and vice of Rome the film shows, but only a colour-supplement approximation of it, just as the righteous attitudes it strikes are false and formal.[102]

More positive was *Variety*, which found the direction and Victor Mature compelling. "With Mature easily winning top acting honors for his splendidly projected Demetrius, he is pressed by Susan Hayward as the evil Messalina, and Jay Robinson, repeating his mad effeminate Caligula."[103] The *New York Times* appreciated that it "got right down to the business of making a good old-fashioned Roman circus film ... equal cuttings of spectacle, action, sex and reverence." [104]

Demetrius and the Gladiators was the sequel to the previous year's *The Robe* [premiered September 1953], based on Lloyd C. Douglas' historical novel. *The Robe* had been given the honor of being the first commercial film in CinemaScope. Richard Burton, Jean Simmons, Victor Mature, Michael Rennie and Jay Robinson starred in a somber and reverent (i.e., unexciting) adaptation. *Demetrius*, originally titled *The Gladiators*, was less successful but remains heaps more fun. Doubtless more people saw it when it first appeared on TV as one of the entries during the first season of *Saturday Night at the Movies* in 1961. Many were the teenagers who couldn't wait to see a "gladiator movie." Even today one gets a charge when the massed gladiators march toward the camera to the accompaniment of Franz Waxman's score (as thrilling as Alfred Newman's for *The Robe*), and when Demetrius grabs a sword and rushes into the arena to take vengeance on Dardanius, following this up with single-handed victory over Dardanius' gang. It's thrilling to see Glycon prod them into the arena. When one protests that it's against the rules, Strabo grabs a whip and yells, "We changed the rules!" That would get big laughs in a theater today. (There's precious little humor in 2000's *Gladiator*.)

A Fox press release quoted co-star Victor Mature as saying that Hayward was "Garbo with a difference ... Garbo doesn't talk. Susan talks but reveals very little about herself." The release admits that Hayward was a guarded personality, a woman who won't be dissuaded once she makes up her mind. For instance, she rejected all pleas to cut her hair. Fox's chief designer Charles LeMaire: "She was saving it for *The Gladiators*.... It's just perfect style—for first century Rome!" And Susan's hairdresser, Emmy Eckhardt, was frequently approached for information, all to no avail. "So, probably unintentionally, Susan Hayward has revealed some of the things 'that make her tick,' after all. She is disciplined, humorous and practical. Much of her true personality remains a mystery. However, since mystery is an active ingredient of glamour, it is possible that mystery is a contrived product of her discipline—or her sense of humor."[105]

Despite the contention by some that this was "a blatant misuse of Susan's time and talents,"[106] Hayward is not mere window dressing but physically and facially fulfills one's fantasy image of the nymphomaniac Empress. In important scenes she saves Demetrius' life, argues with Peter, and tells Caligula Peter has returned. Not every film need be a hard-bitten, realistic drama providing its protagonists Shakespearean depth. In reality, Messalina continued cheating on Claudius, and as the many viewers of the U.K. BBC television series *I, Claudius* (1976) know, the Emperor finally had enough and she was beheaded. In *Demetrius* Messalina says she'll be a good wife. But we know from earlier in the film that she's a liar. A nice touch is her farewell to Demetrius and the expression of grief that touches her face—an expression that we see but Demetrius and Claudius do not.

Early in the film the Emperor abruptly enters Messalina's apartments. Her maidservant alerts her and she sits up in her bed, a vision to behold. Enter CinemaScope: Messalina is now rather distant on the right, while one must almost turn one's head to the left to see Caligula speaking to her from screen left. Pictorially one can only imagine how this could be filmed in a more liberal age, i.e., after the MPAA was instituted in 1968. It could be tastefully done, with the sheer curtains barely concealing a nude Messalina.

Garden of Evil (20th Century–Fox, 1954)

The story: In need of repairs, a ship bound for California stops at a Mexican port. Holing up in the local tavern, passengers Hooker (Gary Cooper), Fiske (Richard Widmark), and Daley (Cameron Mitchell) are astonished to see a beautiful redheaded American woman enter and offer a hefty payment to anyone who will follow her into the interior. Leah Fuller (Hayward) has a husband trapped in a mine. The three Americanos

As Messalina in *Demetrius and the Gladiators* **(20th Century–Fox, 1954).**

and one Mexican, Vicente (Victor Manuel Mendoza), agree to accompany
her. The lengthy journey takes them across dusty plains and through ver-
dant forest. After ascending a hazardous mountain path, they exit into a
land of bizarre beauty. A town has been buried by volcanic ash, its church
steeple visible above the lava. Fuller (Hugh Marlowe) is found alive. Using
brute force, the men extract him. While splinting Fuller's broken leg,

Hooker is told it doesn't matter—the Indians will soon destroy them all. The savages had let Fuller alone, figuring his torment was no more than they could provide. Distant smoke signals and a feather found near the cabin suggest that Fuller is correct. Leah hatches a scheme whereby the men will take her husband and escape. She'll remain behind and tend the fire to make things seem normal. Fiske volunteers to stay with her, but she says he means nothing at all to her. As the men prepare to leave, Hooker knocks Leah unconscious and they all gallop off. During a stop, Fuller convinces Daley to help him onto a horse. As he watches Fuller ride away, Indian arrows find their mark in Daley's back. Shortly thereafter Fuller is found dead—tied upside down to a stone cross. Next to die is Vicente. Hooker, Leah and Fiske make the mountain pass, where they stop and pick off the pursuing savages. Hooker plays card-sharp Fiske to see who'll remain behind while the other two escape. Fiske wins and Hooker leaves with Leah. Beyond the mountain Hooker stops and says he's got to return—Fiske cheated him. Using his carbine to good effect, Hooker makes his way back to a dying Fiske. As the sun sets, Hooker rises from his friend's body. "If the earth was made of gold, I guess men would die for a handful of dirt." He rides back to Leah and they leave the garden of evil.

For decades *Garden of Evil* was forgotten by all but cineastes, yet at its release it received some cogent, if not complimentary, analysis, especially from the *New Republic*'s Martin S. Dworkin, who began his review with a brief analysis of the western genre and later said, "Most revealing is Bernard Herrmann's score, complete with an echo of "Dies Irae" as Susan Hayward pokes around a ruined chapel. The music often sounds good—too good, for it is conceived in a tenor of heroic depth that gives the lie to the goings-on."[107]

The New Yorker wasn't kind either, and was rather condescending to the western genre:

> I suppose one shouldn't expect much in the way of three-dimensional characters in a Western, but the makers of this one have assembled a gang that is more than usually dreary. The hero, played by Gary Cooper, is supposed to have once been a sheriff, and his conversation consists almost entirely of monosyllables. The second in line, portrayed by Richard Widmark, is a gambler who wants to die—just why I failed to discover—and the third (Cameron Mitchell) is a cad who has made a living shooting criminal fugitives in order to get the price on their heads. As the lady in the case, Susan Hayward never quite convinced me that she was capable of winding men, even men like these, around her finger.[108]

The *New York Times* found it "more of a fascinating journey to an exotic area than it is an unusual story.... Miss Hayward, while decorous, is a lady whose character is not quite clearly defined."[109] *Time* also appreciated the scenic aspects: "*Garden of Evil* ... is a western for farsighted people. The foreground—in which four hombres ... trail off after a pert little gold digger (Susan Hayward) in search of gold or whatever else may be in them thar hills—is hardly worth looking at. But the background, the Mexican landscape, is one of the grandest the world has to show, and the gates of the CinemaScope camera are flung wide to show it all."[110] Brian Garfield put it in better perspective in *Western Films: A Complete Guide*: "Exciting with fast action and fabulously scenic Mexican vistas ... and a thrilling score.... The soft-spoken adventurer Hooker is in a number of ways the quintessential Gary Cooper screen character."[111]

Garden of Evil had been filmed on location, and what a location: the "lost world" west of Mexico City. On February 20, 1943, the volcano that became known as Paricutin erupted from a cornfield, its effluvium burying the nearby town and surrounding area until becoming dormant in 1952. The church spires sprouting from the lava field are seen in the film.

Gary Cooper said, "The action, the characters, the romance, the background—everything is meaningless without suspense of outcome.... And threaded through the primary suspense of plot must be secondary moments of suspense climaxed by high action. In other words, the audience must be made to care what happens next.... It is the woman's battle and the primary suspense of the film is whether or not she can hold her own against such gold-hungry, gun-happy characters as Widmark, Cameron Mitchell, Victor Manuel Mendoza—and me."[112]

In a one-minute interview on a dubbing stage, Hayward said, "One could feel that the things that happen to us in the story were real—that men would fight among themselves for a woman, that others would be tempted to steal her gold, that some would go mad from the suspense of ever-present danger. It was the first time I had made a picture entirely on location, and it was a rich and rewarding experience. I believe we have given to *Garden of Evil* a feeling of realism that never could have been achieved on a sound stage."[113]

In keeping with her avowed interest in foreign lands and peoples, Hayward added, "These trips have given me a deeper appreciation and feeling for my work. You sort of get the pulse of the world and are able to achieve a broader understanding of the characters you are asked to portray."[114] But Susan got home for Christmas, although nobody else did. It was likely that Howard Hughes used his influence to circumvent political red tape for foreigners working in Mexico.[115]

Garden of Evil was one of the last of revered film composer Bernard Herrmann's scores to be recorded onto CD, but two versions appeared in 1999, one on the Marco Polo label, the other on Varese Saraband.

With Cameron Mitchell in *Garden of Evil* (20th Century–Fox, 1954).

It's a spare western, hard and pictorially beautiful. Director Hathaway was a master of outdoor films. He'd previously directed Hayward in *Rawhide* (1951).

Problem with Location

After a long and bitter trial, Susan Hayward divorced her husband Jess Barker on August 17, 1954. She received custody of the twins, with

Barker granted visitation rights.[116] Susan's problems with her ex-husband weren't over, however. Barker's attorney filed a motion for a new trial on October 4. The petition presented Barker's objections to Susan taking their twins to Hong Kong for a film (*Soldier of Fortune*), thus necessitating their removal from school and endangering their safety.[117] Superior Judge Herbert Walker denied Susan the ability to take her children to Hong Kong. Barker had said the city was "invested [sic] with Communists and disease." Hayward startled everyone by saying she wouldn't go alone. Sid Rogell, executive production manager, had explained how much preliminary overseas effort had already occurred.[118]

1955

Untamed (20th Century–Fox, 1955)

The story: Come to County Limerick, Ireland, in 1847 to procure horses for his South African compatriots trying to create a new state, Paul Van Riebeck (Tyrone Power) meets Katie O'Neill (Susan Hayward), whose reckless riding causes him to fall with his mount. He takes her horse and forces her to walk his steed back to the estate. He calls her a killer but they share a certain rapport. Nevertheless, he returns to South Africa. Behind him the potato blight devastates Ireland and Katie's farm. She marries Shawn Kildare (John Justin), they have a child and sail for South Africa and a new, hopefully kinder land. Arriving in Capetown, they are mentored by the DeGroot family and apprised of an imminent trek eight hundred miles into the interior where fruitful farmland will be found. Trek leader Simon's son Kurt (Richard Egan) has eyes for Katie, despite his involvement with the fiery Julia (Rita Moreno). Paul and his commandos fail to meet the trekkers at a river crossing as planned. He is, however, cognizant of the danger the Zulu army poses the trekkers. When the Zulus arrive, fifty horsemen ride out to seek peace, but the Zulus charge. Loosing a volley, the riders return to the lager. Things look grim until Paul arrives with ammunition and his own skillful tactics. The Zulus are dispersed, but Katie's Shawn is among the dead. Paul can hardly believe he's met her again. "I, I can hardly believe it. You, Katie, here in Africa, fighting Zulus." Kurt tells Paul he fought at Katie's wagon, meaning he has a claim on her unless there's something between her and Paul. Paul acknowledges no ties. The trek continues until a fertile expansive valley is reached. During a celebratory dance, Katie tells Paul that she really came to Africa to see him. He admits to kindred feelings and they embrace. Kurt confronts them, and he and Paul engage in a battle of whips. Defeated, Kurt vows not to be "tricked" again. Paul and Katie plan a house facing the river while Paul continues to dream of a free state. A small house is finished, but Paul's comrade, Christian (Brad Dexter), arrives to urge Paul to rejoin the commandos before the group disintegrates. Katie professes her love, but Paul leaves while she sleeps. Katie rides into town, tells Paul she hates him and slaps his face. Paul and the commandos ride off. With Kurt in tow, Marge DeGroot (Faye Emerson) visits Katie. Despite their history, Katie hires Kurt to plough the land—and also invites Julia to reside there. During a storm that ravages the farm, lightning strikes Katie's special tree, which falls on Kurt. His right leg is amputated. When gold is found in the hills, Katie trades her possessions with the natives for the gold—and a huge diamond. With the proceeds, she settles in Capetown. But she's not happy. The free state becomes a reality, except for representation in the assembly. In Capetown at his childhood residence, Abendblum, now Katie's manse, Paul meets with the governor. The next day he returns and learns of the existence of Paul, Jr. Why didn't Katie tell him? She retorts that she couldn't find him and says she never wants to see him again. He says he'll return for the child, but she says he must kill her first. Katie loses the manse and heads inland to search for diamonds. Katie encounters Kurt in Colsberg. He is one of many outlaws at large in the land. Paul's commandos approach. Kurt plans an ambush, but Paul detaches Christian with part of the force and the battle is won by Paul's side. Paul's scout Tschaka (Paul Thompson) kills Kurt with a spear. Paul bids adieu to Christian, Tschaka and the commandos and gives Katie a ring. "Where to, Paul?" asks Katie. "Back to the land," he replies.

The *New York Times* said, "The performances of Susan Hayward as the lady, John Justin as her Irish spouse, Tyrone Power as the commando leader and Richard Egan as the fellow who works the farm are mechanical and unrevealing. They are handsome automatons."[119] *Natural History* liked the historical background: "The film gives an insight into the hardships and privations that the early settlers went through in establishing a Dutch Free State in South Africa..."[120] Observing its western-like elements, one writer said it had "an actionful Edna Ferber sort of plot with most of the story devoted to romantic rivalries among the various personnel. It's a lavishly junky movie that's totally predictable—the sort that gave Hollywood a bad name among sophisticates who prefer a bit of substance with their corn."[121]

Like *Raintree County* (1957), *Untamed* would be measured against *Gone with the Wind* and found wanting. With all that's going on, it required another hour for depth. The human emotions seem a bit perfunctory. And what exactly are the commandos doing when Paul's away? Fighting Zulus, guarding the border, creating farmsteads? On the positive side, it does have scope, a wonderful line ("You, Katie, here in Africa, fighting Zulus"), and a fine Franz Waxman music score. The latter was released on the *Film Score Monthly* Golden Age Soundtrack CD label in 2001 and promoted in a full-page color ad in the February 2001 issue of *Film Score Monthly*. The Zulu attack on the wagon lager is exciting, in particular the scene where the Zulus rush forward and the trek horsemen let loose a volley, turn and retreat. Assegais fly at the camera 3-D style.

Publicity

While promoting *Untamed*, Hayward supposedly authored another publicity release concerning misconceptions about Hollywood. She called it a fine place to raise children and argued that there was "no such 'Hollywood atmosphere,' just as Hollywood itself does not exist as a town but is a part of huge sprawling Los Angeles."[122]

Another Fox release commented upon Hayward's divorce and reclusiveness. "In most important respects, her reticence remains, but after all she has testified that her angry husband chased her nude from the house to the swimming pool. Plainly her private life all along has contained some elements of drama not apparent in her reports of family fishing trips and of fly-casting practice on the margin of that same swimming pool." Regarding *Untamed* and its Irish character, which might seem autobiographical, Hayward reportedly said, "No, I wish I were like that. I used to think I knew what I wanted but I don't anymore—nor how to get it if I did. I want to be happy, but who doesn't?"[123]

On December 13 Superior Judge Herbert Walker ordered Hayward to pay ex-husband Barker's attorney $10,000 in order for him to handle Barker's divorce appeal, which had been granted in August.[124]

Chapter 5

Personal Problems, Professional Triumphs

There are girls in Hollywood whose outer hardness conceals only an inner hardness. Miss Hayward, I would say, is not in this class. She has miscalculated too often to be accused of being calculating. She struck me as being intelligent, gifted and blunt—down to earth without being earthy. An acknowledged glamour girl who does not talk with her hips, but in the normal way, and has things to say which are worth hearing.

—Thomas Wiseman, The Seven Deadly Sins of Hollywood[1]

The April 16, 1955, issue of *Cue* featured a smiling, girl-next-door-fetching Susan Hayward on its cover and a one-page article summarizing her busy film schedule. It was predicted that she'd be making a million dollars within five years.[2] But the price of constant work, plus her ex-husband's refusal to let their divorce stand, pushed the actress over the edge that same month.

The Tuesday morning, April 26, banner of the *Los Angeles Times:* "SUSAN HAYWARD FOUND UNCONSCIOUS IN HOME."Hayward had ingested an overdose of sleeping pills. Providentially, she had phoned her mother to inform her of her drastic action. "I think something's wrong with my daughter," Ellen said when telephoning the police, who got to Hayward's 3737 Longridge Avenue Sherman Oaks home at 3:35 a.m.[3]

The equally large *Los Angeles Herald Express* headline read: "ACTRESS

SUSAN HAYWARD TRIES SLEEP PILL SUICIDE." A picture showed an unconscious Hayward being given oxygen. Her stomach was pumped at North Hollywood Receiving Hospital, and she regained consciousness at Cedars of Lebanon Hospital. Her doctor, Dr. Stanley Immerman, concluded that the suicide attempt was caused by Susan's despondency over her marital problems. Her brother Wally agreed and added that she'd also been working too hard for two studios.[4]

Soldier of Fortune (20th Century–Fox, 1955)

The story: Jane Hoyt (Hayward) journeys to Hong Kong in search of her missing photographer husband Louis (Gene Barry). Neither the U.S. Consulate nor the British government are willing to help her. She does obtain some assistance from Inspector Merryweather (Michael Rennie), who shows her cameras she identifies as her husband's. Directed to a dive called Tweedie's, Jane finds Rene Chevalier (Alex D'Arcy), who points her in the direction of Maxine Chan (Frances Fong). Maxine in turn puts her onto Hank Lee (Clark Gable). Hank is a smuggler and soldier of fortune who, to get in Jane's good graces—and hopefully something else—decides to help her, which will entail springing Louis Hoyt from behind the "Bamboo Curtain" of Red China. Tweedie (Tom Tully) learns that Louis is in Canton. In the company of Merryweather, Hank sails his junk to the mainland, secures Louis and pilots his junk back to Hong Kong while using a previously camouflaged heavy weapon to keep at bay a pursuing Communist vessel. Jane and Louis are reunited. Hank tells Jane, "Ya know, all my life I've wanted to meet someone like you, someone I could believe in. I was beginning to think there wasn't anyone. I never thought I'd find out the hard way. Can I trust you to be a little cagier with this? Thanks for knowing you."

The New York Times called Soldier of Fortune "a glib and implausible fiction that would be embarrassing to a grade-B film.... Even if Susan Hayward, who plays the uxorial role, were ten times as beautiful and exciting ... it still wouldn't stand to reason that Mr. Gable would act as he does."[5] Time called it a "tiny melodrama against the vast, eye-filling CinemaScope backdrop of Hong Kong harbor.... Into this storybook East comes plucky Susan Hayward, thrusting her determined chin at consular aides, British policemen and inscrutable Chinese who do not seem sufficiently eager to drop everything and help search for her husband (Gene Barry) behind the Bamboo Curtain."[6]

Released in June 1955, Soldier of Fortune had been set to shoot in Hong Kong. However, Hayward's scenes were filmed on Hollywood sets

With Clark Gable and rear-projected Hong Kong harbor in *Soldier of Fortune* (20th Century–Fox, 1955).

because she couldn't take her children abroad due to a court order and protestations from her ex-husband.[7] Said the film's director, Edward Dmytryk, "Susan Hayward's marital problems would keep her from going to Hong Kong, so we decided to shoot her exterior scenes only in long shots, using a double...."[8] Dale Logue was that double, and she became Hayward's stand-in for location shots in future films *Back Street* and *Where Love Has Gone*.[9] *Soldier of Fortune* is not the poor film some writers say. Some people label any film bad if it's not a masterpiece. *Soldier* is a watchable but not very exciting adaptation of a better novel by Ernest K. Gann, a writer of very popular airplane and sailing yarns frequently made into films, e.g., *Island in the Sky*, *The High and the Mighty*, *Twilight for the Gods*, *Fate Is the Hunter*. The title promises action, but it's really a romance.

Director Dmytryk summed it up nicely: "I read the script and recognized that it was indeed a potboiler, though possibly one of the better ones. It wasn't up to the quality of films I'd been doing lately, but—there was Clark Gable, the King, Susan Hayward, a fine actress, and Hong Kong."[10]

Further Turmoil

In September Susan took her boys on vacation to Hawaii. She had no comment on a paternity suit against her ex-husband.[11]

In November Susan's year of tumult took another unexpected turn that had reporters' typewriters clacking again. "SUSAN HAYWARD BEAT ME UP, CHARGES FILM BEAUTY" screamed the November 4 issue of the *Los Angeles Herald Express*. Starlet Jil Jarmyn, returned from a New Orleans location shoot for the Roger Corman–directed *Swamp Women*, charged that Hayward had tried to beat her up when she entered the home of Donald Barry, Jarmyn's former fiancé. Barry had been making *I'll Cry Tomorrow* with Hayward. A spokesman for Hayward quoted her, "I'm terribly sorry. I am sure she wasn't hurt. It was just a tempest in a small teapot." Jarmyn charged that Susan hit her over the head with a wooden clothes brush, bit her thumb and tore buttons from her blouse. "She was like a wild woman.... Donald quieted her once. He went to the kitchen to make some coffee, then Susan attacked me again. I tried to leave several times. I finally succeeded."[12]

Long-time Hayward admirer and confidante Louella Parsons weighed in. According to the columnist, Hayward told her,

> It's a great big ruckus over nothing. I went, at 9 o'clock in the morning, to have a cup of coffee with Don—it's as simple as that—when this woman, Jil Jarmyn, walked in. She made a very insulting remark—so insulting I cannot even repeat it. I don't take that kind of talk from anyone, so I slapped her, and slapped her hard. She turned on me and we had a real tussle. She hit me and I hit her. It wasn't over Don Barry. My anger was at this woman, whom I never saw before, daring to use such language.[13]

Another columnist took Hayward to task and equated her with Robert Mitchum and Ava Gardner. Although it might have been a frame-up, and he didn't plead guilty, in 1949 Mitchum had served jail-time for conspiracy to possess marijuana. At the 1954 Cannes Film Festival he'd been photographed with a topless starlet on the beach. Gardner was a rebel, oft-married and gallivanting around Europe. The columnist refreshed the readers' memories on how Hayward had been projected as a devoted wife and mother, wholesome and religious:

> There can be little doubt that such ballyhoo was instrumental, along with her undeniable great talent, to catapulting her to ranking stardom. For her to jeopardize that exalted position through continued revolting, wanton escapades not only may prove suicidal to her career, but it is an ungrateful, thoughtless, devastating blow to the creators, the companies and the overall industry that were helpful in establishing her high estate. Producers

should, and probably will, think twice before they seek her to topline more expensively budgeted features, most especially any that are as volatile, per se, as the Roth tome.[14]

I'll Cry Tomorrow was the "Roth tome," and Van Spear was decidedly wrong about producers thinking twice about using Hayward again. Maybe that was because *I'll Cry Tomorrow* was a hit, Hayward's greatest professional triumph to date.

I'll Cry Tomorrow (MGM, 1955)

The story: After failing to get an audition, eight-year-old Lillian Roth (Carole Ann Campbell) asks mom Katie (Jo Van Fleet), "Are you a stage mother?" Katie pushes Lillian to the pavement. Regretting her action, Katie asks Lillian to stop crying, she has all day tomorrow to cry. One day, Katie says, they won't have to audition, Lillian will be in demand. Soon Lillian *is* on stage with the Keith Circuit in Chicago. Then it's back home and Broadway. The years pass. Lillian (Hayward) is on a Paramount set belting out "Sing You Sinners." Although Katie tried to keep Lillian in the dark about his presence, David Tredman (Ray Danton) finally gets through to his childhood friend and Lillian visits him in a nearby hospital. He claims his illness is not serious. "You don't turn back!" cries Katie when in New York she learns that Lillian wants to marry David. But Katie need not worry. David dies. Heartsick, Lillian goes on with the tour in David's honor but berates her mother for daring to think she always knows what's best for her. Lillian's nurse Ellen (Virginia Gregg) gives Lillian a drink because she can't think of anything else that will produce a good night's sleep.

Almost by accident Lillian finds herself married to Wallie (Don Taylor), a soldier and admirer she'd once met. She and Wallie spend most of their free time arguing—and drinking. Freed of her husband after one particularly vicious row, Lillian attends a party and meets Tony (Richard Conte), a self-assured fellow who handles a drunk for Lillian. She doesn't know that Tony beat the guy up in another room.

Lillian tells Katie she can stop drinking whenever she wants, but her hand shakes when she writes out the check for her mother's upkeep. Nevertheless, Lillian can always belt out a tune on stage like "Happiness Is Just a Thing Called Joe."

Tony reenters her life and they marry, but Lillian finds that Tony isn't what he seemed. He's a wife beater. In California, Lillian ditches Tony only to find herself wandering the streets, pawning her fur coat, and being taken advantage of by other men. She finally collapses in front of a Chinese grocery. The owners contact her mother.

Back in New York, Lillian rents a hotel room and considers leaping from the window. But she calls on God's help and falls back into the room. Outside, she notices an Alcoholics Anonymous sign in a window and ventures inside where she meets Jerry (Don Barry) and Selma (Margo). Bert (Eddie Albert), who'd taken to drink after contracting polio, becomes her confidante. Bert, Selma and other AA members watch over Lillian as she struggles through withdrawal.

Accompanied by Bert on the piano, Lillian practices her singing with such tunes as "Red, Red Robin." Lillian tells Bert she's got bookings but also the chance to tell her story on TV. Bert says she'll have to make the decision, she doesn't need him anymore. "Love me, Bert. We belong together," is her reply. In California she marches resolutely down the aisle to share her saga on Ralph Edwards' TV show *This Is Your Life*.

For one of the paramount films in the Hayward canon, some critics carped—though none were wholly negative. Said the *Saturday Review*,

> Susan Hayward is now, without question, our most prominent portrayer of movie drunks. In *Smash-Up*, a few years back, she took to the bottle and skidded down to the row, causing some of us to wonder, during the process, if she wasn't an actress of ability as well as a good-looking young lady. In *I'll Cry Tomorrow*, her latest alcoholic vehicle, she has extended the range of her *Smash-Up* performance, given it more hysterical and haggard overtones, and has added a degree of what I can only term overall twitchiness.[15]

Hayward's performance was compared with Frank Sinatra's heroin addict in that same year's *The Man with the Golden Arm*. Sinatra was felt to be less mannered, more at ease, while "Miss Hayward, on the other hand, is always in there pitching. I had the impression that she was acting throughout, and when I'm aware, too much, that someone is acting I'm not so easily convinsed [sic]. Nevertheless, she goes to great lengths to literally throw herself into the part."[16]

The *New York Times* found the film a "poignant picture of a top vaudeville singer's decline into the valley of alcoholism and her tough but triumphant return.... The one weakness of this picture—as a psychological study, at least—is its failure to make it seem compulsory that the heroine should take to belting booze.... Don Taylor and Richard Conte as washout husbands and Ray Danton as the short-lived fiancé are pretty mechanical figures. They are in the weak part of the film. The strong part is that in which Miss Hayward indicates the actual agonies of Miss Roth."[17]

One harsh review was a retrospective one:

> Whenever she's on screen with Jo Van Fleet—playing her screen mother—

you don't notice her, she's colourless in a plastic part, wrapped in cellophane; whereas Van Fleet, if not exactly flesh and blood, at least does her job in an interesting way (for instance, no reference is made to their being Jewish, but Van Fleet's intonation and mannerisms suggest it). Later in the film, Hayward has to portray an alcoholic—admittedly without help from either script or direction, and she just cannot supply what they lack. Davis, Stanwyck and even Crawford were given equally difficult tasks—their villainesses—but they could always suggest some motivation for their actions.[18]

Like the *Saturday Review* critic, this one may not have read Roth's book. In it Roth comes across as naive and immature. The reader is often perplexed about motivation, whether in her choice of mates or decisions to consume alcohol in vast quantities.

Look had a contrary, positive take, calling *I'll Cry Tomorrow* "one of the year's most remarkable films, told with an unsparing truth that will leave audiences shaken. The story's emotional power is vividly communicated by Susan Hayward in a shattering, intense performance that may win her an Academy Award. Daniel Mann, who directed for MGM, also becomes an Oscar candidate for his sensitive, almost documentary handling of the tragic story."[19]

Library Journal was on the same page:

Lillian Roth's extraordinarily self-revealing book has been translated to the screen in an unprettified version which will seem courageous and powerful to some, and shocking to others.... The role provides Miss Hayward with a tremendous dramatic challenge, in terms of both range and depth, and she is equal to it throughout. She makes the deterioration and eventual complete degradation of a lovely and talented person a really heart-wrenching experience.[20]

Hayward had lobbied for the part after reading Roth's 1954 book. Written in collaboration with Mike Connolly and Gerold Frank, it described Roth's rise to singing-acting fame on stage and in film in the '20s and '30s, her various failed marriages, descent into alcoholism and recovery. The book was the number-six bestseller of 1954, according to *Publishers Weekly*. MGM had originally targeted June Allyson for the film lead. Pert and perky, Allyson specialized in wifely roles opposite James Stewart in *The Glenn Miller Story* (1954) and *Strategic Air Command* (1955), and Alan Ladd in *The McConnell Story* (1955). Playing a "drunk" would have been casting against type. Maybe she could have done it. She did play *The Shrike* (1955). Nevertheless, Hayward seems a better candidate due to her popularity, experience in heavy drama, and her past role miming real singer Jane Froman in *With a Song in My Heart*.

Hayward would not simply mimic Lillian Roth's body language and

On the set of *I'll Cry Tomorrow* (MGM, 1955).

arm movements. Under the tutelage of vocal coach Bobby Tucker and maestro Leon Cepparo, Hayward did her own singing. "The new Voice is sultry and professional and may very well turn out to be a milestone in a screen career already heavy with acting honors."[21]

MGM's musical director-composer Johnny Green had been impressed when testing Hayward:

It would simply be a voice-match job like Eleanor Parker's for Marjorie Lawrence in *Interrupted Melody*, or Susan's own for Froman's in *Song in My Heart*. But we have a regular procedure here whenever voices are to be dubbed. No matter how definitely an actress may be a nonsinger, we try to get a recording track of her talking seriously, talking lightly, laughing, etc. Even if she is tone deaf, even if she can't carry a tune.

We then have a frame of reference—not only timbre and pitch, but also peculiarities or characteristics of speech. If the actress is used to pronouncing it 'wah-ter,' for instance, the double has to sing it that way in the song. When we have picked the double we put her and the actress together for weeks, so that she may acquire the actress' vocal mannerisms.

Susan was terribly interested in who would be her voice. She was also terribly self-conscious about making a tape. That day she was right here in my office; I made everybody get out, put the mike in the middle of the room, and mooched over to the piano by easy stages.

I played a little and Susan hummed a little. Somehow we got onto "Let's Fall in Love." Susan knew the Arlen tune. Finally—"You asked for it!" she said, kicked off her shoes and waded in. When she finished I was all choked up, wet around the eyes.[22]

Hayward called Green a Svengali. "I was shaking all over—stage fright. Johnny cracked jokes and said relaxing things. Then he suggested, 'I'll play the piano and you sing.' Well, you begin to enjoy it and before you know it there you are—a ham. It's kind of fun to go along with it and I'll try to make good."[23]

Hayward told *Look*:

I read her [Lillian Roth] book when I had the flu. I got out of bed, called my agent, said I must have the part—it belonged to me. I felt it was a great story of a very courageous woman, whose problem everyone should understand.... And the wonderful thing is that everything went easy for me, even the drunk scenes. This had never happened to me before. Danny Mann checked every detail. He wouldn't let me cheat with lipstick or even a curl. If he thought my hair wasn't mussed enough, he put water on his hands and mashed it down.[24]

Decades later Susan's son Timothy commented on the film:

I've had a very difficult time watching that movie. That movie is really who she was. Some of those scenes in that film—the little nuances—the way she twists her nose, the way she moves her hands or her head. That's, that's who I saw in front of me. That's the reality of who this person was.[25]

Hayward had made *I'll Cry Tomorrow* for MGM. At Hayward's home studio, Fox, Darryl Zanuck explained why he'd turned the film down.

This is a very interesting solid, downbeat story and, while it has an outstanding performance by Susan Hayward, I considered it to be overrated. Here again it did not quite live up to my expectations from the standpoint of quality, but also here again I believe we made a mistake in passing up this property....

We turned down *I'll Cry Tomorrow*, frankly because we were all afraid of the subject matter and of the fact that Lillian Roth was not a really famous personality. [Producer Julian] Blaustein wanted it but only if he could get Marilyn Monroe for the role....[26]

One can't help but be inspired by Hayward's march down the aisle at the end of the film. *I'll Cry Tomorrow* grossed an impressive $6,000,000.[27]

With Lillian Roth (left), Susan's character in *I'll Cry Tomorrow* (MGM, 1955).

1956

Celebrity chronicler Earl Wilson somewhat gingerly approached Hayward for an interview in January 1956. He was advised not to ask about her troubles. He did, however, broach the Don Barry incident, asking if she had intentions of marrying him. "It never entered my thoughts.... It's a very distasteful subject, and actually I think you're no gentleman to bring it up." He asked what she did want to talk about. "My plans for the future—I do have the possibility of singing and singing well." They also spoke about *I'll Cry Tomorrow* and Lillian Roth and the press. "I always find the press to be pretty fair," was Susan's comment on how it treated her.[28]

The March 20, 1956, issue of *Look* featured Hayward and James Cagney on the cover as the winners of the magazine's fifteenth *Look* Movie Awards. Hayward was pictured inside in a scene from *I'll Cry Tomorrow* ("A Hollywood-trained player since 1939, she gives a performance that does the industry great credit: a many-sided and poignant study of the dissolution of a human being and her fight to be rehabilitated").[29] Susan and Cagney were also pictured standing hand in hand in a circle. Behind them sat past winners of the *Look* awards, and it is a sterling cast indeed, including William Holden, James Stewart, Teresa Wright, Broderick Crawford, Jean Hersholt, producers Walter Wanger and Walt Disney, and cinematographer James Wong Howe. The same issue featured a full-page color ad for *The Conqueror*, Hayward's next released picture.

Hayward cut the ribbon at the "Salute to the United States Air Force" exhibit in Pershing Square on March 7, 1956.[30] Various film stars pitched their films on television, sometimes at the studio's request. Richard Widmark appeared on an episode of *I Love Lucy* to promote his film *Time Limit* (1957). In 1956 Hayward made one of her rare television appearances as a guest on *The MGM Parade*. Host George Murphy spoke with her about her fishing skills and *I'll Cry Tomorrow*. A scene from the film was shown.[31]

In March 1956, Hayward appeared on the TV show *Climax*. She played herself in "The Gay Illiterate," a dramatization of Louella Parsons' autobiography. In December 1956, in another TV appearance she accepted a *Wisdom* magazine award for writer Pearl S. Buck.[32]

Cannes

Hayward went to Cannes, France, where she and Kim Novak were among those smiling for paparazzi.[33] Hayward won the best actress award for her role in *I'll Cry Tomorrow*.[34] Back in Hollywood there were some cheers and at least one rather over-the-top but intriguing compliment:

Miss Hayward's performance in *I'll Cry Tomorrow* WAS a performance. The Academy winner, Anna Magnani's, was not. The work of the Italian actress

At the Cannes Film Festival, 1956.

in Rose Tattoo was Anna Magnani, NOT a performance; nothing different from any of her other portrayals. It was the real life gal, doing the only thing she knows how to do BUT with Susie Hayward, her work in *I'll Cry* was an acting accomplishment that has hardly ever been equaled on our picture screens, requiring as it did an artistry that only an actress of the caliber of Miss Hayward could accomplish.[35]

Hayward's next release was about as far as one could get from the realism of *I'll Cry Tomorrow*. She played a 13th century Tartar princess.

The Conqueror (RKO, 1956)

The story: As Targatai (Leslie Bradley) crosses Mongol territory with his bride Bortai (Hayward), daughter of Kumlek (Ted deCorsia), Mongol leader Temujin (John Wayne) pays a rather good-natured harassing visit. Much impressed with the litter-lounging Bortai, he returns with more of his men and drives off Targatai and his guard. To appraise Bortai more thoroughly, he rips off her gown. Flinging an animal robe over herself, she glowers at him. Back at his camp, Temujin concludes, "I feel this Tartar woman is for me." For her part, Bortai is not keen on the relationship: "I do not dance for jackals!" Intent on reclaiming his bride, Targatai raids the Mongol camp but is killed. Bortai's escape attempt is foiled by Temujin, who forces his attentions upon her and finds his ardor temporarily reciprocated. Back in the burning camp, Temujin hatches a scheme to ply Wang Khan (Thomas Gomez) with gifts while lying to him about a planned attack by Tartars and Merkits. During the festivities in Wang Khan's walled city, dancing girls hold forth. Contrary to recent pronouncements, Bortai leaps onto the floor and dances with veil and sword. At the end of the routine she hurls the sword toward her captor but misses. Wang Khan's shaman (John Hoyt) tells Temujin that his master is old and soft, the time right for a virile younger man to rule the Gobi. Before he can digest this information and act, Temujin is bushwhacked. Escaping, he hides in a cave. After pretending to offer his services to Kumlek, Temujin's brother Jamuga (Pedro Armendariz) is tracked to Temujin's hiding place. Temujin is told Jamuga betrayed him. Having second thoughts about her late captor, Bortai helps Temujin escape. Back at the Mongol camp, Temujin learns that Jamuga did not betray him. Jamuga and Kasar (William Conrad) are sent to Wang Khan to seek an alliance. Wang Khan's shaman has other plans, and Kasar is murdered but Jamuga escapes, only to be captured by Kumlek's men. Meanwhile, Temujin gains easy access to the city. The shaman stabs Wang Khan but does not live to benefit because the dying ruler reveals his shaman's perfidy to Temujin. At the Tartar stronghold, Bortai convinces her father to spare Jamuga, if only to find Temujin. She convinces Jamuga that she loves his brother. Jamuga tells her Temujin is destined for greatness. Temujin gathers his forces, and defeats and kills Kumlek. Though innocent of treason, Jamuga realizes he can no longer live with his brother and plans a quick death for himself. Temujin and Bortai ride into history.

Aiming her sword at John Wayne in *The Conqueror* (RKO, 1956).

The *New York Times* called it "simply an Oriental 'Western.' An illusion persists that this Genghis Khan is merely Hopalong Cassidy in Cathay.... Of course, she [Bortai] is a delectable dish, who, despite heavy dialogue and filmy costumes, is none other than Susan Hayward."[36]

Time: "'This Tartar woman is for me,' drawls Big John through his Fu Manchu mustache as Susan ('much woman') Hayward goes dawdling sensuously through the desert ... the terror of two continents takes almost two full hours to win one girl, so the script just skips the conquest of Asia."[37]

As with many a Hollywood period piece, *The Conqueror* was the victim of bad writing and a concentration on the protagonist's early years, which limits the spectacle youthful audiences and military historians crave. With the resources at hand, and a sterile desert instead of steppe grass serving as the location, invasions of China, Persia and Russia could hardly be pictured. Who would pay for the sets and the thousands of riders?

Hayward looks confounded or befuddled in a few scenes, as if she knows this is malarkey. But remember this: in this era of filmmaking it was hardly unusual for actors to take period parts. Of course, John Wayne as Genghis Khan is a stretch. And a red-haired Tartar woman? It's this strange casting and the writing/dialogue that make *The Conqueror* often ludicrous. There are a few saving graces, one being excellent horsemanship. On one level that's what this movie is: horses galloping, horses falling, horses skidding down desert scree. Another plus is music from one of Hollywood's greatest composers, Victor Young, who'd scored *Shane* and the Hayward films *Reap the Wild Wind* and *My Foolish Heart*. Perhaps RKO wanted to outdo Universal with its mini-epics, including *Sign of the Pagan*, the Attila story with Jeff Chandler and Jack Palance. *The Conqueror* was practically remade in 1965 as *Genghis Khan*, an international co-production that was just as full of hokum as *The Conqueror*.

Hayward does quite well in her dancing girl number. Apparently she thought her legs weren't her best physical attribute and they were veiled. The veils helped the illusion that she was a dancer. Her pantaloons were so high the navel was hidden, of course.[38]

Under billionaire and RKO studio owner Howard Hughes' guidance, *The Conqueror* had been filmed many moons before but was perceived as a work in progress. But editing did not save it from becoming known as an all-time hoot.[39] Yet, according to *Variety* it did gross $4,500,000 in U.S. and Canadian rentals.[40]

Events on the set in Utah's Escalante Desert were pretty wild. According to John Wayne's wife Pilar:

Some movies are lucky. Not this one. During the filming, Duke's costar, Susan Hayward, developed a wild passion for him. She was headstrong and determined. My presence in St. George fed her jealousy, and her heavy drinking diminished her inhibitions.

One night a group congregated at Duke's house for one of those impromptu gatherings that are so much a part of life on location. We were all talking and drinking when Susan came up to me, a wild gleam in her gorgeous eyes. "Take off your shoes," she challenged, kicking her own high heels into a corner, "and fight me for him!" I knew at once the him was Duke, and I didn't know whether to laugh or put up my fists.[41]

Seen now, the ads for *The Conqueror* are hilarious. In some, Wayne (in traditional haircut) holds a sword in his right hand and clasps a distraught Hayward by the waist in his left. "THE MAN with the might to conquer the world! THE WOMAN with the lips to conquer the man!" In another, Hayward is reclining in the foreground while Wayne is pictured in the rear with a fur hat and holding a falcon. "The Warrior Who Shook The World!" is proclaimed. And above Hayward: "This Tartar Woman matches his fury with flame ... meets his fire with ice!" In yet another the tagline is: "She is for ME ... my blood *says take her!*" Wayne, again with traditional haircut, holds Hayward's arms from behind. She's shown wearing the "dancing girl" outfit. Still another has Wayne clasping Hayward on a horse: "SPECTACULAR as its barbaric passions ... and savage conquests."

There was a ten-cent Dell comic book tie-in that featured color photos from the movie on the front, black and white inside the cover. As befit its image with parents, Dell toned down the sex and violence. Thus no frames depict Temujin killing Bortai's father. Neither is Bortai seen dancing. Jamuga does not say he wants to die, but merely predicts his brother's future greatness.

1957

Top Secret Affair (Warner Bros., 1957)

Top Secret Affair co-starred Hayward with another popular leading man, Kirk Douglas.

The story: Having initiated the Joint Atomic International Commission and promoted her daddy's friend, George Radburn, for top spot, *News World* publisher Dorothy Peale (Hayward) is agitated beyond belief when she learns that Redburn has been passed over in favor of Major General Melville Goodwin (Kirk Douglas). Dorothy plans to cast aspersions on Goodwin's character and enlists her underlings, Phil Bentley (Paul Stewart), Lotzie (Michael Fox), and Bill Hadley (Charles Lane), to dig up dirt on the war hero. At the direction of the Army, Goodwin arrives at Peale House for an interview. Loaded questions are buffeted aside, and it's realized that the general will be a hard nut to crack. But Lotzie keeps getting compromising photographs and Dorothy acts the femme fatale.

Goodwin goes for it and they paint the town red. Nevertheless, Goodwin can hold his liquor and it's Dorothy who gets pie-eyed. But Goodwin feels he's been made the fool and tells information officer Gooch (Jim Backus) that he's leaving. But Dorothy, still three sheets to the wind, dares him to come down and teach her a lesson. She falls from the diving board into the pool and Goodwin rescues her. When sober, she wonders how she got into a bathing suit. Goodwin massages her neck, then they engage in some affectionate byplay. The next day Dorothy tells Phil to change their editorial policy and can the incriminating photos. But a reserved Goodwin informs Dorothy that he only loved one other, a French woman who turned out to be a spy during the Korean war. He had her executed. He won't be burned again. Dorothy reverses her editorial policy and the scathing attack on Goodwin is printed. Not knowing that, Goodwin reverses his own position, returns to Dorothy and proposes. She's so obviously shocked he tells her to render her answer the next day. But when the *News World* hits the stand that day, a Senate inquiry into Goodwin's behavior and character is instigated. During the ensuing inquiry, Dorothy admits that her article was unfair and untrue. Nevertheless, she can't disprove the spy affair. At the eleventh hour a declassified Top Secret document is produced that explains how Goodwin was under orders to continue his affair with the French woman, and that the only information he gave her was false. The reporters and veteran protestors against *News World* rise in exaltation. Dorothy exits and is harassed on the way to her car. Goodwin follows her outside, grabs her in a judo-like hold and ushers her to the car. He enters first—as usual. Dorothy shrugs at Phil.

The *New York Times* said, "You're never able to be sure what sort of military character this General Goodwin is. Neither are you able to generate much sympathy or regard for the man-handling woman publisher who suddenly sprouts a fancy for him ... Kirk Douglas and Susan Hayward play the top roles with bruising aggressiveness...."[42] *Time* felt that "the story merely borrowed the names and professions of Marquand's characters and was thrown together as a frothy comedy, presumably on the theory that if a plot is silly enough, it is bound to be funny. It isn't."[43]

Warner Bros. had sought to promote the film through personal details about Hayward:

She is refreshingly natural and lacking in conceit. She has only one vanity—her natural red hair which she washes, brushes and sets herself. She always refused to have it cut short to suit current fashions until *Top Secret Affair*. Then it was her suggestion that her locks be shorn in keeping with the ultra modern business woman she portrayed in the film.

She prefers suits to dresses and is partial to black and white. She is a gourmet and an excellent cook, but maintains her weight at 112 pounds

With Kirk Douglas in *Top Secret Affair* (Warner Bros., 1957).

without dieting. She is an accomplished mimic but is not the "life-of-the-party" extrovert. She is an intelligent conversationalist and well informed on many subjects. Yet she can't make small talk at social gatherings.[44]

Despite being a generally enjoyable comedy with two big stars, *Top Secret Affair* has no reputation at all. Douglas doesn't even mention it in his autobiography, *The Ragman's Son*. Character actor Paul Stewart, always welcome whether villainous (*The Window*) or noble (*Twelve O'Clock High*), delivers the film's best line when observing Hayward leading Backus on a tour of her manse: "Look at her, the gracious Borgia."

Second Marriage

Susan had been divorced from Jess Barker for almost two and one half years when, on February 8, 1957, she eloped with Floyd Eaton Chalkley. They were married by a Justice of the Peace, Stanley Kimball, in Phoenix, Arizona. Chalkley was a former FBI man said to be practicing law in Georgia. That's where they made their home. The marriage seemed to surprise everyone, including Susan's mother and 20th Century–Fox.[45]

Hayward talked to old chum Louella Parsons, who relayed the information to the public:

> Shortly before the ceremony, Susan telephoned me to tell me of her happiness. She said she and her bridegroom will honeymoon in New Orleans and then go to Carrollton, Ga., where Chalkley has a home…. Ever since the red-headed beauty met Chalkley, who is a well known attorney in Carroll [sic], Ga., she has been devoting her time to him when he was in Hollywood. Chalkley was formerly with the FBI and resigned to practice law and became an investigator for individual firms. Because of the secrecy of his work, little has been published about him.[46]

More details on Chalkley's life and the courtship were provided by Chalkley's friend Vincent X. Flaherty, who said he knew him as a "high school, college and professional football and basketball player, and when he got a law degree and became an agent for the Federal Bureau of Investigation." Flaherty said Chalkley left the agency after World War II, picked up other laid-off agents and started an investigating agency, and installed industrial security systems. Flaherty claimed to have urged Chalkley years earlier at a Mocambo nightclub party to dance with Hayward. "Hey, Eaton, why in the world don't you dance with Susan?—mix in, pal, mix in."[47] Flaherty expanded his tale of introducing Eaton to Susan at the Mocambo after she won her Academy Award in 1959.[48]

As Hayward moved to Georgia, attorneys worked out a visitation agreement for ex-husband Jess Barker and the twins. Barker would have one weekend per month, half of the Christmas and Easter vacations, and the first half of their summer vacation.[49]

In October Susan signed with Joseph L. Mankiewicz' independent film production company, Figaro, Inc. The film in question would be based on the life of the late Barbara Graham, executed in California's gas chamber for murder. Walter Wanger would produce. "Producer is elated about Miss Hayward's deal, for, it's noted, actress could have formed her own company, but Figaro offers her production guidance."[50]

Hayward signed again with 20th Century–Fox for five pictures on a non-exclusive basis when her current contract expired the following year. Fox had purchased the rights to the filmization of John P. Marquand's novel *Stopover Tokyo*, and this was thought of as a vehicle for Hayward.[51] In the long run, Joan Collins costarred with Robert Wagner in an unmemorable film.

1958

Hayward was so happy in Carrollton, Georgia, that she expressed a desire to retire from the screen. "It's absolutely true. I'd quit today if I hadn't made some contracts before I was married." She loved the change of seasons and riding. Her sons, 13, were in a military academy near Atlanta. She'd enrolled them there because of talk the public schools would be closed in a segregation dispute.[52] She said, "I don't miss Hollywood in the slightest. I don't even miss my psychiatrist." She said Carrollton residents accepted her "as Mrs. Eaton Chalkley. The townspeople are just as gracious and lovely as they would be to anyone else. I'm never asked for autographs, nor do they make a fuss over me." But she contradicted herself simultaneously, telling another interviewer "she is not retiring from the screen. 'I have six more pictures to make for 20th Century–Fox and two independents coming up.'"[53]

Yet Hayward told another columnist she was seriously thinking of retirement after her contractual obligations were fulfilled. "I'm living. Peacefully and happily at last. I didn't know life could be so wonderful. My husband's Georgia friends have accepted me as one of them and we hardly ever talk about Hollywood."[54]

Hayward's mother died of a heart attack on April 15, 1958. She was seventy years old. Hayward was at the bedside when Ellen succumbed at Mount Sinai Hospital.[55]

The summer had its own problems. While Susan was in Lone Pine, California, making *Thunder in the Sun* (then known as *Between the Thunder and the Sun*), Eaton fell ill. Susan and Eaton's 16-year-old daughter June, who had been visiting the set, took a plane to be with him.[56]

I Want to Live! (United Artists, 1958)

The story: Babs (Hayward) and Peg (Virginia Vincent) have accompanied two men to the New Frisco Club in Las Vegas. A policeman tries to bust Graham's "date" for transporting a woman across state lines. Despite the certainty that she'll be convicted of solicitation, Graham saves her date from a federal charge by claiming she paid for the room. After serving her time, Babs heads for San Francisco, where she is convicted of perjury after giving two men friends an alibi. Before being released, she's given a pep talk by a matron who urges her to try marriage. She has, she says, but does so again with bartender and small-time crook Henry Graham (Wesley Lau). They have a child but split up when he can't shake his dope habit. To get money, Barbara returns to Emmett Perkins (Philip Coolidge), who runs a theft ring. He, she and Jack Santo (Lou Krugman) are tailed to their hideout. Before surrendering, Santo beats Babs up. As a defiant Babs emerges, newspaperman Ed Montgomery (Simon Oakland) asks for an exclusive. She merely shakes her child's toy tiger in his face. Grilled by the police, she declines to become a stoolie and is shocked to be charged with the murder of the elderly Mrs. Monahan. In court, she's identified as the murderess by gang member Bruce King (James Philbrook), whom Babs once spurned as a romantic partner. Babs has no real alibi and allows an inmate to persuade her to pay a friend to supply one. However, Ben Miranda (Peter Breck) turns out to be an undercover policeman who's entrapped her into indicating she was at the scene of the murder. Her lawyer isn't much help. She'd wanted the public defender but he was handling the other defendants. The jury convicts and the judge sentences Babs to death at San Quentin. Leaving the courtroom, she blames Montgomery and the media for playing her up as the murderess from day one. After testing her in Corona prison, psychoanalyst Palmberg (Theodore Bikel) concludes that Barbara Graham is amoral but not violent. She's also left handed, and Bruce King said she held the gun in her right hand. Accepting the possibility of her innocence, Montgomery uses his paper to tell the story of Babs' horrid childhood. Babs' petition to the Supreme Court is denied, and she is transferred to San Quentin. Neither the state courts nor the governor will commute her sentence. It appears that the other gang members on death row aren't fessing up to the crime because they think a woman won't be gassed. Unfortunately, Palmberg dies, leaving too few notes on his latest investigation. While the gas chamber is being readied, matrons, the warden, and guards at San Quentin make Babs' last days comfortable. Stays occur. Babs wants it over and tells her lawyer not to beg. She demands a mask so she won't have to see the newsmen watching the execution. The Captain (Dabbs Greer) advises her on the best way to take it. She responds, "How would you know?" He pats her shoulder. When it's over, Montgomery watches the host of reporters speed away in their cars to file their stories.

Critics were impressed with the film and Susan's performance. Kinder than he was when reviewing *With a Song in My Heart* in 1952, The *New York Times'* Bosley Crowther wrote:

> Susan Hayward has done some vivid acting in a number of sordid roles that have called for professional simulation of personal ordeals of the most upsetting sort. But she's never done anything so vivid or so shattering to an audience's nerves as she does in Walter Wanger's sensational new drama, *I Want to Live....* Anyone who can sit through this ordeal without shivering and shuddering is made of stone. And Miss Hayward plays it superbly, under the consistently sharp direction of Robert Wise, who has shown here a stunning mastery of the staccato realistic style. From a loose and wise-cracking B-girl she moves onto levels of cold disdain and then plunges down to

With Dabbs Greer (left) and Russell Thorson guiding her into the gas chamber in *I Want to Live!* (United Artists, 1958).

depths of terror and bleak surrender as she reaches the end. Except that the role does not present us a precisely pretty character, its performance merits for Miss Hayward the most respectful applause.[57]

The Saturday Review found it "as impassioned an argument against capital punishment as we are ever likely to get from Hollywood.... Its inhumanity, the scientific precision of a state execution, is in itself shocking. When linked to a presumption of innocence, it becomes the forthright indictment of an entire system."[58]

Library Journal was impressed:

> Dominating the film, and on the screen almost every minute, is Susan Hayward.... The direction is terse and realistic and, in the final death house scenes, mounts to unforgettable and almost unbearable tension.[59]

During filming, columnist Sidney Skolsky argued that Hayward amazed the theatrically trained cast members. "She continues to win their respect and admiration daily. They didn't expect a movie star to be an actress. They don't know how she does it. She doesn't seem to have a method." Furthermore, "She and celluloid are compatible and combustible." Of such emotional roles, Hayward said, "I love them. The greater the emotional stress, the more I revel in it."[60]

Note the Hayward trademark: first appearing sitting straight up in bed from outside camera range. It hearkens back to *Demetrius and the Gladiators* when, as Messalina, she sits bolt upright as the Emperor Caligula enters her chamber. Stretching the coincidence, we can find a similarity with her first appearance in *The Conqueror*: lounging in a Tartar wagon.

Producer Walter Wanger had been making a comeback. He had served four months at the Wayside Honor Farm in Castaic, California, for shooting his actress wife Joan Bennett's agent, Jennings Lang, on December 13, 1951. He had suspected Bennett and Lang of adultery. Although he and Bennett reconciled at the time, they divorced in 1962.[61]

At beginning and end:

> You have just seen a FACTUAL STORY. It is based on articles I wrote, other newspaper and magazine articles, court records, legal and private correspondence, investigative reports, personal interviews—and the letters of Barbara Graham.

> Edward S. Montgomery
> Pulitzer Prize Winner
> San Francisco Examiner

I Want to Live! was the movie that caused many baby boomers to question the use of capital punishment. Director Robert Wise said that Mankiewicz urged the filmmakers to make a statement about capital punishment after the gas chamber scene. "We said, 'Joe, if our story hasn't been an indictment of capital punishment, then we failed miserably. We shouldn't have to talk about it now—the picture should have made the point.'"[62]

Wise thought the Babs Graham character needed to be played by someone who'd experienced "a difficult childhood. And at the same time, I wanted this actress to express qualities that normally wouldn't be found in a person coming from this upbringing. I felt Susan Hayward was ideal for this difficult role."[63] Wise also thought Hayward empathized with Graham because both had had public image problems with the press.[64]

Wise confirmed that Hayward kept to herself when not before the camera. "Like many stars, she had her own group on the set—a makeup man or a hairdresser, and a wardrobe woman—and between setups they would stay in the dressing room chatting or playing cards."[65]

Despite the actress' reserve, Wise found that "working with Susan Hayward was a satisfying, stimulating experience. Her characterization and performance were beyond any of our expectations. That she accomplished this with professionalism and lack of phony temperament is a tribute to the actress and the woman."[66]

Wise and Hayward had but one problem: the cinematographer. Wise recalled the issue more recently:

> I saw *I Want to Live!* as having a very realistic, documentary feeling to it. I didn't want it to be too slick and polished. I had seen some of Curly Lindon's work at Paramount and decided he was right for it. Susan Hayward had another cinematographer in mind [Stanley Cortez] and that led to my only set-to with her. The photographer she wanted was very good, but used to making things look lovely and nice; he would not be on my list of candidates at all. We were in a stand-off on this. Finally, her agents told her to see me and try to get this very important matter resolved. I told her the cinematographer she wanted was wrong for the kind of picture I saw this being and held my line on it. She went back to her agents and they advised her to give in to me. She did, but she watched those dailies like a hawk all the way through. After the first couple of days, I thought I might lose Curly because she was complaining that her neck was not looking good, but we found ways of dealing with it that still fit the photographic approach we had for the picture.[67]

Much was made of the jazz score and the musicians: Shelly Manne, Jack Sheldon, Bill Holman, Frank Rosolino. Composer Johnny Mandel was challenged by the "musical treatment of the gas chamber preparations and the execution itself. You know, Bob Wise, the director, fought for music in those scenes. At first, I didn't want to write anything for them. Then, I saw Bob's point. So I wrote a score to be played at a very low level, using the instruments in their freak registers. The reason for this is sim-

With David Niven after the 1959 Academy Awards telecast.

ply that at this point you *have* the audience. There's no need for thunder and lightning."[68]

The nature of the film gave Hayward the opportunity to make one of her infrequent TV appearances. She was interviewed on CBS' *Person to Person* in 1958.[69]

Academy Award at Last

Tangible kudos began flowing Susan's way. She won the best actress award at the International Film Festival held in Mar Del Plata, Argentina.[70] Sardi's Restaurant was the venue for the New York Film Critics award ceremonies and Hayward was there to accept their Best Actress award on January 24, 1959. The proceedings were taped for broadcast on NBC's *Monitor* program and radio's Voice of America.[71]

More significantly, Hayward finally won the Best Actress Academy Award on Monday night, April 6, 1959. The RKO Pantages Theatre in Hollywood was the site. Flanked by co-presenters James Cagney and Kim Novak, who handed her the statuette, Hayward made a brief acceptance speech: "Thank you very much, ladies and gentlemen. And thank you, ladies and gentlemen of the Academy for making me so very, very happy tonight. And my special thanks to Mr. Walter Wanger who made this possible. I thank you." Susan acceded to host Jerry Lewis' request to return from backstage for another bow.[72]

At the post-ceremonies party at the Beverly Hilton, Hayward reinforced her regard for producer Wanger by telling Louella Parsons, "I'll always make a picture for him. I feel I owe him so much."[73]

Years later Hayward confirmed that "the reports were true about what Walter Wanger said when I won the Academy Award. He said, 'Thank God, now we can all relax. Susie finally got what she's been chasing for twenty years.'"[74]

Vincent Flaherty, himself a columnist and old friend of Eaton's, described the pandemonium that attended Hayward's victory. "Going from the theater to the Beverly Hilton, the winner had been mobbed by greater numbers of autograph seekers than ever before. Police had to extricate Susan and Eaton from the Pantages Theater, had to cleave a pathway for them as they entered the Beverly Hilton."[75]

Shortly after the festivities, Susan and Eaton returned to Carrollton, Georgia, but the coverage of her award-winning performance continued for months. She said, "I think I know now ... how an always-left-at-the-post race horse feels after finally winning a race. The tension is off—I'm relaxed for the first time since I started acting. After you finally win one of those Oscars the importance of battling in your environment ceases to be a pres-

Hayward and husband Floyd Eaton Chalkley after the 1959 Academy Awards telecast.

sure." She broached the possibility of retirement again: "But I haven't changed my mind about retiring in a few years. I don't believe I'll do more than five or six more films." (Famous last words. Actors, like writers, musicians and artists, rarely retire.) Hayward also described how the Carrollton residents responded to her return. "They met me at the plane with banners, a parade, four bands, the keys to the city and a special edition of the newspaper."[76]

Hayward would spend most of her time at home during the next few years, puttering around the house or driving into Carrollton for groceries or hardware. Years later a resident recalled observing her in the supermarket:

> Obviously coming from an afternoon social event, she was wearing a pink linen coat over a dress of the same material and was a tiny woman, a fact which surprised me because she was always larger than life on the silver screen. She paid for her groceries and walked out to her car with that distinctive Susan Hayward gait. Her red hair, cut shorter than it usually was in her films, bobbed up and down as she moved.[77]

Chapter 6

Better Than the Material

And I say this, like with great respect. It is a great treat to see you, Miss Hayward. And I say Susan if I may. From the days of the Slate Brothers [nightclub] this woman came to see me when I really needed a fan. And it is a delight to see you on the screen and may I say from the bottom of my heart, you are one of our greatest actresses and I adore you.

—*Don Rickles on* The Joey Bishop Show *(February 1968)*[1]

I Want to Live! was Susan Hayward's crowning achievement—and a success she never duplicated. She apparently turned down the female lead in *Elmer Gantry*, the 1960 film that brought Burt Lancaster his Best Actor Academy Award. In the 1960s Hayward's roles tended toward wronged or suffering women, twice in empty, little-impact, color remakes of better black and white films of the 1930s and 1940s. They were beneath her talent and by decade's end would seem hopelessly archaic.

I Want to Live! can even be used to give credence to the "Oscar jinx" theory. Although many Hayward admirers seem loathe to accept this conclusion, a strong argument can be made that not one of Susan's projects after her Academy Award triumph was a superior film. Yes, the budgets were adequate. Sometimes the surrounding cast was fine, although as the decade progressed, Hayward rarely paired off with as strong leading men as she had in the past. Occasionally, as in *The Honey Pot*, a film was rather opulent. But even there Hayward's character died halfway through and the film was not quite up to director Joseph L. Mankiewicz standards. Hayward was almost always better than the material.

1959

Thunder in the Sun (Paramount, 1959)

The story: Arriving in Independence, Missouri, fifty-two French Basques engage the services of scout Lon Bennett (Jeff Chandler) to guide them and their precious grapevines to California. Although he has second thoughts about taking a mere seven wagons through hostile territory, he's committed because he's already spent the Basques' money. When Lon arrives at the nighttime camp, he ogles red-haired Gabrielle (Hayward), who dances atop a makeshift table. Despite her betrothal to expedition leader Andre (Carl Esmond), she is not off limits as far as Lon is concerned. When two local hooligans appear and manhandle the vines, Lon drives them off with his six shooter. Andre (Carl Esmond) is killed when a sentry follows Lon's advice to shoot first. Without Andre, some of the party feel lost, but Gabrielle stiffens their resolve. As next of kin, Andre's brother Pepe (Jacques Bergerac) is now betrothed to Gabrielle. When an expected watercourse is found dry, rationing must begin—for people and horses but not the vines. After a knock-down, drag-out fight with Pepe that he barely wins, Lon enforces his order to clear the wagons of furniture and everything not absolutely essential. Water is found at the foot of the mountains. The next day a prairie fire starts when one of the wagon's burning pots falls into the sage. Lon must rescue Gabrielle, who was saving vines. Out of the smoke into the fire: smoke signals signify an impending Indian attack. Pepe makes Lon agree to a rather unorthodox plan: the Basques, experts at mountain warfare, will enter the pass and attack the Indians while the wagons roar through. Although some of the party are killed, the Basques rule the day, routing the Indians with their physical expertise and piercing war cries. When Gabrielle sees the casualties, including Fernando (Fortunio Bonanova), she screams it's all her fault. But Fernando's widow reasons with her. Lon shows her and Pepe a view toward the fertile valley they've targeted. Pepe makes Lon understand that Gabrielle is Lon's. Lon carries Gabrielle back toward the wagons.

The *New York Times* said, "If Oscars were handed out for plain physical endurance, Susan Hayward might rate still another one for *Thunder in the Sun*, which creaked into neighborhood theatres yesterday, wagon-train style.... Miss Hayward sets her jaw grimly and does a workmanlike job in a role that would have flattened a less determined actress."[3] According to Brian Garfield, "the studio edited this one to death, and it's jerky and poor as a result."[4]

Thunder in the Sun had been made before Susan won the Academy Award and was rushed into release to benefit from that publicity. It co-starred Hayward with another Brooklyn native, Jeff Chandler (né Ira Grossel). Despite the intriguing Basques-cross-America angle, *Thunder in the Sun* is not an exceptional western. It features a novel incident but a not novel execution. What's the year, anyway? The Basques are supposed to be fleeing a Napoleonic wars–ravaged Europe. That ended in 1815. With his rifle and revolver, Chandler's scout seems of a post–Civil War (1861–65) era. It's one of those Hollywood films where the all-too-obviously-to-be-jilted pseudo-lover observes the leading man and woman in a clinch. (Recall the Hayward-Power-Egan triangle in *Untamed*.) At least as irri-tating are the plethora of studio sets and rear-projection shots. All night-time encampments are obviously filmed on a soundstage. Compare this fakery with Hayward's *Garden of Evil*, where on-location was the order of the day. The film does have its moments, however, especially the Basque mountain fighters leaping from rock to rock and bewildering their native American foes with their shrills cries. There may be three firsts in the action department: Chandler cuts an Indian's throat and we see the blood; Chandler swings his rifle to unhorse an Indian; Hayward knees Chandler in the groin. Hayward has another of her trademark sitting-up-in-bed scenes, this time in the wagon with her back bare.

Woman Obsessed (20th Century–Fox, 1959)

The story: After her husband Tom (Arthur Franz) dies fighting a for-est fire, Mary Sharron (Hayward) finds the north woods a harsh environ-ment in which to raise son Robbie (Dennis Holmes). Shoeing the horse and plowing the fields become overwhelming tasks. Help appears in the form of Fred Carter (Stephen Boyd), a lumber mill worker who says Tom once did him a favor. From Dr. (Theodore Bikel) and Mrs. Gibbs (Flo-rence MacMichael), Mary learns that Tom was the only person to act civilly toward's Carter's wife, a former "loose woman" who died in a house fire six years previously. This is perhaps the reason Carter doesn't laugh, which her son has brought to Mary's attention. Fred proves his worth in more ways than one, rescuing Mary and Robbie from certain death by freezing when they're caught in a blizzard. When Mary wakes up and dis-covers that she has been disrobed before being put into bed, she asks Fred if everything is all right. Immediately regretting her veiled accusation, she apologizes. Fred merely says he can't imagine her ever doing anything wrong. After the spring planting, Fred takes Mary and Robbie to the car-nival where Fred and Mary learn more about each other. Mary had been a teacher, Fred a poor youth with little education. Back home, Fred tells Mary there's talk in town about him living there, and he insinuates that he'd like to marry her. She counters that she sees him as a friend only, and he storms out. Upon discovering that Robbie wouldn't mind a stepfather, Mary reconsiders. After the wedding, Robbie is distraught when a cougar mauls a deer and Fred shoots it to put it out of its misery. Worse, Fred tries to show Robbie how to gut it. When Robbie falls unconscious, Fred labels him a coward. Confronting each other, Mary and Fred exchange slaps. Dr. Gibbs arrives, as does Sergeant Le Moyne (Ken Scott). The latter senses problems and tells Mary to fire off two flares if she needs help. Fred tells Dr. Gibbs that Robbie is a coward. That evening Mary tells Fred he's never going to touch her again, but when she locks the bedroom door an enraged Fred breaks it down. The next day Robbie threatens to hurl a pitchfork at Fred but doesn't, which only reinforces Fred's low opinion of the boy. When Fred is in town, Mary reveals to Dr. Gibbs that she's pregnant but that the child was not conceived in love. In town, Fred picks a fights with Henri (James Philbrook) and is arrested by Sergeant Le Moyne. After being released, he tells Mary he's gonna make himself scarce. She reveals that she's selling the farm. When Robbie doesn't return home and a storm comes up, Mary rushes outside to find him. After collapsing from pain, she is found by Fred, who learns of her condition. When the road is blocked by fallen trees, Fred carries Mary the remaining six miles into town. She's miscarried but can have more children, says Dr. Gibbs. Fred says he'll find Robbie despite the raging torrent that now separates the farm from civilization. Dr. Gibbs reveals to Mary that Fred's brother was a coward who let his wife die in that fire. Meanwhile, Fred swims the river and tracks Robbie. Falling into quicksand, he assumes Robbie will leave him there. Instead, Robbie saves him. When Mary arrives at the farm she finds a spic and span homestead. Confronting Fred, Mary asks for his forgiveness, saying she really did want his child. He says maybe he won't leave until after dinner. They embrace.

While *Newsweek* called it "the kind of heartthrobs some will love,"[5] The *New York Times* was harsher: "It is hard to say what goes with Miss Hayward when she gets into these rugged outdoor films. Her good sense and concern as a dramatic actress appear to go by the board. She rigs herself out in fancy garments, tosses her head and breathes hard. Fresh air seems to unhinge her. She behaves more reasonably in jails ... [It's an] utterly foolish film."[6]

The Snow Birch was the working title. A mixture of outdoor scenes with sets, some fuzzy close-ups of wild animals, and occasional back projection during wagon-riding militate a mite against verisimilitude. Although it's beneath the talents of the cast, the story is not really bad.

Viewed today, it looks like a textbook case of spousal abuse, although Hayward's character makes plans to solve her dilemma. Theodore Bikel, always a welcome film presence, was reunited with Hayward after their *I Want to Live!* success. Here merely a hunk to fistfight with Boyd, James Philbrook had also played a significant role in that film. Going back much further, Florence MacMichael had been a scene stealer in the Hayward-Holden *Young and Willing* (1943). Co-star Stephen Boyd would make more impression the same year as Charlton Heston's nemesis Messala in *Ben-Hur*.

During filming, Hayward was interviewed by Arlene Dahl, another titian-haired Hollywood glamour queen (star of such films as *Woman's World* and *Slightly Scarlet*), wife of Fernando Lamas, and makeup entrepreneur. Dahl wanted to find out if Susan's Georgia sojourn had changed her "beauty routine." Hayward responded at length, discussing food, mascara, and hair, telling Dahl she rode horseback every day. According to Dahl, Susan "long ago discovered the look she likes best for herself, and she knows how to keep it with a minimum of effort."[7]

Nearly Cleopatra

With epics much in the air, especially since 1956 (*Around the World in 80 Days*, *Giant*, *The Ten Commandments*, *War and Peace*), 20th Century–Fox decided to renew its acquaintance with the intriguing queen of the Nile. Theda Bara had starred in the company's 1917 silent version.[8]

The Fox casting department had listed possibilities for the title role. On February 16, 1959, producer Walter Wanger wrote, "For Cleopatra, they have listed Brigitte Bardot, Marilyn Monroe, Jennifer Jones, Kim Novak, Audrey Hepburn, Sophia Loren, Gina Lollobrigida, and Susan Hayward."[9] Obviously the studio posed every hot property—and their young contract actresses like Christine Carere—whether the actress was appropriate for the role or not. Although Hayward was 41 at the time, she remained beautiful and had experience with period roles. More importantly, she was under contract to Fox.

On October 8, 1959, Wanger wrote:

> October 8, 1959. [Spyros] Skouras has taken a poll of everyone at the New York office, and they all want Susan Hayward to play Cleopatra. He told me he is going to announce Susan for the role immediately.
>
> Skouras seems determined to have a contract actress—and Susan is under contract—play Cleopatra because he hasn't much faith in the potential gross of the picture. "It can't gross really big unless it is produced at a limited cost," he told me. "Only biblical pictures can do big business today."[10]

Apparently Skouras took the term "biblical" literally and was thinking of *The Robe* (1953) and *The Ten Commandments* (1956). Successful Roman and medieval epics like *Spartacus* (1960) and *El Cid* (1961) were in the future, however, so he didn't have their grosses to go on. Skouras was perhaps envisioning a moderate-sized film, say a *Land of the Pharaohs* (1955). And that film's lead, Joan Collins, was preparing herself for a shot at playing Cleopatra. But neither she nor Hayward got the role. Elizabeth Taylor did and the rest is history.

1960

Hayward announced the Best Actor Academy Award and presented it to her *President's Lady* co-star Charlton Heston at the April 4, 1960, Academy Award show. Heston had won for *Ben-Hur*.

1961

Susan didn't appear on film again until 1961. She told husband Eaton she wanted to retire and fish. In Fort Lauderdale she had three boats. However, Eaton is said to have talked her into doing more films and may, according to some, have come to like basking in the glamour of the Hollywood set. "Susan was tremendously in love with the man, and so permitted him to have inordinate influence over her professional life."[11]

The Marriage-Go-Round (20th Century–Fox, 1961)

The story: Dean of Women Content Delville (Hayward) and her cultural anthropology professor husband Paul (James Mason) give lectures before their respective female and male audiences. Content's subject is domestic relations, her husband's marriage, specifically monogamy. Content relates the story of their recent houseguest, Katrin Sveg (Julie Newmar), daughter of an old Swedish friend. Strange to say, from a pigtailed sprite they'd known a decade before, she'd become a veritable Amazon. As Paul informs his class, it wasn't long after her arrival when Katrin offered to bear his child. After all, her father was a Nobel Prize winner, her mother a great beauty, and Paul a genius. Paul tells Content of this proposition and she consults close friend Ross Barnett (Robert Paige), a professor of Indo-European languages. She races home, where Paul and Katrin have been dancing the evening away. Content invites Katrin to the pool where the university's swimming team practices. Team members go ga-ga over the Swede, and she engages them in wrestling and dancing, and demonstrates her expertise at diving. As Content watches Paul watching Katrin, her brow furrows. At home she confronts Katrin and lays down the law of a rather straight-laced society. Katrin is unimpressed. After all, she's bigger, stronger, and better looking. She'll win out. Later Paul learns from Katrin that her father Nils is never going to appear. He's busy with research in Iceland. After Katrin kisses him, Paul orders her out. Paul can't get a word in to tell Content that Nils isn't coming, and she tells him to let Katrin stay. What's more, he should take her to that lecture on chromosomes. However, the lecture is not that night, as Content learns when she goes to the lecture hall. Ross arrives and translates the letter she'd found in Paul's coat pocket. She believes Paul lied about Nils arriving. At home, she finds him kissing Katrin. Katrin excuses herself, and Paul and Content have it out. Content plans to return to her mother and Brooklyn. While Content packs, Paul convinces Katrin that she really is searching for a husband and he wouldn't be a good one. After all, he knows all about his wife: her measurements, clothing sizes, and so on and couldn't stand learning that all over again. Katrin sees the light, although she's not sure she needs a husband just yet. She agrees to leave, but Content misconstrues what is merely a goodbye kiss. Paul must argue, then beg her forgiveness and say he values their marriage above all else. Content is content. She tells her class, and Paul tells his, that all is well in this monogamous society.

The *New York Times* called it a "giddily light and witty film…. Susan Hayward is likewise excellent…. Being a dandy with poison-tipped sarcasm, and plenty of looks herself, she easily holds her own against the menace [Julie Newmar] and makes the standard moral ending bearable."[12] *America* said, "Far from advocating antisocial behavior, the picture is foursquare behind monogamy and regards the would-be husband borrower simply as a screwball, albeit a particularly unsettling one. Nevertheless, it is too much of a one-joke movie; it does seem static and eventually distasteful."[13]

Nineteen-sixty-one is the release date cited by most publications, but occasionally one will see nineteen-sixty. One suspects a limited December 1960 release took place to make sure it was in contention for Academy Awards. It's a solid pseudo-bedroom comedy of manners and morals. Mason has great expressions upon first greeting and scanning Amazonish Newmar. Feminists and others will cringe just a trifle, as when Mason tells Newmar she needs the care of a husband. Hayward is all professionalism. Her best moment is striking a match on the butt of Newmar's nude statuette. Naturally it's dated in the biology realm. Mason tells Newmar quite correctly for the time that she can't have a baby without a man. (The "test-tube baby," or in vitro fertilization, wouldn't occur until 1978.) Hayward's hair is shorter at the end than at the beginning. Mostly dressed staidly for seminar lectures, Hayward has one glamorous moment: wearing a peach-colored nightgown, she wakes to find Mason missing from the *other* bed.

The Marriage-Go-Round was to be Hayward's last Fox film. She had no qualms about leaving and commented,

> Let's face it—what have I done here in the last five years. One, *Soldier of Fortune*, in which I played a mish-mash; and two, *A Woman Obsessed*, about which I have no comment. The picture I'm doing is all right, but the studio has nothing planned for me. They used to plan things when Darryl Zanuck was in charge. But since he left—nothing. It's the old question of being a stepchild everyone takes for granted.[14]

Sister Florence Makes News

Susan's sister Florence made headlines. She was due in court to battle for custody of her 17-year-old son and a baby girl born December 24, 1960. Florence said she was destitute. Susan and her husband had no comment, according to their attorney. Florence said she hadn't seen Susan since their mother's funeral in April 1958. She pleaded for work. "I can sew ... and I can do general housework and I can work as a saleswoman. If someone would only give me a job I could earn money enough to support my two children."[15]

Back in 1959 a *Saturday Evening Post* article had covered Hayward's career and personal trials.[16] Fans had detected errors, and in the August 15 issue four registered their complaints and corrections, proving that Hayward's public was loyal and numerous.[17] The *SEP* article spurred the entertainment editor at the *Los Angeles Mirror–News* to indicate that the *SEP* writer's inability to talk directly to Hayward was no aberration and presented his own less than complimentary piece that month. Florence apparently visited the *Los Angeles Mirror–News* entertainment editor from time to time. He described "Susan's embittered older sister, Florence Marrener, who wanders the fringes of Skid Row with her teen-age son."[18] Hayward's reluctance to speak about her relationship with her sister makes Hayward the bad person. Robert Wise, her director on *I Want to Live!*, hinted at problems. One day during shooting Hayward had failed to appear. That evening producer Walter Wanger told Wise that Hayward had had a family problem involving her sister. The next day Hayward was back on the set. According to Wise, "She never said anything about it, and, of course, I respected her for her reluctance to talk about a personal problem, and I never pressed her on it. I just considered that it was something she couldn't help, that it was a situation that might happen to all of us, and we went on and did our day's work."[19]

In the May 1961 issue of *Confidential*, Florence's name was given as the author of "My Sister, Susan Hayward, Has Millions—But I'm on Relief." Florence gave the whole family history but got a lot of little things wrong about her sister's career, e.g., that she never made a film for Warner Bros., and that *Beau Geste* was her first film. The article is not full of spleen, however. Florence just can't figure out why Susan came to ignore her and their mother. She gives Susan credit for giving their mother money to live on. She thinks the break between herself and Susan probably occurred when they were in New York for a premiere and Florence invited relatives back to their hotel room. When Susan arrived with friends, she pitched a fit and didn't take Florence back to Hollywood. "I wish she just had a little more love in her heart."[20]

Ada (MGM, 1961)

The story: Chiefly notable for his crooning and guitar pickin' prowess, down-home boy Bo Gillis (Dean Martin) finds himself running for governor. During a break between stump speeches, Bo is introduced to Ada Dallas (Hayward). In the privacy of a hotel room Bo finds that Ada is not your typical hooker. She has wit and brains as well as a face and figure. In no time a'tall he's proposin' and she's acceptin'. This disturbs Bo's publicity man Steve (Martin Balsam), and his wily and ultimately ruthless political mentor, Sylvester Marin (Wilfrid Hyde-White). But Ada is given a fictional background and the quest for the governorship proceeds. After Sylvester engineers an exposé of the opposing candidate's wife's addiction to narcotics (which leads to her suicide), Bo is assured of a win. Bo and Ada visit the state house, and Bo tells Ada he's scared of not being able to handle the job. Ada replies that he can because he has help—her. One fly in the ointment is Colonel Yancey (Ralph Meeker), the state police chief who's too big for his britches according to Ada. Ada has Steve procure her an invite to a tea given by the town's upstanding ladies. Although she is unmasked for not being from good stock, Ada intimidates the grand dames by suggesting that their families' state contracts will be in jeopardy if they don't play ball—and attend *her* teas. Bo finds his job consists of merely signing bills passed to him by Sylvester. When his lieutenant governor, Ronnie Hallerton (Frank Maxwell), expresses misgivings about a state park bill obviously designed to pad the coffers of administration friends, Bo approaches Sylvester, who lectures him on how things really are. Bo counters by saying that Sylvester can't do anything without Bo's right arm—to sign the bills. Sylvester blackmails Ronnie into resigning and seeks help from Ada. In return, she demands the lieutenant-governorship. Leaving the capitol, Bo repairs to his limousine. His driver indisposed, he gets behind the wheel, turns the ignition—and is hurled from the car by an explosion in the trunk. Hospitalized, Bo is visited by Ada, who finds he thinks she's responsible for the assassination attempt. At home she is sworn in as acting governor. Afterward Steve berates her but she accuses him of never doing anything for Bo except write a few speeches that were never made. After a meeting in which she antagonizes some of Sylvester's yes men, Ada visits Sylvester and says she's presenting three bills that will harm the corrupt politicos in his pocket. To counter her, he has Yancey tape her when she offers her former madam $10,000 in hush money. In the state house, Ada finalizes plans with legislators she hopes will get her bills through. A raucous session ensues in which Joe Adams (Larry Gates) makes the first move on Ada's behalf. Bo and Steve observe from the visitors balcony, as does Sylvester. Yancey arrives and one of Sylvester's men attempts to play the incriminating tape, but Bo rises from his seat and demands the right to defend his wife. He makes a stirring speech and the session ends after votes that will start the process of reform. Bo and Ada walk from the state house together.

The *New York Times* was not impressed, calling the film "an incredibly naive fable.... He [Dean Martin] is no more convincing as a character than is Susan Hayward as his wife, and her performance as a gold-hearted former tramp is brazen, blatant and absurd."[21] *Time* was more disposed to its attractions, labeling it "a cute idea—maybe too cute. But the screenplay ... develops it into a pleasant political comedy, and Daniel (*Butterfield 8*) Mann directs the show with tact and skill. He makes the most of Martin's charm, the least of Hayward's flim-flamboyance."[22]

Ada is a consistently interesting, entertaining film that is rather more pertinent now than when released—after Watergate and impeachment and media investigations of political figures. It may be Hayward's most polished film after *I Want to Live!* It could have benefited from a bit more insight into the Hayward character's background and aspirations. Location scenes were filmed in Sacramento. It was recognized for its strengths in James Robert Parish's *Prostitution in Hollywood Films*, who found it "driven forward by a gutsy performance from high voltage actress Susan Hayward,"[23] and called it a "sleek study of political corruption."[24]

Having divorced himself from his wildly popular films with comedian Jerry Lewis after 1956's *Hollywood or Bust*, Dean Martin had done credible dramatic work in *The Young Lions* (1958), *Some Came Running* (1959), *Rio Bravo* (1959), and *Career* (1959), as well as making lighter fare such as *Who Was That Lady?* (1960).

Various Hayward trademarks can be found, e.g., whacking Ralph Meeker, and being confronted while wearing nought but a slip. Did any actress ever look better in a white one?

Back Street (Universal-International, 1961)

The story: At the Lincoln, Nebraska, airport USO canteen, U.S. Marine Paul Saxon (John Gavin) observes a redhead dancing with another serviceman. Unable to get a flight, he finds a hotel and encounters the redhead again. She's clothes designer Rae Smith (Hayward), who's there to show the prominent Mr. Venner (Alex Gerry) her illustrations. Venner, however, is more intent on putting the make on her. Paul comes to her rescue by pretending to be her fiancé. At her house, which she shares with sister Janie (Virginia Grey), Rae discusses Paul. He shows up and asks her to accompany him on a picnic. By the lakeside Rae sketches his face and learns that Paul is heir to the Saxon department stores. They kiss and she admits that it's crazy but she loves him. Paul tells Rae he's got to go home and straighten things out. Rae guesses it's another woman. "Goodbye, Marine, goodbye." Paul has second thoughts at the airport and calls Rae's home. Via Janie, Rae learns that Paul has two tickets, but on her way to the airport her car runs out of gas. Three weeks pass and Janie tells Rae she should be satisfied with Curt (Charles Drake). Finally Rae learns that Paul is married. Jeannie tells Rae to sell the store and go to New York to try to break into the big time. In New York Rae uses her chutzpah to get a job with Dalian (Reginald Gardiner), and before long the company is "Dalian et rae." One day Paul spots her on the street. She rejects his request for lunch and dinner, but he comes to her apartment. She maintains that she can't be the "other woman," but he says he loves her. Rae tells Dalian she has to get away, and he takes her to their Rome office. Rae's old flame Curt arrives, and she entertains him and the Claypools (Hayden Rorke, Mary Lawrence) at a restaurant where she once again meets Paul. This time he's with his inebriated wife Liz (Vera Miles). Rae tells Curt she wants to see more of him. Liz tells Paul she's sick of him but won't give him a divorce because she won't be an ex–Mrs. Saxon. Out walking, Paul observes Rae leaving the shop. She agrees to a quiet talk and admits to loving him still. At his home, Paul finds that Liz has guessed correctly about his afternoon whereabouts. Rushed to the hospital after taking a multitude of sleeping pills, Liz recovers and, with Paul, moves to Paris.

Rae follows Paul to Paris and takes up residence in the country home Paul buys for her. During a formal showing at Dalian et rae, Rae meets Liz. After learning from her friends that Paul is seeing someone, Liz hires a private investigator. At the airport Paul, Jr. (Richard Eyer) overhears a woman behind the counter say Rae Smith goes everywhere Paul does. Later he tells Rae to leave his father alone. Rae tells Paul to help his son. At the Fall Fashion Preview by Dalian et rae for a children's hospital benefit, Liz bids $10,000 for a gown and says in front of everyone that it should be delivered to the *other woman*, Rae Smith. Rae tells Paul everything's over, that his children matter more than her. It's become cheap and dirty and they can't change it; all the old clichés are true. Paul says to stay put, he'll be back and never leave again. Paul drives into Paris and confronts Liz. They drive off together. He says he'll sue for divorce. She responds that she'll never give him up and wrecks the car. Liz is killed, while Paul is paralyzed and in critical condition. Paul manages to indicate to his son that he should phone Rae. Paul says goodbye to Rae and succumbs. Rae sits alone at home near a photo of Paul in his Marine uniform. She recalls their first picnic and pictures herself making it to the Lincoln airport in time to leave with him. There's a knock on the door. It's Paul, Jr. and sister Caroline. Paul, Jr. asks if they can visit once in a while because nobody else is left. Rae hugs them both while staring at her sketch of Paul.

The *New York Times* said, "This little woman of Miss Hayward's is just the figment of someone's cheap and tacky dreams ... and the film itself is a moral and emotional fraud."[25] *Time* said, "In this third film version of the book—Ross Hunter's full-color, wide-screen, $2,500,000 overproduction in which the bathrooms look like the lobby of the Beverly Hilton—the fallen woman falls, not into the pit of shame, but into the lap of luxury. She still suffers, but on silk."[26]

Back Street had been filmed better in 1932 and 1941. The soundtrack album notes were overly complimentary, to say the least, terming this version the "most moving." (Oddly, one musical selection is a dead ringer for the main theme from *Goodbye, Again*, an Ingrid Bergman film of the same year—but from a different studio and composer.) This version is a typical glossy, refurbished soap from producer Ross Hunter.

Back Street is one of the films comedienne Carol Burnett obviously was thinking about when she said, "I want to be ... Susan Hayward, Olivia de Havilland, Joan Crawford, all those suffering ladies in one movie and do a total takeoff on all those pictures. I'd love it. Of course laughing so much...."[27]

Hayward looks much younger than her years and more or less fits the character. Perhaps this was why she favored cinematographer Stanley

Back Street (Universal-International, 1961) publicity shot with John Gavin.

Cortez. John Gavin was tall, dark and handsome, with the square jawed-look that most famous male stars are mistakenly said to possess.[28] Gavin was to have been a new Rock Hudson. But it may have been this movie which led to his description as "wooden." He is certainly not very convincing.[29] It's rather a mystery as to exactly what time period *Back Street* describes. It begins at the Lincoln, Nebraska, airport, apparently at the close of World War II. Then it's postwar Europe, pretty well-heeled and reconstructed. But no dates are actually given and the audience doesn't really know how much time is passing, other than through the growth of Gavin's children, who don't age all that much. Talk about symbolism not lost on the audience: when Rae and Paul go to the Italian beachfront house and embrace, the camera moves to the rocky, stormswept shore below!

1962

I Thank a Fool (MGM/Eaton Productions, 1962)

The story: Stephen Dane (Peter Finch) successfully prosecutes Dr. Christine Allison (Hayward) for a mercy killing by lethal injection. After serving eighteen months in prison, Christine is out but has no job prospects. Then a job offer arrives with Miss Heather (Athene Seyler), who drives her to a rather posh country residence. Christine's prospective employer is none other than Stephen Dane, who wants Christine to attend to his unbalanced wife Liane (Diane Cilento). The story is that Liane sustained a head injury in a car crash that took the life of her beloved father, Captain Ferris. But it's not long before Christine hears conflicting stories. Liane tells Christine that someday she'll return to her home in Ireland. Liane does manage to escape her confines from time to time, as when she absconds with a car and goes to the town fair with the stable hand, Roscoe (Kieron Moore). Stephen has to convince Christine to stay, and relates his own tale of confinement in a prisoner of war camp. One day the supposedly deceased Captain James Ferris (Cyril Cusack) appears and tells Christine he'd agreed to pretend death to keep Liane from trauma. Christine takes Liane to the Dublin ferry. In Ireland they drive to the Ferris homestead. Along the way Liane directs Christine's attention to a cliff from which her mother fell to her death. At the farm Captain Ferris is found tipsy and in the company of his girlfriend. Stephen appears. When her father tells her she should go, Liane runs from the house and injures herself near the cliff. Doctors think she might need to be committed. Stephen says Liane told him about all the sick things that took place at her home. That evening Christine gives Liane sleeping pills and keeps the bottle in her room. But in the morning the bottle has disappeared and Liane is dead. At the inquest Christine comes to the conclusion that Stephen has used her to kill Liane. But during an adjournment Christine notices that Captain Ferris has the watch he'd once given Liane. As he attempts to thrust suspicion aside, the townsfolk overhear the conversation. Soon the police arrive, and the flustered Ferris backs into an unstable fence and falls to his death in the playground. When Christine leaves the village, Stephen requests—and is granted—a lift.

Newsweek said, "The only worthwhile things about this picture are the splendid sets by Sean Kenny.... Otherwise, Susan Hayward, as a doctor who might have killed her lover (we're never sure), is merely twitchy...."[30] London's *Times* said, "It belongs to the genre in which the plot never stops thickening and significant entrances are made through French windows.[31] The *New York Times* said, "Poor Susan Hayward. If she isn't playing a drunkard or a kook or something of the sort in films, it appears she has to be involved with characters who are drunkards or kooks or some sort of psychopaths.... Miss Cilento, Miss Hayward and Mr. Finch go through their roles without conviction.... Miss Hayward might have done herself better if she had played the coroner."[32]

Had the filmmakers known what was up with fright films and veteran actresses, they could have converted this into another *What Ever Happened to Baby Jane?* (1962) or *Hush ... Hush, Sweet Charlotte* (1965). Nevertheless, it's a fairly satisfying mystery, though a trifle overlong. There are rarely seen environs of London and a sterling cast. Besides London, locations included Liverpool and Crookhaven, Ireland.

1963

Stolen Hours (United Artists, 1963)

The story: American Laura Pember (Hayward) leaves her guests at her English estate to retrieve her younger sister Ellen (Diane Baker) at the airport. On the way Laura has a spell of distorted vision and almost drives into the wrong lane. Arriving home, Laura takes some medication and rests in her room. Her friend, race car driver Mike Bannerman (Edward Judd), arrives with Dr. John Carmody (Michael Craig). Mike hopes John can make a surreptitious physical examination of Laura, who even Ellen thought had lost weight. John observes that Laura is sensitive to light. Investigating further, he finds that she has little feeling in her right hand. Eventually Laura realizes that John is a physician and tosses a drink in his face. Having second thoughts, she soon apologizes and agrees to undergo tests. Those tests reveal that she needs brain surgery. After the operation, surgeon Dr. Eric McKenzie (Paul Rogers) tells John he's satisfied that Laura will have a pain-free six months, perhaps a year. But her malady will return. When the time comes she'll lose her sight and death will swiftly follow. John, Mike and Ellen decide not to tell Laura. Initially skeptical of her ability to be a good wife, Laura breaks down and says yes to John's marriage proposal. Visiting his office one afternoon she finds her file and learns the bad news. She hides the knowledge from John until she can bear it no longer and berates him. Later she recants and they marry, honeymooning in the Carmody house on a Cornish bluff. Laura convinces John to relocate his practice here. Laura takes to Peter, a youngster who enlists her support in the spring outdoor races. After bringing the children back to the house, Laura realizes that her vision is clouding. She hides this from John, who's off to tend a pregnant townswoman. Ellen realizes Laura's condition but is forced to go with him. Laura retires to her bedroom, lets Peter describe the view from the window, then lays on her bed. Peter covers her and says goodbye.

Reviewers were unkind.

Moira Walsh, in *America*, carped, "I am not a great admirer of the films of yesteryear, and I harbor no happily nostalgic memories of Bette Davis dying gallantly in *Dark Victory* after a glamorously misspent life. I am sure, however, that it was a better movie than this color remake with Susan Hayward. Twenty-five years ago it was possible to put a little sincerity and conviction into naive stories about regeneration or high society or both. Today the story is simply preposterous—all treacly, pseudoglamorous surface, and not an ounce of muscle or substance."[33]

The *New York* Times posed the question, What's wrong, you may ask with Miss Hayward? Why isn't she able to give as strong a performance as Miss Davis memorably gave? Well, for one thing, she postures. She strikes dramatic attitudes ... her generous producers and the director, Daniel Petrie, have not done as much as they might to have saved her from the tastelessness of extravagance." [34] Said the London *Times*, "Naturally it would be a brave woman indeed who was prepared to step into Miss Bette Davis's shoes, but Miss Susan Hayward, perhaps alone of the stars who do not already quite qualify for the label 'veteran,' has both the stature and the stamina, and the new film is most engaging, even if it does not altogether wipe its predecessor from memory.... Miss Hayward is beautiful and brave in a succession of ravishing gowns...."[35]

Like Bill Travers, Michael Craig and Edward Judd were dependable leading men of the period. Craig and Judd were well known to constant moviegoers on both sides of the Atlantic. Craig had played an American Civil War POW who escaped and landed on the *Mysterious Island* (1961) to confront Captain Nemo. Judd was the male lead in the well received *The Day the Earth Caught Fire* (1962). As for Hayward, she is radiant and healthy. Was any actress ever more photographed as she reached up and

Stolen Hours (United Artists, 1963).

put her arms around her man? There is an excellent main title sequence decorated with dandelions. On the negative side, there is no evidence of intravenous sustenance for Laura after the surgery! How could the surgeon be so sure Laura would experience no pain, go blind and die within an hour? Such negative comments aside, this version of *Dark Victory* (1939) has a certain charm, if that's the correct word. Perhaps the aftermath of Laura's death should have been shown: the return home of John and Ellen, the trauma of grieving, the recovery, memorial statements made above the cliffs. Like *I Thank a Fool*, this was also set in England. It was originally titled *Summer Flight*.

1964

Where Love Has Gone (Paramount, 1964)

The story: Sculptress Valerie Hayden (Hayward) witnesses her daughter Dani (Joey Heatherton) stab and kill Valerie's boyfriend. Valerie's ex-husband, architect Luke Miller (Michael Connors), returns from Arizona to San Francisco to console his daughter as she's taken to Juvenile Hall. There he flashes back to his first meeting with Valerie, when he was on leave from World War II and about to receive the Congressional Medal of Honor. He criticized her artwork but received an invitation to dinner from Valerie's mother (Bette Davis). Mrs. Hayden knew the Miller family was of good stock and makes a proposition that Luke marry Valerie and become a vice president of the firm. Outraged by her presumptuous behavior, Luke storms out, taking Valerie with him. Both realize they are attracted to each other. They marry and receive an elegant penthouse as a wedding gift. Unknown to Valerie or Luke, Mrs. Hayden uses her influence to keep Luke from getting loans to start his company. Eventually he accepts the vice presidency she'd offered. But life is no bowl of cherries and he takes to booze as he wines and dines clients. Valerie has a child, Dani, which is some consolation. Mrs. Hayden had also used her influence with art critic Sam Corwin (DeForest Kelley) to get Valerie a prestigious prize. When Valerie can no longer take Luke's boozing, she begins to hit her old haunts, including the "Sex-Sational Floor Show." Corwin makes references to her past promiscuity. As Luke descends into alcoholism and Valerie into one-night stands, they argue and Mrs. Hayden admits to making a mistake about Luke. A divorce is granted. Back to the present: Luke visits Marian Spicer (Jane Greer), Dani's probation officer. Dani tells her father she loves all the wrong people. Marian visits Valerie to learn more about Dani's background. Valerie discovers that Dani is not a virgin. Dani sees Dr. Jennings (Anne Seymour), a psychologist. Mrs. Hayden receives a blackmail threat: love letters for money. She seeks Luke's help, and Luke consults Sam Corwin. Meanwhile, Valerie finds that her dead boyfriend's pal Rafael (Anthony Caruso) has the incriminating letters. She turns the tables on him by bugging his apartment and photographing him. Valerie's mother wants custody of Dani, but Val swears she'll never mangle Dani's life as she has hers. More letters surface and Sam buys them for Luke. Val tells Luke they can learn to love each other again and thus keep Dani. Luke says it's too much responsibility for one man. Marian asks the court to put Dani in a state home. Luke produces letters and says he thinks that Dani was trying to kill Valerie when her mother's lover stepped in front of her. Valerie speeds off to her home, slashes the portrait of her mother and stabs herself to death. After the gravesite service, Luke berates Mrs. Hayden for her parenting skills and walks slowly back toward Valerie's grave.

The *New York Times* said, "It is cheap, gaudy, mawkish and artificial—offensive to intelligence and taste.... Never mind Susan Hayward. We've become quite accustomed to seeing her expending her pyrotechnic talents on lurid and fatuous roles."[36] *Newsweek* said, "One watches *Where Love Has Gone* in disbelief, wondering how, in a movie from a major studio, there could be such universal and serene ineptitude.... Still, Bette Davis is splendid.... And one must credit Miss Hayward at least for slashing a terrible portrait of Bette to shreds."[37]

Studio hopes had been high that this would duplicate the success of the other Harold Robbins novel preceding this to the screen, *The Carpetbaggers* (1964), which, despite being a rather boring potboiler, nevertheless made lots of money. Robbins' *Where Love Has Gone* inspiration was obviously the 1958 murder of Lana Turner's boyfriend, mob-connected Johnny Stompanato, by her 14-year-old daughter Cheryl.[38]

This was a strained shoot, what with Bette Davis playing Hayward's mother. Reportedly Davis threw her wig in Hayward's face when the latter suggested a change in blocking a scene. Hayward is supposed to have called Davis a bitch. Co-star Mike Connors said,

> Bette felt insecure up against a ten-years-younger woman, Susan, who was better-looking, and, moreover, the real star of the film, the person the proceedings revolved around. And Susan, who was sullen and defensive anyway, found that hers and Davis's temperaments were too much alike for pleasant socializing off-camera. I remember it, and so did Eddie Dmytryk, as an atmosphere of armed truce—and a mean, icy truce it was, too![39]

Director Dmytryk, who'd been enthusiastic about Hayward back when making *Soldier of Fortune*, said:

> The first mistake was Susan. She had serious misgivings about playing a

Where Love Has Gone (Paramount, 1964), with Michael Connors.

promiscuous woman. Yet, for some now-unremembered reason, Marty Rackin felt she was the only actress for the part, and he made a number of character concessions to win her agreement. The concessions improved the moral tone of the script, but diminished its dramatic possibilities.[40]

Dmytryk also said that Bette Davis was no diplomat and fed scuttlebutt on the set that she was rewriting scenes:

> Unlike her opponent, Susan was an insecure actress, and suspicions immediately flooded her mind. Her agent was soon at the studio, and the three of us were in Rackin's office. We discovered that Susan's contract specified that she was bound only to the script she had originally read, and, good or bad—and even [John Michael] Hayes admitted it lacked quality—that's all she was going to do. And that's all she did.[41]

At least the movie has good lines, such as Hayward's "I've never regarded carpentry as an art form." And Mike Connors to her: "You're not a woman, you're a disease!" Locations were in San Francisco, and the opening shots of the city over the credits are quite good.

It's not clear why Hayward's character is promiscuous. That is, Corwin makes suggestive comments about her past but we're really at a loss to understand how she could have been a nymphomaniac and gotten "better" so fast.

Again, in keeping with making this what might be called a "Susan Hayward vehicle," Hayward's leading man is not on her level. Mike Connors would soon find his niche in the long-running TV private eye show *Mannix*.

A hot young teen property due to her steamy dancing and singing on such TV programs as *The Andy Williams Show*, and later gyrating in boots and leotard on the deck of the aircraft carrier U.S.S. *Ticonderoga* (December 1965) with Bob Hope on tour in Vietnam, Joey Heatherton is at this stage inadequate as an actress. Dani is supposed to be 15. Heatherton was 20 when the film was released.

There should have been more characters to put it on the level of good, entertaining trash.

The movie receives some analysis for its depiction of bogus sexuality: "And Susan Hayward in *Where Love Has Gone* (1964) is a society sculptress, 'one of the truly greats', whose nymphomania is handily implied by the statues of male nudes which she sculpts from models picked up on the San Francisco waterfront. The only model one actually glimpses, bolting from her bedroom, is wearing sweater and slacks: it may not be the Greek ideal of male beauty, but it at least allows Hollywood to combine artistic integrity, the sex drive and censor-proof suggestiveness, all in the one shot."[42]

Some blame Susan's husband Eaton, as well as producer friend Marty Rackin, for her choice of roles at this time. They didn't let her instincts keep her from "rolling in the cinematic gutter."[43]

1967

The Honey Pot (United Artists, 1967)

The story: Wealthy Cecil Fox (Rex Harrison) hires sometimes-actor William McFly (Cliff Robertson) to assist him in a rude trick to be played on three former lovers. Texan Lonestar Sheridan (Hayward), Princess Dominique (Capucine), and movie star Merle "Bunny" McGill (Edie Adams) are informed that Cecil is dying. Cecil knows all will want to be prominently featured in his will. Sure enough, all three rendezvous at Cecil's villa. Lonestar Sheridan thinks she's secured her spot at the top of the will when she states that she'd been Cecil's common law wife. Cecil informs Bunny that Lonestar is correct only if he dies intestate. Cecil feigns immobility and McFly rescues him when Lonestar tries to cart him off to the hospital. Lonestar mysteriously dies in the night from a sleeping pill overdose. "Now all the fun's gone," says Cecil. The police inspector (Adolfo Celi) investigates. Cecil reveals his scam to Lonestar's secretary cum nurse, Sarah (Maggie Smith). He tells Sarah he knows she's larcenous, too. Sarah thinks McFly murdered Lonestar and uses the dumbwaiter to ascend to Cecil's quarters. She says McFly killed Lonestar. Cecil gives Sarah cryptic information about how he'll live more in the next ten minutes than other people will in their whole lives. Cecil is soon found dead. McFly reads the will and it is revealed that Cecil was himself virtually penniless. With the inspector's help, the guests learn that Cecil killed Lonestar to inherit *her* fortune. Sarah has McFly and the inspector sign Cecil's will as a keepsake for her, then the inspector discloses that this lets her inherit Lonestar's wealth because Lonestar was indeed Cecil's common law spouse. McFly is aghast, but Sarah says she'll pay for his law school degree and they'll marry. Initially reluctant, McFly races after her as the inspector looks on and the voice of Cecil Fox opines that it's nice for young people to get together at the end.

Variety called it "an elegant, sophisticated screen vehicle for more demanding tastes.... The playing is all of a superior caliber, and the director has chosen his cast well and paced them properly to counterpoint his theses. Harrison is a natural as the scheming millionaire.... Susan Hayward, Capucine and Edie Adams are fine as his vastly opposite onetime companions."[44] The *New York Times* said it was "more artifice than art."[45]

Originally titled *Anyone for Venice*, *The Honey Pot* had its location scenes filmed in Venice. It was sophisticated and opulent, interesting but not compelling, and in its own way as out of kilter with its time as Hayward's potboilers earlier in the decade.

Documentary

Susan was among a sterling cast in *Think 20th*, a 30-minute 20th Century–Fox 1967 studio promotional item which also featured Julie Andrews, Richard Attenborough, Candice Bergen, Michael Caine, Bette Davis, Patty Duke, Judy Geeson, Rex Harrison, Charlton Heston, Deborah Kerr, Steve McQueen, Jill St. John and others in Fox pictures. Richard Fleischer directed, Darryl F. Zanuck narrated.[46]

Tragedy

Bad fortune had struck during the location shooting of *The Honey Pot*. Susan's husband Eaton became ill. Returning to the United States, he was treated for an undisclosed illness for three weeks in Ft. Lauderdale.

The Chalkleys had purchased a winter home in Ft. Lauderdale.[47] Susan was at his side when he died at home on January 9[48] after being discharged from hospital.[49] Hepatitis was the cause of Chalkley's death.[50] He'd been infected during World War II during a blood transfusion.[51] Some biographers attribute Eaton's death to heavy drinking which brought on more hepatitis attacks.[52]

A few years later Hayward said, "Eaton Chalkley was quite a man. He was rugged and he was fair. There was an awful lot of strength to him. When I first met him, I knew my sleepless nights and nervous days were all behind me."[53]

Her Carrollton, Georgia, home had lost its charm with her husband's death, and Hayward moved to Fort Lauderdale. "After my husband's death I sold all the machinery and the cattle, but if someone wants to buy the farm, it's there, for sale."[54] She liked the fishing opportunities that Ft. Lauderdale provided. "I love it here. Of all the places I've lived, this is the place to be. I'm really a back-to-nature sort, very simple. I yearn to get out of doors."[55]

Valley of the Dolls (20th Century–Fox, 1967)

Like *The Honey Pot*, which was directed by Joseph L. Mankiewicz, the director who'd guided her in 1949's *House of Strangers*, Susan chose to do *Valley of the Dolls* because of its director, Mark Robson. He'd piloted her through the success of 1949's *My Foolish Heart*. Said Hayward, "Nowadays I simply won't do a picture unless I know the director and his work. The thing that appealed to me in *Valley of the Dolls* was the fact Mark Robson is directing.... I made *The Honey Pot* because Joe Mankiewicz directed. He's brilliant and he has heart. I can honestly say I've enjoyed every minute of my career. It is not art to me: it is work and darned good work, but it has never been my entire life."[56]

The story: Anne Welles (Barbara Parkins) leaves Lawrenceville in New England and takes a secretarial position with a New York theatrical law firm. At a Broadway rehearsal she observes veteran stage star Helen Lawson (Hayward) canning newcomer Neely O'Hara (Patty Duke). Helen admits that Neely is talented and might steal her own thunder. But firm attorney Lyon Burke (Paul Burke), whom Anne finds herself attracted to, secures Neely a singing gig on the Joey Bishop–hosted telethon, which leads to club shows followed by a full-scale Hollywood contract. Meanwhile, showgirl cum actress Jennifer North (Sharon Tate) marries singer Tony Polar (Tony Scotti) over the objections of his sister Miriam (Lee Grant). Anne, meanwhile, is hired away from the law firm by Kevin

Gillmore (Charles Drake) and finds success as the Gillmore Girl in TV cosmetic commercials. She plans to marry Gillmore until Lyon reappears. She and Lyon have a rocky relationship, and Anne begins taking "dolls," i.e., pills. Unable to deal with fame and two marriages, Neely becomes a full-blown alcoholic and drug addict, and finds herself at the same sanitarium where Tony Polar is dying of Huntington's chorea. Jennifer, who'd appeared in French nudie films to pay his medical bills, commits suicide by pills after learning she has breast cancer. Neely recovers and attempts a theatrical comeback at Lyon's urging. Back in New York she once again faces her nemesis, Helen Lawson. After verbal sparring, the two engage in a cat fight and Neely accidentally pulls off Helen's wig. She drops it in the toilet before tossing it out onto the floor. Instead of slinking out the stage door, Helen merely wraps a kerchief over her head. "I'll go out the way I came in." Neely's victory over Helen doesn't translate into confidence that she can face the audience, and, like Helen, Neely wants to can a newcomer who might steal the limelight. But after a row with her manager, Lyon, Neely gets drunk and her understudy goes on. After a late night binge in a nearby bar, Neely wanders around outside the theater wondering what's happened and calling on Anne, Jennifer, Lyon—and God— before collapsing in an alley. Having freed herself of dolls, Anne returns to her home in New England. Lyon rolls up, but Anne is noncommittal about a permanent relationship and leaves Lyon mystified while she revels in a snowscape walk.

Time said Susan was "a brassy voiced Broadway zircon in the rough."[57] *Variety* said, "Few assets, many liabilities mark this sex-teasing, talky sudser.... Susan Hayward, who replaced Judy Garland in cast, does an excellent job in giving acting depth to the role of the older legit star, ever alert to remove threats to her supremacy. Her scenes with Miss Duke are particularly lively."[58] The *New York Times* found it an "unbelievably hackneyed and mawkish mishmash of backstage plots and 'Peyton Place' adumbrations.... Our old friend, Susan Hayward, stands out as if she were Katharine Cornell. Her aging musical comedy celebrity is the one remotely plausible character in the film."[59]

Said biographers La Guardia and Arceri, "That scene in the ladies' room ... reveals a Susan Hayward who is almost too good for this movie. She plays three different kinds of anger, shifting with great ease from one to another, and employs a body choreography (such as staring at the ceiling at exactly the right angle seconds after her young rival enters the powder room) which Patty Duke cannot match. Duke tears off her wig and soaks it in the john, forcing Susan's Helen to consider rushing out the back exit. Susan's reading of the line 'I'll go out the way I came in' was a reading only three decades in the business could create: at first embarrassment, melting into an ironic smile, melting into hard-cord determination. No other performance in the movie comes close to Susan's."[60]

In retrospect, "*Valley of the Dolls* was to the late sixties what *The Carpetbaggers* had been to the first half of the decade: the trash masterpiece which everyone went to see, even though they knew better; the irresistibly sleazy, great-bad movie which provided garishly gaudy scenery, unbelievably exaggerated dialogue, a lusciously lurid plot, silly stabs at a serious message, and cartoon characterizations by a cast of ordinarily competent actors."[61]

Filmed in New York, New England and Hollywood, *Valley* was based on Jacqueline Susann's best-selling novel which traced the modeling and acting careers of three young women who, to varying degrees, become hooked on pills, the "dolls."[62] The film was a huge moneymaker for Fox despite the critical lambasting. Released in December 1967, it was the number four grosser of the ensuing year at $20,000,000, following *The Graduate*, *Guess Who's Coming to Dinner?* and the *Gone with the Wind* reissue.[63] Some find it a cult movie, i.e., a movie so bad it's fun to belittle and laugh at. Despite the synopsis, which makes it sound like heaps of vicarious fun, others find it too boring to warrant the label of "cult movie." Yet there are a few scenes that must elicit yucks, most involving the Duke character. Especially outrageous is the sanitarium scene where Duke's singing generates a response from the practically comatose Tony, who perks up and wheels his chair into the center of the room as he chimes in.

Hayward had replaced Judy Garland, who was near the end of her career and life. Said Jacqueline Susann, "Susan did a good workmanlike job ... but she could have walked away with it. Judy Garland had the part for 10 days. Then Judy lost her nerve. She took to her dressing room. She got on something. That was that. I originally wanted Bette Davis for the role. When the studio chose Hayward, it thought the public would associate Susan as a singer because of her Jane Froman movie."[64] (Judy Garland died in 1969 after a life and career of incredible highs in films such as *The Wizard of Oz*, *Meet Me in St. Louis* and *A Star Is Born*, and lows involving suicide attempts, bad marriages).

Choreographer Robert Sidney later recalled, "I loved Susan, but she was a very predatory person. She'd go for the jugular, too, if she had to."[65] This was in reference to the reel and real conflict that developed between Hayward and Patty Duke. Said Duke about the animosity: "Maybe it was even the scene we were doing. The situation was created that we didn't really like each other and we were going to do the best we could to sabotage each other."[66]

In keeping with her standard approach to acting, Hayward had no comments about replacing Garland.[67] Said choreographer Bob Sidney,

Valley of the Dolls (**20th Century–Fox, 1967**).

"She's the only actress I know who never had any comment about any other actress."[68]

Had it been a year later, when the MPAA rating system was introduced and nudity and spicy language permitted, *Valley of the Dolls* might have had real zip. There are flashes of nudity, or what today would be called "partial nudity": Parkins silhouetted in her apartment as she disrobes for bed, Tate twisting around and pressing up against her lover in one of the nudie films. It's not even clear that the Parkins character is taking that many pills. Jennifer took none until her suicide.

Duke is over the top and out of her depth, chewing scenery. And even in 1967 the plot and incidents seem archaic, as if this was about the '20s or '30s rather than the late '60s. The best thing about *Valley* was the "Theme from Valley of the Dolls" sung by Dionne Warwick.

Missing Out

Nineteen-sixty-seven could have supplied Hayward with a better role had she taken it. She, Patricia Neal and Doris Day were supposedly considered for the role of Mrs. Robinson in *The Graduate*. Anne Bancroft got the role and scored big.

1968

There were two primary reasons Susan made a TV appearance in February 1968 on the late night talk show *The Joey Bishop Show*.[69] She agreed to appear only if her Ft. Lauderdale neighbor, Jack Frost, could come on and play the organ. It was also a chance to plug *Valley of the Dolls*, albeit after its initial release. Hayward came from Florida but said she'd lived many years in California and "I have no complaints about California, really. I love it."

Audience members asked questions. Susan humorously asked Joey, "Do I have to answer truthfully?" A man wondered what other television had she done and she replied, "I have never done a television show in my life—that I can recall. I have been interviewed, like, by a newsreel or, if people come to Lauderdale on a premiere, something like that, but this is the first time I've ever been in front, would you believe, of an audience in my life. Last time was Girls' Commercial High School. It's true!"

Another man asked who her favorite leading man was. Susan responded, "Well, I can say absolutely and completely, my all-time favorite leading man is John Wayne." She cited Chuck Connors as her second favorite, meaning, one supposes, she liked his work, because they'd not worked together.

Susan told Gilda from Boston that of her own films, *I'll Cry Tomorrow* was probably her favorite. Later she said her favorite song in that film was "Happiness Is Just a Thing Called Joe."

A woman said, "Your eyes have so much love. What is your philosophy of life?"

Susan replied, "I don't think I've ever thought about it."

Another woman asked: "What keeps you so happy?"

Susan said, "I think, I think life has been good to me, and so how can I be unhappy?"

Susan's friend, producer Martin Rackin, was in the audience, and they joked about how he'd always called her "Hooligan."

Joey presented Susan with a photo album, she said she'd give to her grandchildren. She viewed the photos and recited the names of actors and movie titles. She was also shown a picture of herself advertising Chase candy.

Sitting beside Susan was comedian Don Rickles. For perhaps the only time in his career, the master of the skewering barb was in awe and held his tongue. Joey said that Susan wanted Don on that night.

A scene from *Valley of the Dolls* was shown and Susan said afterward, "Tough old broad. Very tough old broad. On the screen. *I'm* not." She told Don she took the role because "I needed gasoline for my boat."

Susan introduced organist Frost, who played two numbers. Susan says, "I want to tell you one thing, Joey. Whenever Jack comes over to my house—it's a very nice house; it's right on a canal, and I say, 'Jack, c'mon over, bring your wife, we'll have a party.' And I call everybody up and we knock the walls out, and everybody calls the police and the police stay and enjoy it, too."

The segment concluded as Joey asked Susan to dance with him to the tune "Do I Hear a Waltz?"

Late in 1968, Susan Hayward lost an important mentor. Walter Wanger, the producer so very instrumental in Hayward's career, died of a heart attack on November 18.

Also in 1968, Susan was talked into giving the stage a try. She knew she could sing and dance a little, as witnessed by her roles in *With a Song in My Heart* and *I'll Cry Tomorrow*. She trained in New York for *Mame*. The "challenge of working on a real stage before real people instead of on a sound stage before a camera was simply irresistible." Choreographer Onna White, who'd done the Broadway version of *Mame* and the 1968 film version of *Oliver!*, helped her train. There was talk that if Hayward did well, she might garner the lead in the film version.[70] Others thought it would go to Barbra Streisand, Angela Lansbury or Rosalind Russell, who'd done the role in the 1958 non-musical film *Auntie Mame*.[71] As it transpired, the film role went to Lucille Ball in 1974.

Hayward trained hard to get into shape. According to some biographers, her drinking had taken a toll on her figure and shocked choreographer Onna White, who put Susan through a tough regimen to put tone back into her muscles.[72]

Loretta Swit was in the cast and later said, "The whole cast was such a fan. We got up and we applauded when she walked in. And she was so surprised. And she kept trying to quiet us down."[73]

On December 27, 1968, *Mame* opened in Caesar's Palace in Las Vegas. There was initial success. The *Los Angeles Times'* C. Robert Jennings said, "But she is a curiously affecting Mame. I was even moved by her scenes with Patrick. Having cursed and cried through countless miles of celluloid for so long, it is not surprising that she was best on lines like 'Oh, hell' and 'That word, darling is *Bastard*' and 'Who gives a *damn* about money, I've lost my child. Oh, Vera, what are we gonna do?' Hokey, sure, but just glutted with Susan Hayward's own very special brand of sexiness and suffering. I guarantee you will never see the likes of it again."[74]

Success was short-lived because Hayward's vocal chords gave out. "My doctors insisted I leave *Mame* and do nothing but rest my voice for several months. I love the show and the cast, and I hate to walk out on Caesars Palace. What really breaks my heart is I've never copped out on any role or anybody in my 30 years as a performer." [75] A few years later Hayward put a different spin on her exit: "I tried the stage—the Las Vegas production of *Mame*—but that was only because Marty Rackin insisted. I could not wait for the run to get finished. Talk about being bored! The same old lines, the same old songs every night. Not for me, Baby, not for me."[76]

According to some biographers, despite her willingness to shape up for *Mame*, once in Las Vegas she reverted to liquor and cigarettes.[77] And a doctor found small tumors on her vocal cords, giving her a good reason to exit the show.[78]

Chapter 7

Bowing Out

Take a chance, girl. Take your lumps—and learn to say goodbye.
—Darrin McGavin in Say
Goodbye, Maggie Cole *(1972)*

Having rested her vocal cords, in April of 1969 "Hayward sold her Miami manse and bought an apartment house there [Ft. Lauderdale condominium]. But she's raring for Hollywood pick action again and has so notified her agents here."[1]

Before Hayward could get any action a fire struck her Ft. Lauderdale condo. The cause was thought to be a cigarette dropped on a living room chair. There was plenty of smoke damage but nothing valuable lost.[2] Hayward had called in the fire and was preparing to lower herself from the balcony with knotted bed sheets when the firemen got to her.[3] Several months later Hayward left Florida and leased a Beverly Hills home preparatory to resuming her screen career.[4]

1972

The Revengers (National General, 1972)

The story: Former Civil War officer and Colorado rancher John Benedict (William Holden) returns from a hunting trip to find his family dead, killed by Comanches led by the renegade Tarp (Warren Vanders). Chasing Tarp into Mexico, Benedict masquerades as a mine owner and deals with a prison warden (Raul Prieto) for six convicts, Hoop (Ernest Borgnine), Job (Woody Strode), Quiberon (Roger Hanin), Chamaco (Jorge Luke), Zweig (Rene Koldehoff), and Cholo (Jorge Martinez De Hoyos). With this disparate gang Benedict tracks Tarp to his den of thieves. Tarp escapes, however, and Benedict has trouble holding his motley crew together. Shot by Chamaco, Benedict is left for dead as his gang splits up. Benedict finds succor at the homestead of Elizabeth (Hayward), who's trying to carve a new life for herself from the wilderness. Despite the affection that grows between them, Benedict cannot be dissuaded from his quest. Unfortunately, he is captured by the now–ex–prison warden. Remorseful over plugging Benedict, Chamaco and his chums bust Benedict free from his captor. Meanwhile, Tarp is being detained by an army lieutenant (Scott Holden). Comanches attack the post to rescue Tarp but are driven off by Benedict and his men, who use dynamite to good effect. In the melee Chamaco is mortally wounded. Benedict gets the drop on Tarp but finds him a broken man. Realizing that he's become almost as savage as Tarp, Benedict lets him be and turns for home.

Variety was on target, saying it "meets the demands of screen westerns as a shooting gallery, but story-wise, despite a premise that could have elevated feature into a slick actioner, plunges into a sough of indecisive writing in need of 15 to 20 minutes' shearing." As for Hayward, "Much of the footage deals with Holden's relations with his gang ... and an overly-long sequence in which Susan Hayward plays a frontier nurse, neither pertinent to plot and more of a detriment than an asset despite femme's pretty puss."[5]

The *New York Times* called it "a workmanlike movie, snugly directed by Daniel Mann, with a solid craggy and dusty sweep of Mexican background.... Furthermore, the story shoehorns into the middle a brief, tender vignette involving a wounded Holden and a frontier nurse, played by Susan Hayward. Miss Hayward is a fine, honest actress but entirely incredible as this gentle altruist who sheds wisdom way out in the middle of nowhere."[6]

Some audience members had high hopes for this western because it re-teamed Holden, Borgnine and Mexico, and thus superficially recalled their 1969 masterpiece, *The Wild Bunch*. But quality of that nature was an illusory desire. *The Revengers* (1972) was not directed by a master of the western form such as Sam Peckinpah, but rather by another Brooklyn native and one of Hayward's favorites, Daniel Mann. He'd directed her in *I'll Cry Tomorrow* and *Ada*. As any veteran moviegoer could see, *The Revengers* was not merely a shadow of *The Wild Bunch* but a variation on several similarly plotted films. In *The Bravados* (1958) Gregory Peck returns home to find his wife dead, whereupon he leaves neighbor ranch lady Joan Collins in the dust and takes the warpath against an outlaw gang he mistakenly thinks murdered his wife. In *The Comancheros* (1961) John Wayne leaves Joan O'Brien back at the farm while he quashes renegades and Indians. Three years after *The Revengers* came *The Outlaw Josey Wales* (1975), in which Clint Eastwood kills the Comancheros and Union Army raiders who wiped out his family.

Producer Martin Rackin had been instrumental in attracting Hayward to the film:

> I was making a picture called *The Revengers* in Mexico and I had a great cameo part, opposite William Holden. The telephone bit again: "Hey, Hooligan, how about another shot at getting out of Sun City?" She came to Mexico and did a superb job for me in my picture. While she was there, I got the feeling she *might* be ready to return to the industry permanently. So I put her with my publicist, Jay Bernstein, who put her with Norman Brokaw, one of the top agents at William Morris.[7]

Actually Mary Ure, wife of Robert Shaw, was originally scheduled for the role of Elizabeth. Another inducement for Hayward to accept the role was William Holden, with whom she'd costarred in *Young and Willing* (1943):

> I'm looking forward to *The Revengers*, because I'll be working with old friends. I've known Bill Holden for 20 years, since we worked together at Paramount when we were both getting started in the business. And I like the idea of going on location to make a picture. Life on location with an outdoor picture is so simple and relaxed. I won't have to dress up or even wear makeup. *The Revengers* is going to be a work of love.[8]

Hayward told her interviewer she maintained her weight at 110 or lower by eating six eggs a day. In three days she could lose five pounds. She expressed interest in making TV movies or "a television series if the part were right."[9] She wanted to continue working: "No, I'm not thinking in terms of bringing glamour back to the screen, because I won't try to be glamorous. I'll try to be real. But I think you can be real without being repulsive."[10]

Hayward completed her role in *The Revengers* in November 1971.[11] In 1972 she told an interviewer, "My life in Hollywood today ... is not too different from what it used to be. I never was a party-goer. I see the friends I saw in the past, and I'm working."[12] By then Hayward had signed with the William Morris Agency and taken the plunge into TV movies.

Heat of Anger (CBS TV movie, 1972)

The story: Construction magnate Frank Galvin (Lee J. Cobb) is incriminated in the death of construction worker Ray Carson (Ray Simms), who'd been having an affair with Galvin's 18-year-old daughter Chris (Jennifer Penny). Galvin family friend and attorney Jessie Tate Fitzgerald (Hayward) hires young Augustus Pride (James Stacy) to be her associate counsel in the pending trial. Frustrated by Galvin's recalcitrance to come clean, Pride threatens to quit the case until he learns that Galvin can't remember details about his confrontation with Carson. At the trial Jessie reveals that Galvin is not Chris' natural father. Lillian McWhorter (Lucille Benson), one of Carson's schoolteachers, indicates that even as a youth Ray was a risk taker. This is seconded by Mrs. Carson (Tyne Daly) who admits that Ray had multiple romantic flings and had to keep proving things to himself. Despite these pluses for her side, Jessie worries that District Attorney Kagel (Fritz Weaver) is too relaxed. In the elevator Kagel reviews Galvin's criminal past and says he will entertain a voluntary manslaughter plea. Galvin tells Chris he and her mother are leaving the state. Chris calls Jessie, who, with Pride, convinces Galvin not to jump bail. In order to beat Kagel to the punch, Jessie has Pride grill Galvin on his checkered past. Galvin recalls his confrontation with Ray and says he didn't get up after Ray knocked him down because he was sick of fighting. But Ray taunted him and, high on his own juice, backed up and fell from the building. The jury finds Galvin not guilty. As Pride watches a recap on TV, Jessie stops by and asks if she can call on him again. He says yes and she leaves. He prepares coffee because he senses she'll return to argue her case for a long-term partnership.

Reviewer Leonard Maltin found it a "Familiar blend of courtroom stereotypes.... Good cast cannot redeem script. Average."[13]

Hayward had replaced Barbara Stanwyck on this project when the latter had a kidney removed. The original title was *Fitzgerald and Pride*. As well as being a TV movie, it was a pilot for a prospective series.[14] Hayward had wondered if she could still memorize lines but found acting came back naturally.[15] Observing her in the makeup chair, a *TV Guide* reporter covered Hayward's return to Hollywood: "The familiar long red hair cascaded; the small but sensual body jutted; a miracle of nature or science had made the familiar upturned-nose face almost as unwrinkled as it was when she slunk through *Demetrius and the Gladiators* with Victor Mature nearly 20 years ago."[16]

Hayward seemed to be enjoying herself. But *Heat of Anger* was no more than an average TV movie that would be totally forgotten but for her presence. The music is obtrusive. The camera zooms in too much too

The Revengers (National General Pictures, 1972), with William Holden.

fast. Despite these flaws, *Heat of Anger* could have made a decent TV series. It didn't, but Hayward immediately found herself in another TV movie for which five thousand dollars were allotted for her swank attire.[17]

Say Goodbye, Maggie Cole (ABC TV movie, 1972)

The story: Medical researcher Dr. Maggie Cole (Hayward) watches in disbelief as her husband, Dr. Benjamin Cole (Richard Anderson), suffers a coronary and crashes his small plane. Seeking a change of venue, Maggie spurns Hank Cooper's (Dane Clark) efforts to keep her on staff and takes a short-term general practitioner's job in Chicago. She'll fill in for Dr. Lou Grazzo (Darren McGavin) while he's on vacation. But Grazzo never leaves, telling her he'll go "Soon as my car's serviced." Taking the advice of luncheonette counter girl Lisa Downey (Michelle Nichols), Maggie rents a room at Grandma Downey's (Jeanette Nolan). When Maggie discovers that Lisa has leukemia, she asks Hank Cooper to send her an experimental drug, a "vial of hope." Initial hope for Lisa fades and Maggie is distraught. Grazzo finds her and tells her to stop running and to face up to the fact of her husband's death. Maggie returns to the hospital.

Lisa wakes and calls for mommy. Maggie says, "I'm here" and clasps the dying girl's hand. "I really loved that girl, Lou," Maggie tells Grazzo. She says she'll stay on at the practice, returns to the hospital desk and signs off on the cause of Lisa's death.

The *Los Angeles Times* said, "The movie is a showcase for Miss Hayward's talents, and while this is good for Miss Hayward and for those who would like to make her into a permanent weekly fixture, it is bad for the movie ... the plot doesn't so much wander as sprawl. We not only know Maggie Cole's struggles, but the problems of everyone at the local drugstore.... Also Miss Hayward and McGavin spend so much time hinting at women's lib issues that until the end they forget about each other as people, let alone man and woman."[18] Said another reviewer, "Impressive performances by Hayward and McGavin in touching, realistic drama. Above average."[19]

Much is implausible. It would be very difficult to use an experimental drug for the first time on a human just by phoning the lab and having it shipped in. Is it plausible that a researcher will be allowed to practice medicine when she hasn't done so in fifteen years? There are perfunctory patient diagnoses. Patients don't ask questions. Hayward is a bit too glamorous in her attire, what with necklaces and perfect hair. Dialogue marks it as a film of its time: "Square," "skinhead," "hip with the lip." Nevertheless, like *Heat of Anger,* this too could have succeeded as a TV series. Perhaps it was the downbeat ending that prevented it.

In any case, Hayward might not have been able to play the part. The use of Dilantin in *Say Goodbye* would be an ironic predictor of things to come. Hayward would soon be too ill to work.

As for her TV movie experience, Hayward said, "I love doing television movies. You work like a slave, but it's fun. And the shooting schedules run thirteen days straight, which I like because I have a great deal of self-discipline when I'm working. I feel a sense of responsibility. I'm always on time and I like to get the work done right on schedule."[20]

"[Teleplay author Sandor Stern] basically wrote the story for Susan," wrote Dianne Thomas in the *Susan Hayward Collectors' Club Newsletter.* 'He had been inspired by Susan's life after Eaton's death.... By Susan knowingly accepting this somewhat biographical role—it appears to have been a catharsis, a sort of therapy for her. Filming certain scenes would surely bring back memories of Eaton and the grief of losing him, yet she agreed to make the TV movie. Therefore, I believe she was in effect saying: 'Hey, world. I'm back again, just as strong or stronger than before. I've been hit hard, but now I'm bouncing back, ready to work again and to go on with life.'"[21]

Veteran chronicler of Academy Award winning movies and actors

Robert Osborne was granted a lot of information by Hayward at this time. She provided her views on 35 topics, from actors in politics to fans, from *I'll Cry Tomorrow* to morality, from the awards to working. Of fans she said she never understood why they put actors rather than a medical person on a pedestal. She didn't keep scrapbooks. She did believe in capital punishment. "John Wayne is my favorite leading man of all time. Why? He's so big and so rugged and so strong and can do practically anything, yet he's very gentle. I've always adored him, always, but then so has the whole world."[22]

The End of a Life

Hayward was becoming severely ill and the newspapers were picking up on it. Her son Timothy told Dorothy Manners that when she exited the hospital, "she has a lot of continued rest and care ahead, but she'll be in familiar surroundings and that means a lot to her and to us.' And to the rest of us who are pulling for this lovely lady who has been so very ill."[23] One article suggested Hayward was doing so well she was thinking of moving to Mexico.[24]

Though hardly healthy enough to do it, Susan agreed to present the Best Actress Academy Award at the ceremonies on April 2, 1974, at the Dorothy Chandler Pavilion in Los Angeles.

Designer Nolan Miller created a high-necked, long-sleeved green sequined gown to hide Hayward's now lean figure. Said Miller, "We're going out and getting you the goddamnedest red Susan Hayward wig that anyone has ever seen!" as well as jewelry from Van Cleef and Arpel's.[25]

Makeup artist Frank Westmore wrote that Hayward requested his expertise the afternoon of the ceremony:

I was distressed at what I saw. Susan had been undergoing radioactive cobalt treatments for a malignant brain tumor, and the damaging rays had destroyed her beautiful red hair, her eyebrows, even her eyelashes. The basic pert and beautiful face was still there, but I had to reconstruct her as she had been thirty years before. I worked feverishly for four hours, until she had to leave for the Music Center presentation site at 6 p.m. I was never more proud of my craftsmanship than when I saw Susan walk out on that stage, leaning on Charlton Heston's arm, as she announced that the winner was Glenda Jackson. She looked not much different from the Susan Hayward of 1945, and that's how the world will remember her.[26]

But Hayward needed Dilantin injections to go on stage with her *President's Lady* co-star Charlton Heston.[27]

Hayward's entrance was the second surprise of the evening, follow-ing a rare public appearance by Katharine Hepburn, who had wanted to present producer Lawrence Weingarten with the Irving G. Thalberg Memorial Award.

> Then came Electrical Charge Number Two. Susan Hayward had shown up to help Charlton Heston award the Best Actress of the year trophy and to prove to the world some of those recurrent rumors about the state of her health were exaggerated. "Ladies and gentlemen, this is not an illusion. It's Susan Hayward," said [David] Niven. She walked to the podium—some-what tentatively—with Heston, looking as gorgeous as she was in the oil fields of Tulsa. Deliberately cutting off a potential standing ovation, Hay-ward was home and into the business at hand. The cameras caressed her too briefly but her moment, like Hepburns [sic], was also a knockout."[28]

Hayward presented the Academy Award designated for Glenda Jack-son for her role in *A Touch of Class* to the film's producer-director, Melvin Frank. He gave Hayward a kiss.

Ironically, Hayward and Katharine Hepburn had never met until the Academy Award show. But afterward Hepburn came to call.

> Because Kate is such a private person, she won't like my writing of the good she does in her own quiet way. She takes care of people; helps them; reads and cooks for blind friends; shares her indomitable spirit with those who need it most.
> In the last days of Susan Hayward's life, Kate visited her regularly, bring-ing courage and comfort. She never told me about it. Susan's hairdresser did.[29]

One reporter said Hayward described her continued survival as "a miracle of faith." She was said to have told the William Morris Agency to find more work, beginning with a commercial.[30] In retrospect, this seems a smokescreen. Hayward was private, but the manner in which she was enabled to attend the Academy Award show indicated she couldn't work. But perhaps she was optimistic about the possibility of remission.

In July Hayward was admitted to Atlanta's Emory University Hos-pital for a biopsy to determine if her brain tumor was malignant or benign.[31] She left the hospital shortly thereafter and returned to California. Dr. George Tindall, Emory University Hospital neurosurgeon, would not breach confidentiality to discuss the biopsy result.[32] Hayward was back at Emory in October.[33] After she left later that month for California her doctor said she'd shown "considerable improvement" from "non-surgical treatment."[34]

Improvement was only relative. Edythe Marrenner Chalkley died at home at 2:25 p.m. on March 14, 1975.[35] Century City Hospital was listed as place of death on her Certificate of Death. The immediate cause: cerebral seizure and bronchial pneumonia. The final illness lasted one week. This itself was the result of tumor metastasis that had lasted approximately two and a half years. Susan was listed as 57 years old, as having been an actress for 36 years and having been born on June 30, 1917.

Some obituaries perpetuated the myth of the *Saturday Evening Post* cover having influenced David Selznick to test her for the Scarlett O'Hara role in *Gone with the Wind*. *Variety* got it right, however, indicating that it was the modeling photos inside that attracted attention. But it contained its own misinformation, e.g., *The Conquered* instead of *The Conqueror*, and a birth date of 1919.[36]

Susan Hayward was buried in Carrollton, Georgia, where she'd spent those happy years with second husband Eaton. The Reverend Thomas Brew and the Reverend Danny McGuire conducted the final rights in Our Lady of Perpetual Help Catholic Church across from Susan's Carrollton estate.[37] She was buried beside Eaton.[38] It was reported that there were 500 mourners.[39]

Hayward's California physician, Dr. Lee Siegel, indicated that she'd undergone chemotherapy for two and a half years. He described her as a rare case because most people would have died between six weeks to three months. "But she had a tremendous desire to live…. She was a terrific fighter" who survived so long because of her "fighting spirit, the chemotherapy and her religious faith."[40]

Hayward bequeathed her furs to friend Carmen Perugini. Her brother Wally was granted $200,000 to be paid in monthly installments by the United California Bank, acting as trustee. Jewelry as well as the bulk of the estate was to be held in trust for her sons until they turned 35. Hayward requested that her sons give their father, Jess Barker, nothing.[41] In a codicil Hayward wrote, "I Susan Chalkley being of sound mind wish to exclude my sister Florence from any benefits from my will, or from any benefits that may accrue from my estate."[42] That codicil was added after Florence disputed the will and asked for $20,000. "I, Florence Marrenner, was the victim of a deliberate continuing, determined effort of ill will and evil motives, by the decedent, my sister."[43] Florence's claim was rejected and, as executors, Hayward's sons signed off on it.[44]

An advertisement in the June 6, 1976, *Los Angeles Times* announced that on June 13 Hayward's furniture, art, paintings, china, personal effects and an organ, among other items, were auctioned off by the firm of Arthur B. Goode on North La Cienega Blvd. In 1984 Hayward's jewelry was auctioned off by Sotheby's.[45]

How to Succeed—the Hayward Way

Edythe Marrenner grew up in poverty but, through moxie and persistence, looks and talent, achieved professional success. As Susan Hayward she overcame tactlessness and an uncompromising nature that threatened to make her an "under-used" actress in a brief career.[46]

Elements of her character are what attracted her audience. Men desired her beauty and perhaps the challenge of confronting a tigress. Women wished to emulate her independence—manifested in screen characters who offered to light their male partner's cigarette, hailed their own taxi, and waded into a fight when necessary. Susan Hayward was no shrinking violet—on screen or off.

Hayward's personal life became as rocky as that of some of her screen characters. An ugly divorce battle with her first husband was partly responsible for a suicide attempt. Hard on the heels of those incidents was a headline-making incident when Hayward engaged a starlet in a veritable catfight. The security and love she felt with her second husband was short-lived due to his untimely death. Cancer shortened her own life. Nevertheless, she had her sons, a few special friends and, though she seems not to have fully appreciated or even realized it, the adoration of a mass audience.

In the final analysis, we can only know Hayward from her screen roles. As a columnist wrote shortly after Hayward's death, "I never knew Susan Hayward, never even saw her in person. And that, I suppose, is the only way you ever really get to know a movie star. When she died not long ago, there were few memory-filled eulogies from former co-workers. They probably knew her too well to know how memorable she was."[47]

Appendix: Chronology

June 30, 1917	Born Edythe Marrenner in Brooklyn, New York
June 1935	Graduates Girls' Commercial High
1936	Becomes model for Walter Thornton Agency
October 30, 1937	Appears in *Saturday Evening Post* "Merchant of Venus" modeling spread
November 1937	Moves to Hollywood
December 1937	Hollywood screen test as Edith Marrener
1937–1938	Scarlett O'Hara stand-in during *Gone with the Wind* casting tests, signs contract with Warner Bros., changes name to Susan Hayward, gets bit parts
1938	First noticeable speaking role in *Girls on Probation*
1939	Released from Warner Bros. contract, signs with Paramount
1939	"Official" screen debut in *Beau Geste*
October 7, 1939	Appears on cover of *Saturday Evening Post*
July 23, 1944	Marries actor Jess Barker
February 19, 1945	Gives birth to twins Timothy and Gregory
1945	Signs contract with producer Walter Wanger
1948	Nominated for Best Actress Academy Award for *Smash-Up! The Story of a Woman* (1947)
1948	Walter Wanger sells Hayward contract to 20th Century–Fox

1950	Nominated for Best Actress Academy Award for *My Foolish Heart* (1949)
August 10, 1951	Places hand and footprints in cement at Grauman's Chinese Theatre
1951	Proclaimed "Queen of Glamour" by Motion Picture Photographers' Association
1952	Ranked number nine in Quigley Publications exhibitors poll
February 9, 1953	Wins *Photoplay* Gold Medal award for *With a Song in My Heart*
1953	Nominated for Best Actress Academy Award for *With a Song in My Heart* (1952). Wins Foreign Press Association's Golden Globe as Best Actress—Musical/Comedy for *With a Song in My Heart,* and voted World Film Favorite—Female. Wins *Photoplay* Gold Medal award for *With a Song in My Heart*
1953	*Picturegoer* and *Motion Picture* awards for Best Actress of 1952
1953	Ranked number nine in Quigley poll
1954	Divorces Jess Barker
April 26, 1955	Attempts suicide via sleeping pills
1956	Nominated for Best Actress Academy Award for *I'll Cry Tomorrow* (1955). For *I'll Cry Tomorrow* receives Cannes Film Festival Best Actress Award, New York Film Critics Best Actress Award, and Golden Globe as Best Actress—Drama
1956	Ranked number five in *Boxoffice* popularity poll
February 9, 1957	Marries Floyd Eaton Chalkley
January 24, 1959	Wins New York Film Critics Best Actress Award for *I Want to Live!* (1958)
April 6, 1959	Wins Best Actress Academy Award for *I Want to Live!*
1959	Ranked number 10 in Quigley poll
January 9, 1966	Husband Eaton Chalkley dies
December 27, 1968	Opens in *Mame* at Caesar's Palace, Las Vegas
April 2, 1974	Presents Best Actress Academy Award for Glenda Jackson

| March 14, 1975 | Susan Hayward dies in Beverly Hills, California |
| Autumn 1999 | Voted Favorite Film Actress of 1950s–1960s in *Access Hollywood* website poll |

Filmography

Ada (MGM, 1961; 108 min.) Producer, Lawrence Weingarten. Director, Daniel Mann. Assistant Director, Al Jennings, Michael Messinger. Screenplay, Arthur Sheekman, William Driskill. Based on *Ada Dallas* by Wirt Williams. Photography, Joseph Ruttenberg. Editor, Ralph E. Winters. Assistant Editor, Rita Roland. Music, Bronislau Kaper. Song: "May the Lord Bless You Real Good" by Warren Roberts, Wally Fowler; Sung by Dean Martin. Orchestra Conductor, Robert Armbruster. Recording Supervisor, Franklin Milton. Sound, Conrad Kahn. Makeup, William Tuttle. Art Direction, George W. Davis, Edward Carfagno. Set Decoration, Henry Grace, Jack Mills. Costume Design, Helen Rose. Hairstyles, Mary Keats. Special Visual Effects, Lee LeBlanc. Cast: Ada Dallas (Susan Hayward), Bo Gillis (Dean Martin), Sylvester Marin (Wilfrid Hyde-White), Colonel Yancey (Ralph Meeker), Steve Jackson (Martin Balsam), Ronnie Hallerton (Frank Maxwell), Alice Sweet (Connie Sawyer), speaker (Ford Rainey), Al Winslow (Charles Watts), Joe Adams (Larry Gates), Warren Natfield (Robert F. Simon), Harry Davers (William Zuckert), clubwoman (Mary Treen).

Adam Had Four Sons (Columbia, 1941; 81 min.) Producer, Robert Sherwood. Associate Producer, Gordon S. Griffith. Director, Gregory Ratoff. Assistant Director, Norman Deming. Screenplay, William Hurlbutt, Michael Blankfort. Based on the novel *Legacy* by Charles Bonner. Editor, Francis D. Lyon. Photography, Peverell Marley. Music, W. Franke Harling. Musical Director, C. Bakaleinikoff. Art Direction, Rudolph Sternad. Set Decoration, Howard Bristol. Gowns, David Kidd. Executed by Coyla. Cast: Emilie Gallatin (Ingrid Bergman), Adam Stoddard (Warner Baxter), Hester (Susan Hayward), Jack Stoddard (Richard Denning), Molly Stoddard (Fay Wray), David Stoddard (Johnny Downs), Chris Stoddard (Robert Shaw), Phillip Stoddard (Charles Lind), Young Jack (Billy Ray), Young David (Steven Muller), Young Chris (Wallace Chadwell), Young Phillip (Bobby Walberg), Cousin Phillippa (Helen Westley), Vance (June Lockhart), Otto (Pietro Sosso), Dr. Lane (Gilbert Emery), Photographer (Renie Riano), Sam (Clarence Muse).

Among the Living (Paramount, 1941; 68 min.) Producer, Sol C. Siegel. Associate Producer, Colbert Clark. Director, Stuart Heisler. Screenplay, Lester

179

Cole, Garret Fort. Based on a story by Brian Marlow and Lester Cole. Editor, Everett Douglas. Photography, Theodor Sparkuhl. Music, Gerard Carbonara. Sound Recording, Hugo Grenzbach, Gene Garvin. Art Direction, Hans Dreier, Haldane Douglas. Cast: John and Paul Raden (Albert Dekker), Millie Pickens (Susan Hayward), Dr. Ben Saunders (Harry Carey), Elaine Raden (Frances Farmer), Bill Oakley (Gordon Jones), Peggy Nolan (Jean Phillips), Pompey (Ernest Whitman), Mrs. Pickens (Maude Eburne), Sheriff (Frank M. Thomas), Judge (Harlan Briggs), Tom Reilly (Archie Twitchell), Woman in café (Dorothy Sebastian), Minister (William Stack).

And Now Tomorrow (Paramount, 1944; 84 min.) Producer, Fred Kohlmar, Director, Irving Pichel. Screenplay, Frank Partos, Raymond Chandler. Based on the novel by Rachel Field. Editor, Duncan Mansfield. Photography, Daniel L. Fapp. Music, Victor Young. Art Direction, Hans Dreier, Hal Pereira. Special Effects, Farciot Edouart. Cast: Dr. Mark Vance (Alan Ladd), Emily Blair (Loretta Young), Janice Blair (Susan Hayward), Jeff Stoddard (Barry Sullivan), Aunt Em (Beulah Bondi), Dr. Weeks (Cecil Kellaway), Angeletta Gallo (Helen Mack), Joe (Darryl Hickman), Peter Gallo (Anthony Caruso), Dr. Sloane (Jonathan Hale), Bobby (Conrad Binyon), Patient (Minerva Urecal), Hester (Connie Leon), Emily age 7 (Ann Carter), Dr. Vance age 12 (Merrill Rodin), Janice age 4 (Eleanor Donahue), Carrie (Constance Purdy), Maid of Honor (Doris Dowling), Best Man (Ronnie Rondell), Receptionist (Mae Clark), Charlie (Doodles Weaver), Clerk (Byron Foulger), Nurses (Mary Field, Hazel Keener), Waiter (Jack M. Gardner), Truck driver (Jimmie Dunde), Mr. Meade (Alec Craig).

Back Street (Universal-International, 1961; 107 min.) Producer, Ross Hunter. Director, David Miller. Assistant Director, Phil Bowles, James Welch. Screenplay, Eleanore Griffin, William Ludwig. Based on the novel by Fannie Hurst. Photography, Stanley Cortez. Eastman Color by Pathé. Editor, Milton Carruth. Music Supervision, Joseph Gershenson. Title Song, Frank Skinner, Ken Darby. Sound, Waldon O. Watson. Art Direction, Alexander Golitzen. Set Decoration, Howard Bistol. Unit Production Manager, Lew Leary. Gowns Design, Jean Louis. Makeup, Bud Westmore. Hairstyles, Larry Germain. Original Oil Paintings, Alison Hunter. Dialogue Director, Leon Charles. Cast: Rae Smith (Susan Hayward), Paul Saxon (John Gavin), Liz Saxon (Vera Miles), Curt Stanton (Charles Drake), Janie (Virginia Grey), Dalian (Reginald Gardiner), Caroline Saxon (Tammy Marihugh), Mrs. Evans (Natalie Schafer), Paul Saxon, Jr. (Robert Eyer), Mrs. Panworth (Karen Norris), Marge Claypole (Mary Lawrence), Charley Claypole (Hayden Rorke), Miss Hatfield (Doreen McLean), Mr. Venner (Alex Gerry), Airport clerk (Joe Cronin), Hotel clerk (Ted Thorpe), Proprietor (Joseph Mell), Sailor (Dick Kallman), Showroom model (Joyce Meadows), Paris airport employee (Lilyan Chauvin), Harper's Bazaar models (Joanne Betay, Vivianne Porte, Isabelle Felder, Melissa Weston, Bea Ammidown).

Beau Geste (Paramount, 1939; 114 min.) Producer and director, William A. Wellman. Screenplay, Robert Carson. Based on the novel by Percival Christopher Wren. Editor, Thomas Scott. Photography, Theodor Sparkuhl, Archie Stout. Music, Alfred Newman. Orchestrations, Edward Powell. Sound Recording, Hugo Granzbach, Walter Oberst. Technical Adviser, Louis Van Der Ecker. Art Direction, Hans Dreier, Robert Odell. Cast: Beau Geste (Gary Cooper), John Geste (Ray Milland), Digby Geste (Robert Preston), Sergeant Markoff (Brian Donlevy),

Rasinoff (J. Carrol Naish), Isobel Rivers (Susan Hayward), Schwartz (Albert Dekker), Hank Miller (Broderick Crawford), Buddy McMonigal (Charles Barton), Major Henri de Beaujolais (James Stephenson), Lady Patricia Brandon (Heather Thatcher), Augustus Brandon (G. P. Huntley, Jr.), Lieutenant Dufour (James Burke), Renouf (Henry Brandon), Renault (Arthur Aylesworth), Renoir (Harry Woods), Voisin (Harold Huber), Maris (Stanley Andrews), Beau age 12 (Donald O'Connor), John age 10 (Billy Cook), Digby age 12 (Martin Spellman), Augustus age 12 (David Holt), Isobel age 10 (Ann Gillis), Lieutenant Martin (Harvey Stephens), Krenke (Barry Macollum), Bugler (Ronnie Rondell), Burdon the Butler (Frank Dawson), Cordier (George Chandler), Glock (Duke Green), Recruiting office colonel (Thomas Jackson), Sergeant-Major (Jerome Storm), Sergeant (Joseph Whitehead), Corporal (Harry Worth), Corporal Golas (Nestor Paiva), Arab scouts (George Regas, Francis McDonald), Legionnaire Roberts (Carl Voss), Legionnaire Williams (Joe Bernard), Legionnaire Paul (Robert Perry), Legionaire Fenton (Larry Lawson), Legionnaire Clements (Henry Sylvester), Legionnaire Virginia (Joseph William Cody), Trumpeter Leo (Joe Colling), Port Said café girl (Gladys Jean).

Canyon Passage (Universal, 1946; 90 min.) Producer, Alexander Golitzen. Director, Jacques Tourneur. Assistant Director, Fred Frank. Screenplay, Ernest Pascal. Dialogue Director, Anthony Jowitt. Based on the story by Ernest Haycox. Editor, Milton Carruth. Photography, Edward Cronjager. Technicolor. Technicolor Director, Natalie Kalmus. Special Photography, D. S. Horsley. Technicolor Associate, William Fitsche. Music, Frank Skinner. Sound Director, Bernard B. Brown. Technician, William Hedgcock. Art Direction, John B. Goodman, Richard H. Riedel. Set Decoration, Russell A. Gausman, Leigh Smith. Costumes, Travis Banton. Makeup, Jack B. Pierce. Hair Stylist, Carmen Dirigo. Cast: Logan Stewart (Dana Andrews), Camrose (Brian Donlevy), Lucy Overmire (Susan Hayward), Hi Lennet (Hoagy Carmichael), Honey Bragg (Ward Bond), Ben Dance (Andy Devine), Caroline (Patricia Roc), Jonas Overmire (Stanley Ridges), Mrs. Overmire (Fay Holden), Johnny Steele (Lloyd Bridges), Vane Blazier (Victor Cutler), Lestrade (Onslow Stevens), Marta (Rose Hobart), Mrs. Dance (Dorothy Peterson), Clenchfield (Halliwell Hobbes), Gray Bartlett (James Cardwell), Neil Howison (Ray Teal), Liza Stone (Virginia Patton), Asa Dance (Tad Devine), Bushrod Dance (Denny Devine), Cobb (Fancis McDonald), Judge (Erville Alderson), Stutchell (Ralph Peters), Teamster (Jack Rockwell), Miners (Joseph P. Mack, Gene Stutenroth, Karl Hackett, Jack Clifford, Daral Hudson, Dick Alexander), MacIvar (Wallace Scott), Indian spokesman (Chief Yowlachi).

Comet Over Broadway (Warner Bros./First National, 1938; 69 min.) Associate Producer, Bryan Foy. Executive Producers, Hal B. Wallis, Jack L. Warner. Directors, Busby Berkeley, John Farrow. Assistant Director, Russell Saunders. Screenplay, Faith Baldwin, Mark Hellinger, Robert Buckner. Editor, James Gibbon. Photography, James Wong Howe. Music, Ray Heindorf, M. K. Jerome, Heinz Roemheld. Musical Direction, Leo F. Forbstein. Sound, Charles Lang. Art Direction, Charles Novi. Makeup, Robert Cowan. Hairstyles, Ruby Felker. Gowns, Orry-Kelly. Cast: Eve Appleton (Kay Francis), Bert Ballin (Ian Hunter), Bill Appleton (John Litel), Grant (Donald Crisp), Tim Adams (Minna Gombell), Jackie (Sybil Jason), Emerson (Melville Cooper), Janet Eaton (Leona Maricle), Wilton Banks (Ian Keith), Mrs. Appleton (Vera Lewis), Brogan (Ray Mayer),

Willis (Chester Clute), Haines (Nat Carr), Harvey (Edward McWade), Benson (Clem Bevans), Amateur actresses (Susan Hayward, Fern Barry).

The Conqueror (RKO, 1956; 110 min.) Producer, Director, Dick Powell. Presented by Howard Hughes. Associate Producer, Richard Sokolove. Screenplay, Oscar Millard. Editors, Robert Ford, Kenneth Marstella. Editorial Supervision, Stuart Gilmore. Photography, Joseph LaShelle, Leo Tover, Harry J. Wild, William Snyder. Technicolor. CinemaScope. Music, Victor Young. Sound, Bernard Freericks, Terry Kellum. Art Direction, Albert D'Agostino, Carroll Clark. Photographic Effects, Linwood Dunn, Albert Simpson. Cast: Temujin (John Wayne), Bortai (Susan Hayward), Jamuga (Pedro Armendariz), Hunlun (Agnes Moorehead), Kumlek (Ted de Corsia), Wang Khan (Thomas Gomez), Kasar (William Conrad), Shaman (John Hoyt), Tartar Captain (Leo Gordon), Chepei (Lee Van Cleef), Bogurchi (Peter Mamakos), Wang's captain of the guard (Richard Loo), Guard (Ray Spiker), Girls in bath (Jarma Lewis, Pat McMahon), Sibilant Sam (George E. Stone), Honest John (Phil Arnold), Scribe (Torben Meyer), Wang Khan wives (Pat Lawler, Pat Tiernan), Drummer boy (John George), Mongol (Weaver Levy), First chieftain (Michael Granger), Second chieftain (Fred Aldrich), Third chieftain (Paul Hoffman), Fourth chieftain (Lane Bradford), Merkit Captain (Carl Vernell), Jalair (Gregg Barton), Subuya (Fred Graham), Sorgan (Ken Terrell), Hochin (Jeanne Gerson), Mongol guards (Michael Wayne, Norman Powell), Mongolian warriors (Chivwit Indian tribe).

David and Bathsheba (20th Century–Fox, 1951; 116 min.) Producer, Darryl F. Zanuck. Director, Henry King. Screenplay, Philip Dunne. Editor, Barbara McLean. Photography, Leon Shamroy. Music, Alfred Newman. Orchestration, Edward Powell. Choreography, Jack Cole. Sound, E. Clayton Ward, Roger Heman. Art Direction, Lyle Wheeler, George Davis. Set Decoration, Thomas Little, Paul S. Fox. Wardrobe Direction, Charles LeMaire. Costume Design, Edward Stevenson. Makeup, Ben Nye. Biblical Technical Adviser, Dr. C.C. McCown. Special Photographic Effects, Fred Sersen. Cast: David (Gregory Peck), Bathsheba (Susan Hayward), Nathan (Raymond Massey), Uriah (Kieron Moore), Abishai (James Robertson Justice), Michal (Jayne Meadows), Ira (John Sutton), Joab (Dennis Hoey), Goliath (Walter Talun), Adulteress (Paula Morgan), King Saul (Francis X. Bushman), Jonathan (Teddy Infuhr), David as a boy (Leo Pessin), Specialty dancer (Gwyneth [Gwen] Verdon), Absolom (Gilbert Barnett), Priest (John Burton), Old shepherd (Lumsden Hare), Egyptian Ambassador (George Zucco), Amnon (Allan Stone), Samuel (Paul Newlan), Jesse (Holmes Herbert), Executioners (Robert Stephenson, Harry Carter), Jesse's first son (Richard Michelson), Jesse's second son (Dick Winters), Jesse's third son (John Duncan), Court announcer (James Craven).

Deadline at Dawn (RKO, 1946; 83 min.) Producer, Adrian Scott. Executive Producer, Sid Rogell. Director, Harold Clurman. Assistant Director, William Dorfman. Screenplay, Clifford Odets. Based on a novel by William Irish. Editor, Roland Gross. Photography, Nicholas Musuraca. Music, Hans Eisler. Musical Director, C. Bakaleinikoff. Sound, Earl A. Wolcott, James G. Stewart. Art Direction, Albert D'Agostino, Jack Okey. Set Decoration, Darrell Silvera. Gowns, Renie. Special Effects, Vernon L. Walker. Cast: June Goffe (Susan Hayward), Gus (Paul Lukas), Alex (Bill Williams), Bartelli (Joseph Calleia), Helen Robinson (Osa Massen), Edna Bartelli (Lola Lane), Lester Brady (Jerome Cowan),

Sleepy Parsons (Marvin Miller), Collarless man (Roman Bohnen), Man with gloves (Steven Geray), Babe Dooley (Joe Sawyer), Mrs. Raymond (Constance Worth), Lieutenant Kane (Joseph Crehan).

Demetrius and the Gladiators (20th Century–Fox, 1954; 101 min.) Producer, Frank Ross. Director, Delmer Daves. Assistant Director, William Eckhardt. Screenplay, Philip Dunne. Based on the novel *The Robe* by Lloyd C. Douglas. Editors, Dorothy Spencer, Robert Fritch. Photography, Milton Krasner. Technicolor. CinemaScope. Technicolor Color Consultant, Leonard Doss. Music, Franz Waxman. Themes from *The Robe*, Alfred Newman. Musical Director, Alfred Newman. Vocal Direction, Ken Darby. Choreography, Stephen Papich. Sound, Arthur L. Kirbach, Roger Heman. Art Direction, Lyle Wheeler, George W. Davis. Set Decoration, Walter M. Scott, Paul S. Fox. Makeup, Ben Nye. Special Photographic Effects, Ray Kellogg. Cast: Demetrius (Victor Mature), Messalina (Susan Hayward), Peter (Michael Rennie), Caligula (Jay Robinson), Lucia (Debra Paget), Paula (Anne Bancroft), Claudius (Barry Jones), Strabo (Ernest Borgnine), Glycon (William Marshall), Dardanius (Richard Egan), Cassius Chaerea (Charles Evans), Kaeso (Everett Glass), Macro (Karl Davis), Albus (Jeff York), Slave girl (Carmen de Lavallade), Varus (John Cliff), Specialty dancers (Barbara James, Willetta Smith), Senator (Selmer Jackson), Cosin (Douglas Brooks), Decurion (Fred Graham), Magistrate (Dayton Lummis), Chamberlain (George Eldredge), Prisoner (Paul Richards).

The Fighting Seabees (Republic, 1944; 100 min.) Producer, Albert J. Cohen. Director, Edward Ludwig. Second Unit Director, Howard Lydecker. Screenplay, Borden Chase, Aeneas MacKenzie. Story, Borden Chase. Editor, Richard Van Enger. Photography, William Bradford. Music, Walter Scharf. Songs, "Song of the Seabees," music and lyrics by Peter De Rose, Sam M. Lewis; "Where Do You Work-A, John?" music and lyrics, Mortimer Weinberg, Charley Marks, Harry Warren. Special Lyrics, Ned Washington. Sound, Tom Carman, Howard Wilson. Art Direction, Duncan Cramer. Set Decoration, Otto Siegel. Gowns, Adele. Technical Advisers, Lt. Commander Hubert Hunter, Lt. Commander William A. McManus. Special Effects, Theodore Lydecker. Cast: Wedge Donovan (John Wayne), Constance Chesley (Susan Hayward), Lieutenant Commander Robert Yarrow (Dennis O'Keefe), Eddie Powers (William Frawley), Johnny Novasky (Leonid Kinsky), Sawyer Collins (J. M. Kerrigan), Whanger Spreckles (Grant Withers), Ding Jacobs (Paul Fix), Yump Lumkin (Ben Welden), Lieutenant Kerrick (William Forrest), Captain Joyce (Addison Richards), Joe Brick (Jay Norris), Juan (Duncan Renaldo), Johnson (Tom London), Seabee (Hal Taliaferro), Refueling officer (Crane Whitley). With William Hall, Charles D. Brown, Roy Barcroft, Chief Thundercloud.

The Forest Rangers (Paramount, 1942; 86 min.) Producer, Robert Sisk. Director, George Marshall. Screenplay, Harold Shumate. Based on a story by Thelma Strabel. Editor, Paul Weatherwax. Photography, Charles Lang. Process Photography, Farciot Edouart. Technicolor. Technicolor Direction, Natalie Kalmus. Color Camera, William V. Skall. Music, Victor Young. Songs, Frank Loesser, Joseph Lilley, Frederick Hollander. "I've Got Spurs That Jingle, Jingle, Jingle" by Thomas Lilley. Sound Recording, Harry Mills, Richard Olson. Art Direction, Hans Dreier, Karl Hedrick. Special Photographic Effects, Gordon Jennings. Cast: Don Stuart (Fred MacMurray), Celia Huston (Paulette Goddard),

Tana Mason (Susan Hayward), Jammer Jones (Lynne Overman), Twig Dawson (Albert Dekker), Mr. Huston (Eugene Pallette), Frank Hatfield (Regis Toomey), Jim Lawrence (Rod Cameron), Terry McCabe (Clem Bevans), George Tracy (James Brown), Mr. Hanson (Jimmy Conlin), Rangers (Kenneth Griffith, Keith Richards).

Garden of Evil (20th Century–Fox, 1954; 100 min.) Producer, Charles Brackett. Associate Producer, Saul Wurtzel. Director, Henry Hathaway. Assistant Director, Stanley Hough. Screenplay, Frank Fenton. Based on a story by Fred Freiberger, William Tunberg. Editor, James B. Clark. Photography, Milton Krasner, Jorge Stahl, Jr. Technicolor. CinemaScope. Music, Bernard Herrmann. Songs: "La Negra Noche," by Emilio D. Uranga, "Aqui" by Ken Darby and Lionel Newman. Sound, Nicolas de la Rosa, Jr., Roger Heman. Art Direction, Lyle Wheeler, Edward Fitzgerald. Set Decoration, Pablo Galvan. Wardrobe Direction, Charles LeMaire. Costume Design, Tavilla. Makeup, Ben Nye. Hair Styles, Helen Turpin. Cast: Hooker (Gary Cooper), Leah Fuller (Susan Hayward), Fiske (Richard Widmark), Luke Daly (Cameron Mitchell), John Fuller (Hugh Marlowe), Vicente Madariaga (Victor Manual Mendoza), Singer (Rita Moreno), Captain (Fernando Wagner), Priest (Arturo Soto Rangel), Waiter (Manuel Donde), Bartender (Antonio Bribiesca), Victim (Salvado Terroba).

Girls on Probation (Warner Bros., 1938; 63 min.) Executive Producers, Jack L. Warner, Hal B. Wallis. Director, William McGann. Assistant Director, Elmer Decker. Screenplay, Crane Wilbur. Editor, Frederick Richards. Dialogue Director, Harry Seymour. Photography, Arthur Todd. Art Direction, Hugh Reticher. Sound, Leslie G. Hewitt. Gowns, Howard Shoup. Cast: Connie Heath (Jane Bryan), Neil Dillon (Ronald Reagan), Tony Rand (Anthony Averill), Hilda Engstrom (Sheila Bromley), Judge (Henry O'Neill), Kate Heath (Elisabeth Risdon), Roger Heath (Sig Rumann), Jane Lennox (Dorothy Peterson), Mrs. Engstrom (Esther Dale), Gloria Adams (Susan Hayward), Terry Mason (Larry Williams), Mr. Engstrom (Arthur Hoyt), Ruth (Peggy Shannon), Marge (Lenita Lane), Prisoner (Janet Shaw), Dave Warren (James Nolan), Todd (Joseph Crehan), Prosecutor (Pierre Watkin), Public Defender Craven (James Spottswood), Head Matron (Brenda Fowler), Matrons (Kate Lawson, Maude Lambert).

The Hairy Ape (United Artists, 1944; 92 min.) Producer, Jules Levey. Associate Producer, Joseph H. Nadel. Director, Alfred Santell. Assistant Director, Sam Nelson. Screenplay, Robert D. Andrews, Decla Dunning. Based on the play by Eugene O'Neill. Editor, Harvey Manger. Supervising Editor, William Ziegler. Director of Photography, Lucien Andriot. Music, Michel Michelet. Musical Director, Eddie Paul. Sound, Corson Jowett. Art Direction, James Sullivan. Set Decoration, Howard Bristol. Makeup, Bob Mark. Hairstyles, Nina Roberts. Special Effects, Harry Redmond. Cast: Hank Smith (William Bendix), Mildred Douglas (Susan Hayward), Tony Lazar (John Loder), Helen Parker (Dorothy Comingore), Paddy (Roman Bohnen), Long (Tom Fadden), Chief Engineer MacDougald (Alan Napier), Gantry (Charles Cane), Aldo (Raphael Storm), Portuguese proprietor (Charles La Torre), Concertina player (Don Zolaya), Waitress (Mary Zavian), Police captain (George Sorrel), Doctor (Paul Welgal), Musician (Egon Brecher), Refugee wife (Gisela Werbsek), Young girl (Carmen Rachel), Water tender (Jonathan Lee), Third Engineer (Dick Baldwin), Head guard (Ralph Dunn), Lieutenant (William Halligan), Doorman (Tommy Hughes), Bartender (Bob Perry).

Heat of Anger (CBS TV movie, Metromedia Partners Corporation; Stonehenge Productions, 3/3/1972; 75 min.) Producer, Ron Roth. Executive Producer, Dick Berg. Assistant to the Producer, Jerry Wineman. Production Manager, Joe Wonder. Production Executive, Art Stolnitz. Production Administrator, Elliot Friedgen. Post Production Supervisor, Gary Gerlich. Production Associate, Alan Sacks. Director, Don Taylor. Assistant Directors, Howard Roessel, Jack Stubbs. Teleplay, Fay Kanin. Legal Advisory Panel, Richard Caballero, Sanford H. Mendelson. Director of Photography, Robert C. Moreno. Editor, John F. Link II. Assistant Film Editor, Peter D. Rosten. Music Editor, John Mick. Supervising Sound Effects Editor, Charles L. Campbell. Sound Effects Editor, Roger Cornett. Recording Supervisor, Robert J. Litt. Sound Mixer, Jack Lilly. Chief Electrician, John Baron. Art Direction, Lawrence G. Paull. Miss Hayward's Wardrobe, Nolan miller. Hairstyles, Sheri Wilson. Makeup, Tom Tuttle. Casting, Gary Shaffer. Cast: Jessie Tate Fitzgerald (Susan Hayward), Augustus Pride (James Stacy), Frank Galvin (Lee J. Cobb), Vincent Kagel (Fritz Weaver), Chris Galvin (Jennifer Penny), Stella Galvin (Bettye Ackerman), Obie (Mills Watson), Ray Carson (Ray Simms), Mr. Stoller (Jack Somack), Fran (Lynette Mettey), Jean Carson (Tyne Daly), Courtroom artist (Arnold Mesches), Lillian McWhorter (Lucille Benson), Judge Randall Berkley (Noah Keen), Carmen Garcia (Inez Pedroza).

Hit Parade of 1943 (aka *Change of Heart*; Republic, 1943; 90 min.) Producer, Albert J. Cohen. Director, Albert S. Rogell. Screenplay, Frank Gill, Jr. Additional dialogue, Frances Hyland. Editor, Thomas Richards. Photography, Jack Marta. Music Directors, Walter Scharf, Jule Styne, Harold Adamson. Songs, J. C. Johnson, Andy Razaf. Songs, "A Change of Heart," "Do These Old Eyes Deceive Me," "Tahm Boom Bah," "Harlem Sandman," "Who Took Me Home Last Night?", "That's How to Write a Song," music by Jule Styne, lyrics by Harold Adamson; "Yankee Doodle Tan," music by J. C. Johnson, lyrics by Andy Razaf; "Autumn Leaves in the Gutter, Never Again Will They Flutter" (composer unidentified). Susan Hayward dubbed by Jeanne Darrell. Orchestrations, Marlin Skiles. Dances, Nick Castle. Art Direction, Russell Kimball. Set Decoration, Otto Siegel. Wardrobe, Adele Palmer. Optical Effects, Consolidated Film Industries. Cast: Rick Farrell (John Carroll), Jill Wright (Susan Hayward), Toni Jarrett (Gail Patrick), Belinda Wright (Eve Arden), Bradley Cole (Melville Cooper), J. MacClellan Davis (Walter Catlett), Janie (Mary Treen), Westinghouse (Tom Kennedy), Joyce (Astrid Allwyn), Brownie (Tim Ryan), Themselves (Jack Williams, the Harlem Sandman, Dorothy Dandridge, Pops and Louis, Music Maids, 3 Cheers, Chinita, Golden Gate Quartette, Freddy Martin and Orchestra, Count Basie and Orchestra, Ray McKinley and Orchestra).

Hollywood Hotel (Warner Bros., 1938; 109 min.)Executive Producers, Jack L. Warner, Hal B. Wallis. Associate Producers, Sam Bischoff, Bryan Foy. Director, Busby Berkeley. Assistant Director, Russ Saunders. Screenplay by Jerry Wald, Maurice Leo and Richard Macauley. Based on a story by Jerry Wald and Maurice Leo. Dialog Director, Gene Lewis. Editor, George Amy. Director of Photography, Charles Rosher. Musical Director, Leo F. Forbstein. Orchestrations, Ray Heindorf. Musical Numbers Photography, George Barnes. Assistant Dance Director, Matty King. "Satan's Holiday" music, Joe Venuti. Arranger, Benny Goodman. Songs: "Can't Teach My Heart New Trick," "I'm a Ding Dong Daddie from Dumas," "I'm

Like a Fish Out of Water," "I've Hitched My Wagon to a Star," "Let That Be a Lesson to You," "Silhouetted in the Moonlight," "Sing You Son of a Gun," "Horray for Hollywood." Words and music by Richard Whiting and Johnny Mercer. "California, Here I Come" words and music by Al Jolson, Buddy DeSylva and Joseph Mayer. "Dark Eyes," Russian folk song, arranged by Raymond Paige. Sound, Oliver S. Garretson, David Forrest. Unit Manager, Bob Fellows. Art Direction, Robert Haas. Gowns, Orry-Kelly. Cast: Ronnie Bowers (Dick Powell), Virginia Stanton (Rosemary Lane), Mona Marshall (Lola Lane), Chester Marshall (Hugh Herbert), Fuzzy (Ted Healy), Alexander Dupre (Alan Mowbray), Herself (Louella Parsons), Jonesy (Glenda Farrell), Bernie Walton (Allyn Joslyn), Georgia (Johnnie Davis), Himself (Perc Westmore), Dot Marshall (Mabel Todd), Alice (Frances Langford), Himself (Jerry Cooper), Himself (Ken Niles), Himself (Duane Thompson), Colored man (Clinton Rosemond), Desk Clerk (John Ridgely), The Russian (Fritz Feld), Hat check girl (Carole Landis), Seamstress (Georgia Cooper), Announcer at Cathay Theatre premiere (Ronald Reagan), Waiter (Joe Romantini), Girl at end of line (Edythe Marrenner/Susan Hayward), Raymond Page and His Orchestra, Benny Goodman and His Orchestra.

The Honey Pot (United Artists, 1967; 131 min.; review version 150 min.) Producers, Charles K. Feldman, Joseph L. Mankiewicz. Director, Joseph L. Mankiewicz. Script Continuity, Yvonne Axworthy. Executive Production Manager, Attilio D'Onofrio. Assistant Director, Gus Agosti. Screenplay, Joseph L. Mankiewicz. Based on a play by Frederick Knott, a book by Thomas Sterling, and a play by Ben Jonson. Editor, David Bretherton. Photography, Gianni Di Venanzo. Color by DeLuxe. Music, John Addison. Choreography, Lee Theodore. Sound Editor, Jim Groom. Sound Mixer, David Hildyard. Art Direction, Boris Juraga. Production Design, John De Cuir. Makeup, Amato Garbini. Cast: Cecil Fox (Rex Harrison), Mrs. Sheridan, aka Lone Star Crockett (Susan Hayward), William McFly (Cliff Robertson), Princess Dominique (Capucine), Merle "Bunny" McGill (Edie Adams), Sarah Watkins (Maggie Smith), Inspector Rizzi (Adolfo Celi), Volpone (Hugh Manning), Cook (Mimmo Poli), Tailor (Antonio Corevi), Massimo (Luigi Scavran), Mosca (David Dodimead), Revenue agents (Cy Grant, Frank Latimore).

House of Strangers (20th Century–Fox, 1949; 101 min.) Producer, Sol Siegel. Director, Joseph L. Mankiewicz. Screenplay, Philip Yordan. Based on the novel by Jerome Weidman. Editor, Harmon Le Maire. Photography, Milton Krasner. Music, Daniele Amfitheatrof. Art Direction, Lyle Wheeler, George W. Davis. Set Decoration, Thomas Little, Walter M. Scott. Special Effects, Fred Sersen. Cast: Gino Monetti (Edward G. Robinson), Irene Bennett (Susan Hayward), Max Monetti (Richard Conte), Joe Monetti (Luther Adler), Pietro Monetti (Paul Valentine), Tony Monetti (Efrem Zimbalist, Jr.), Maria Domenico (Debra Paget), Helena Domenico (Hope Emerson), Theresa Monetti (Esther Minciotti), Elaine Monetti (Diane Douglas), Lucca (Tito Vuolo), Victoria (Albert Morin), Waiter (Sid Thomack), Judge (Thomas Browne Henry), Prosecutor (David Wolfe), Woman juror (Ann Morrison), Danny (John Kellogg), Nightclub singer (Dolores Parker), Bit man (Mario Siletti), Pietro's opponent (Tommy Garland), Guard (Charles J. Blynn), Bat boy (Joseph Mazzuca), Cop (John Pedrini), Third applicant (Argentina Brunetti), Bit man (Maurice Samuels), Cop (George Magrill), Neighbors (Mike Stark, Herbert Vigran), Referee (Mushy Callahan), Preliminary fighters (Bob Cantro, Eddie Saenz), Doorman (George Spaulding), Taxi driver (John "Red" Kullers), Detectives (Scott Landers, Fred Hillebrand).

I Can Get It for You Wholesale (20th Century–Fox, 1951; 91 min.) Producer, Sol C. Siegel. Director, Michael Gordon. Screenplay, Abraham Polonsky. Adaptation, Vera Caspary. Based on the novel by Jerome Weidman. Editor, Robert Simpson. Photography, Milton Krasner. Music, Sol Kaplan. Musical Direction, Lionel Newman. Orchestration, Earle Hagen. Sound, Winston H. Leverett, Roger Heman. Art Direction, Lyle Wheeler, John De Cuir. Set Decoration, Thomas Little. Wardrobe Direction, Charles LeMaire. Makeup, Ben Nye. Special Photographic Effects, Fred Sersen. Cast: Harriet Boyd (Susan Hayward),Teddy Sherman (Dan Dailey), Noble (George Sanders), Cooper (Sam Jaffe), Marge (Randy Stuart), Four Eyes (Marvin Kaplan), Savage (Harry Von Zell), Ellie (Barbara Whiting), Hermione Griggs (Vicki Cummings), Ray (Ross Elliott), Kelley (Richard Lane), Mrs. Boyd (Mary Phillips), Fran (Benna Bard), Bettini (Steve Geray), Pulvermacher (Charles Lane), Ida (Jan Kayne), Terry (Marion Marshall), Models (Jayne Hazard, Aline Towne), Miss Marks (Eda Reis Merin), Louise (Marjorie Hoshelle), Nurse (Doris Kemper), Secretary (Elizabeth Flournoy), Bartender (Jack P. Carr), Mrs. Cooper (Tamara Shayne), Tiffany Joe (Ed Max), Speaker (David Wolfe), Elevator man (Harry Hines), Blondes (Diana Mumby, Shirlee Allard, Beverly Thompson).

I Married a Witch (United Artists/Masterpiece Productions, 1942; 82 min.) Producer and director, Rene Clair. Screenplay, Robert Pirosh, Mark Connelly. Based on a story by Thorne Smith completed by Norman Matson. Editor, Eda Warren. Photography, Ted Tetzlaff. Music, Roy Webb. Sound Recording, Harry Mills, Richard Olson. Art Direction, Hans Dreier, Ernest Fegté. Set Decoration, George Sawley. Costumes, Edith Head. Makeup, Wally Westmore. Special Photographic Effects, Gordon Jennings. Cast: Wallace Wooley (Fredric March), Jennifer (Veronica Lake), Dr. Dudley White (Robert Benchley), Estelle Masterson (Susan Hayward), Daniel (Cecil Kellaway), Margaret (Elizabeth Patterson), J. B. Masterson (Robert Warwick), Tabitha (Eily Malyon), Town crier (Robert Greig), Martha (Viola Moore), Nancy (Mary Field), Harriet (Nora Cecil), Allen (Emory Parnell), Vocalist (Helen S. Rayner), Justice of the Peace (Aldrich Bowker), Justice of the Peace's wife (Emma Dunn).

I Thank a Fool (MGM/Eaton Productions, 1962; 100 min.) Producer, Anatole De Grunwald. Associate Producer, Roy Parkinson. Director, Robert Stevens. Assistant Directors, David Tomblin, Derek Parr, Tony Wallis. Screenplay, Karl Tunberg. Editor, Frank Clarke. First Assistant Editor, Jim Atkinson. Assembly Editor, Philip Barnikel. Photography, Harry Waxman. Camera Operator, Jack Lowin. Second Unit Photography, Douglas Adamson. Focus, Chic Anstiss. Boom Operator, Bill Baldwin. Sound Camera Operator, Ron Matthews. Music, Ron Goodwin. Recording Supervisor, A. W. Watkins. Sound Recording, Cyril Swern. Sound Editor, Gordon Daniel. Dubbing Mixer, J. B. Smith. Col Cons, Joan Bridge. Art Direction, Sean Kenny. Assistant Art Direction, Michael Knight. Set Dresser, Pamela Cornell. Draughtsmen, Colin Grimes, Alan Tomkins. Production Design, Sean Kenny. Title Design, Chamers & Partners. Production Manager, Basil Somner. Location Manager, Ted Wallis. Continuity, Betty Harley. Production Secretary, Elizabeth Woodthorpe. Dress Design, Elizabeth Haffenden. Wardrobe Supervision, Dora Lloyd. Wardrobe Mistress, Dolly Smith. Wardrobe

Master, Charles Monet. Makeup, Tony Sforzini. Hairdresser, Joan Johnstone. Special Effects, Tom Howard. Casting Director, Irene Howard. Property Buyer, John Bigg. Still Photography, Davis Boulton. Rigger, T. Wilkie. Grip, L. Kelly. Cast: Christine Allison (Susan Hayward), Stephen Dane (Peter Finch), Liane Dane (Diane Cilento), Captain Ferris (Cyril Cusack), Roscoe (Kieron Moore), Aunt Heather (Athene Seyler), Ebblington (Richard Wattis), Woman in Black Maria (Miriam Karlin), O'Grady (Laurence Naismith), Judge (Clive Morton), Coroner (J. G. Devlin), Irish doctor (Richard Leech), Irish barmaid (Marguerite Brennan), Nurse Drew (Brenda De Banzie), Polly (Yolande Turner), Wardresses (Judith Furse, Grace Arnold), Sleazy doctor (Peter Sallis), Restaurant manageress (Joan Benham), Landlady (Joan Hickson).

I Want to Live! (United Artists, 1958; 120 min.) Producer, Walter Wanger. Director, Robert Wise. Assistant Director, George Vieira. Screenplay, Nelson Gidding, Don M. Mankiewicz. Based on newspaper articles by Ed Montgomery and the letters of Barbara Graham. Script Supervisor, Stanley Scheuer. Editor, William Hornbeck. Settings, Edward Haworth. Photography, Lionel Lindon. Music, John Mandel. Jazz Combo: Gerry Mulligan, Shelly Manne, Red Mitchell, Art Farmer, Frank Rosolino, Pete Jolly, Bud Shank. Set Decoration, Victor Gangelin. Costume Design, Wesley Jeffries, Angela Alexander. Hair Stylists, Emmy Eckhardt, Lillian Hokom Ugrin. Makeup, Tom Tuttle, Jack Stone. Casting, Lynn Stalmaster. Production Manager, Forrest E. Johnston. Cast: Barbara Graham (Susan Hayward), Ed Montgomery (Simon Oakland), Carl Palmberg (Theodore Bikel), Peg (Virginia Vincent), Emmett Perkins (Philip Coolidge), Jack Santo (Lou Krugman), Henry Graham (Wesley Lau), Bruce King (James Philbrook), District Attorney (Bartlett Robinson), Richard G. Tribow (Gage Clark), Ben Miranda (Peter Breck), Al Matthews (Joe De Santis), Father Devers (John Marley), San Quentin Warden (Raymond Bailey), San Quentin Nurse (Alice Backes), San Quentin Captain (Dabbs Greer), San Quentin Matron (Gertrude Flynn), San Quentin Sergeant (Russell Thorson), Sergeant (Stafford Repp), Lieutenant (Gavin MacLeod), Undercover vice squad cop (Lew Gallo).

I'd Climb the Highest Mountain (20th Century–Fox, 1951; 88 min.) Producer, Lamar Trotti. Director, Henry King. Screenplay, Lamar Trotti. Based on a novel by Corra Harris. Editor, Barbara McLean. Photography, Edward Cronjager. Technicolor Consultant, Monroe W. Burbank. Music, Sol Kaplan. Musical Direction, Lionel Newman. Orchestration, Edward Powell. Sound, Eugene Grossman, Roger Heman. Art Direction, Lyle Wheeler, Maurice Ransford. Set Decoration, Thomas Little, Al Orenbach. Wardrobe Direction, Charles LeMaire. Costume Design, Edward Stevenson. Makeup, Ben Nye. Technical Adviser, Rev. Wallace Rogers. Special Photographic Effects, Fred Sersen. Cast: Mary Thompson (Susan Hayward), William Asbury Thompson (William Lundigan), Jack Stark (Rory Calhoun), Jenny Brock (Barbara Bates), Mr. Brock (Gene Lockhart), Mrs. Billywith (Lynn Bari), Glory White (Rugh Donnelly), Mrs. Brock (Kathleen Lockhart), Salter (Alexander Knox), Mrs. Salter (Jean Inness), Dr. Fleming (Frank Tweddell), George Salter (Jerry Vandiver), Bill Salter (Richard Wilson), Martha Salter (Dorothea Carolyn Sims), Pike boys (Thomas Syfan, Crady Starnes), Martin twins (Kay and Fay Fogg).

I'll Cry Tomorrow (MGM, 1955; 117 min.) Producer, Lawrence Weingarten. Director, Daniel Mann. Assistant Director, Al Jennings. Screenplay, Helen

Deutsch, Jay Richard Kennedy. Based on the book by Lillian Roth, Mike Connolly, and Gerold Frank. Editor, Harold F. Kress. Photography, Arthur E. Arling. Music, Alex North. Songs sung by Hayward: "Sing You Sinners, "When the Red, Red Robin Comes Bob, Bob, Bobbin' Along," "Happiness Is a Thing Called Joe," "The Vagabond King Waltz." Arranged and conducted by Charles Henderson. Recording Supervisor, Dr. Wesley C. Miller. Art Direction, Cedric Gibbons, Malcolm Brown. Set Decoration, Edwin B. Willis, Hugh Hunt. Costumes, Helen Rose. Makeup, William Tuttle. Hair Styles, Sydney Guilaroff. Special Effects, Warren Newcombe. Cast: Lillian Roth (Susan Hayward), Tony Bardeman (Richard Conte), Burt McGuire (Eddie Albert), Katie Roth (Jo Van Fleet), Wallie (Don Taylor), David Tredman (Ray Danton), Selma (Margo), Ellen (Virginia Gregg), Jerry (Don Barry), David as a child (David Kasday), Lillian as a child (Carole Ann Campbell), Richard (Peter Leeds), Fat man (Tol Avery).

Jack London (United Artists, 1944; 92 min.) Producer, Samuel Bronston. Director, Alfred Santell. Assistant Director, Sam Nelson. Screenplay, Ernest Pascal. Based on *The Book of Jack London* by Charmian London. Dialogue Director, Edward Padula. Editor, William Ziegler. Photography, John W. Boyle. Musical Director, Fred Rich. Sound, Ben Winkler. Art Direction, Bernard Herzbrun. Set Decoration, Earl Wooden. Wardrobe, Maria Donovan, Arnold McDonald. Special Effects, Harry Redmond. Unit Manager, Ben Berk. Cast: Jack London (Michael O'Shea), Charmian Kittredge (Susan Hayward), Freda Maloof (Osa Massen), Professor Hilliard (Harry Davenport), Old Tom (Frank Craven), Mamie (Virginia Mayo), George Brett (Ralph Morgan), Mammy Jenny (Louise Beavers), Kerwin Maxwell (Jonathan Hale), Captain Tanaka (Leonard Strong), Scratch Nelson (Regis Toomey), Lucky Luke Lannigan (Paul Hurst), Mike (Hobart Cavanaugh), Mailman (Olin Howlin), French Frank (Albert Van Antwerp), Whiskey Bob (Ernie Adams), Red John (John Kelly), Captain Allen (Robert Homans), Richard Harding Davis (Morgan Conway), James Hare (Edward Earle), Fred Plamer (Artur Loft), English correspondent (Lumsden Hare), American correspondent (Brooks Benedict), Geisha (Mei Lee Foo), Hiroshi (Robert Katcher), American Consul (Pierre Watkin), Japanese general (Paul Fung), Interpreter (Charlie Lung), Japanese official (Bruce Wong), Japanese sergeant (Eddie Lee), Spider (John Fisher), Victor (Jack Roper), Axel (Sven Hugo Borg), Pete (Sid Dalbrook), Commissioner (Davison Clark), Literary guests (Harold Minjir, Roy Gordon, Torben Mayer), Bit child (Charlene Newman), Bit father (Edmund Cobb), Theodore Roosevelt (Wallis Clark), William Lieb (Charles Miller), Japanese Ambassador (Richard Loo), Cannery foreman (Dick Curtis), Cannery woman (Sarah Padden), Indian maid (Evelyn Finley), Chairman's secretary (Rose Plummer).

The Lost Moment (Universal-International, 1947; 89 min.) Producer, Walter Wanger. Director, Martin Gabel. Assistant Director, Horace Hough. Screenplay, Leonardo Bercovici. Based on the novel *The Aspern Papers* by Henry James. Editor, Milton Carruth. Photography, Hal Mohr. Music, Daniele Amfitheatrof. Orchestrations, David Tamkin. Sound, Charles Felstead, Jesse Moulin. Art Direction, Alexander Golitzen. Set Decoration, Russell A. Gausman, Kenneth Swartz. Hairstyles, Carmen Dirigo. Gowns, Travis Banton. Makeup, Bud Westmore. Agnes Moorehead Makeup, George Bau. Cast: Lewis Venable (Robert Cummings), Tina Borderau (Susan Hayward), Juliana Boderau (Agnes Moorehead),

Amelia (Joan Lorring), Father Rinaldo (Eduardo Ciannelli), Pietro (Frank Puglia), Charles (John Archer), Maria (Minerva Urecal), Vittorio (William Edmunds).

The Lusty Men (RKO, 1952; 113 min.) Wald-Krasna Productions. Producer, Jerry Wald. Associate Producer, Thomas S. Gries. Director, Nicholas Ray. Screenplay, Horace McCoy, David Dortort. Based on a story by Claude Stanush. Editor, Ralph Dawson. Photography, Lee Garmes. Music, Roy Webb. Musical Direction, C. Bakaleinikoff. Sound, Phil Brigandi, Clem Portman. Art Direction, Albert S. D'Agostino, Alfred Herman. Set Decoration, Darrell Silvera, Jack Mills. Wardrobe, Michael Woulfe. Makeup, Mel Berns. Hair Stylist, Larry Germain. Cast: Louise Merritt (Susan Hayward), Jeff (Robert Mitchum), Wes Merritt (Arthur Kennedy), Booker Davis (Arthur Hunnicutt), Al Dawson (Frank Faylen), Buster Burgess (Walter Coy), Rusty (Carol Nugent), Rosemary Maddox (Maria Hart), Grace Burgess (Lorna Thayer), Jeremiah Watrus (Burt Mustin), Ginny Logan (Karen King), Red Logan (Jimmy Dodd), floozy (Eleanor Todd).

The Marriage-Go-Round (20th Century–Fox, 1961; 98 min.) Producer, Leslie Stevens. Director, Walter Lang. Assistant Director, Eli Dunn. Screenplay, Leslie Stevens. Editor, Jack W. Holmes. Photography, Leo Tover. Color by DeLuxe. Music, Dominic Frontiere. Conductor, Dominic Frontiere. Song "Marriage-Go-Round" by Alan Bergman, Marilyn Keith, Lew Spence; Sung by Tony Bennett. Sound, E. Clayton Ward, Frank W. Moran. Art Direction, Duncan Cramer, Maurice Ransford. Set Decoration, Walter M. Scott. Makeup, Ben Nye. Costumes, Charles LeMaire. Hairstyles, Helen Turpin. Cast: Content Delville (Susan Hayward), Paul Delville (James Mason), Katrin Sveg (Julie Newmar), Dr. Ross (Robert Paige), Flo (June Clayworth), Henry (Joe Kirkwood, Jr.), Mamie (Mary Patton), Crew Cut (Trax Colton), Professor (Everett Glass), Sultan (Ben Astar).

My Foolish Heart (RKO, 1949; 98 min.) Producer, Samuel Goldwyn. Director, Mark Robson. Screenplay, Julius J. Epstein, Philip G. Epstein. Based on "Uncle Wiggily in Connecticut" by J. D. Salinger. Editor, Daniel Mandell. Photography, Lee Garmes. Sound Recorder, Fred Lau. Music, Victor Young. Musical Direction, Emil Newman. Musical Arrangements, Leo Shuken, Sidney Cutner. Lyrics, Ned Washington. Sound, Fred Lau. Special Photographic Effects, John Fulton. Art Direction, Richard Day. Set Decoration, Julia Heron. Makeup, Blagoe Stephanoff. Hair Stylist, Marie Clark. Costumes, Mary Wills. Miss Hayward's Gowns, Edith Head. Cast: Walt Dreiser (Dana Andrews), Eloise Winters (Susan Hayward), Henry Winters (Robert Keith), Lew Wengler (Kent Smith), Mary Jane (Lois Wheeler), Mrs. Winters (Jessie Royce Landis), Ramona (Gigi Perreau), Miriam Ball (Karin Booth), Miriam's escort (Tod Karns), Sergeant Lucey (Philip Pine), Nightclub singer (Martha Mears), Dean Whiting (Edna Holland), Usher (Jerry Paris), Grace (Marietta Canty), Receptionist (Barbara Woodell), Mrs. Crandall (Regina Wallace).

$1,000 a Touchdown (Paramount, 1939; 71 min.) Producer, William C. Thomas. Director, James Hogan. Assistant Director, Harry Scott. Story and screenplay, Delmer Daves. Editor, Chandler House. Photography, William Mellor. Music, Ralph Rainger, Leo Robin. Art Direction, Hans Dreier. Cast: Marlowe Mansfield Booth (Joe E. Brown), Martha Madison (Martha Raye), Henry (Eric Blore), Betty McGlen (Susan Hayward), Bill Anders (John Hartley), Bangs

(Syd Salyor), Lorelei (Joyce Mathews), Mr. Fishbeck (George McKay), Brick Benson (Matt McHugh), Popcorn vendor (Tom Dugan), King Richard (Hugh Sothern), Hamilton McGlen, Sr. (Josef Swickard), Two Ton Terry (Adrien Morris), Cabbie (Dewey Robinson), Guard (William Haade), McGlen's first son (Jack Perrin), McGlen's second son (Phil Dunham), Duke (Constantine Romanoff), Stage manager (Charles Middleton), Hysterical woman (Dot Farley), Coach (Emmett Vogan), McGlen's sons wives (Fritzie Brunnette, Gertrude Astor), Buck (John Hart), Babe (Wanda McKay), Blondie (Cheryl Walker), Big Boy (Wayne "Tiny" Whitt).

Our Leading Citizen (Paramount, 1939; 89 min.) Executive Producer, William Le Baron. Producer, George Arthur. Director, Al Santell. Assistant Director, Russell Mathews. Screenplay, John C. Moffit. Story, Irvin S. Cobb. Editor, Hugh Bennett. Photography, Victor Milner. Art Direction, Hans Dreier, Roland Anderson. Sound, Earl Haymann, Don Johnson. Cast: Lem Schofield (Bob Burns), Judith Schofield (Susan Hayward), Clay Clayton (Joseph Allen, Jr.), Aunt Tillie Clark (Elizabeth Patterson), J.T. Tapley (Gene Lockhart), Shep Muir (Charles Bickford), Mr. Stoney (Otto Hoffman), Jim Hanna (Clarence Kolb), Jerry Peters (Paul Guilfoyle), Tonia (Fay Helm), Mrs. Barker (Kathleen Lockhart), Druscilla (Hattie Noel), Miss Swan (Kathryn Sheldon), Police chief (Jim Kelso), Maid (Frances Morris), Director (Harry C. Bradley), Frederick the butler (Thomas Louden), Charles the butler (Olaf Hytten), Janitor (Phil Dunham), Doctor (Gus Glassmire).

The President's Lady (20th Century–Fox, 1953; 96 min.) Producer, Sol C. Siegel. Director, Henry Levin. Assistant Director, Joseph E. Rickards. Screenplay, John Patrick. Based on the novel by Irving Stone. Editor, William B. Murphy. Photography, Leo Tover. Music, Alfred Newman. Orchestration, Edward Powell. Sound, Eugene Grossman, Roger Heman. Art Direction, Lyle Wheeler, Leland Fuller. Set Decoration, Paul S. Fox. Wardrobe Direction, Charles LeMaire. Costume Design, Renie. Makeup, Ben Nye. Cast: Rachel Donaldson Robards (Susan Hayward), Andrew Jackson (Charlton Heston), John Overton (John McIntire), Mrs. Donelson (Fay Bainter), Lewis Robards (Whitfield Connor), Charles Dickinson (Carl Betz), Mrs. Phariss (Gladys Hurlbut), Moll (Ruth Attaway), Captain Irwin (Charles Dingle), Mrs. Stark (Nina Varela), Mrs. Robards (Margaret Wycherly), William (Robert B. Williams), Colonel Stark (Ralph Dumke), Dr. May (Dayton Lummis), Jane (Trudy Marshall), Cruthers (Howard Negley), Clark (Harris Brown), Jacob (Zon Murray), Samuel (James Best), Colonel Green (Selmer Jackson), Mrs. Green (Juanita Evers), Minister (George Melford), House servant (George Hamilton), Slave girl (Vera Francis), Jason (Jim Davis), Innkeeper (Leo Curley), Mary (Ann Morrison), Uncle Alfred (William Walker), Square dance caller (Sherman Sanders), Lincoya age 8 (Ronald Numkena), Colored boy (Rene Beard), Phariss' driver Henry (Sam McDaniel), Chief Justice Marshall (George Spaulding), Judge McNairy (Willis B. Bouncey).

Rawhide (20th Century–Fox, 1951; 89 min.) Producer, Samuel G. Engel. Director, Henry Hathaway. Screenplay, Dudley Nichols. Editor, Robert Simpson. Photography, Milton Krasner. Music, Sol Kaplan. Musical Direction, Lionel Newman;. Orchestration, Edward Powell. Song, "A Rollin' Stone," Music by Lionel Newman. Lyrics by Bob Russell. Sound, Eugene Grossman, Roger Heman. Art Direction, Lyle Wheeler, George W. Davis. Set Decoration, Thomas Little, Stuart Reiss. Wardrobe Direction, Charles LeMaire. Costume Design, Travilla. Makeup, Ben Nye. Special Photographic Effects, Fred Sersen. Cast: Tom Owens (Tyrone Power), Vinnie Holt (Susan Hayward), Zimmerman (Hugh Marlowe), Yancy (Dean Jagger), Sam Todd (Edgar Buchanan), Gratz (George Tobias), Tevis (Jack Elam), Luke Davis (Jeff Corey), Tex Squires (James Millican), Fickert (Louis Jean Heydt), Gil Scott (William Haade), Dr. Tucker (Milton R. Corey, Sr.), Wingate (Ken Tobey), Cilchrist (Dan White), Miner (Max Terhune), Billy Dent (Robert Adler), Callie (Judy Ann Dunn), Chicering (Howard Negley), Mr. Hickman (Vincent Neptune), Mrs. Hickman (Edith Evanson), Flowers (Walter Sande), Hawley (Dick Curtis).

Reap the Wild Wind (Paramount, 1942; 124 min.) Producer and director, Cecil B. DeMille. Associate Producer, William H. Pine. Associate Director, Arthur Rosson. Screenplay, Alan LeMay, Charles Bennett, Jesse Lasky. Based on a story by Thelma Strabel. Editor, Anne Bauchens. Photography, Victor Milner, William V. Skall. Underwater photography, Dewey Wrigley. Technicolor. Music, Victor Young. Sound Recording, Harry Lindgren, John Corps. Art Direction, Hans Dreier, Roland Anderson. Special Effects, Gordon Jennings, W. L. Pereira, Farciot Edouart. Cast: Stephen Tolliver (Ray Milland), Captain Jack Stuart (John Wayne), Loxie Claiborne (Paulette Goddard), King Cutler (Raymond Massey), Dan Cutler (Robert Preston), Drusilla Alston (Susan Hayward), Captain Phillip Philpott (Lynne Overman), _Tyfib_ mate (Charles Bickford), Commodore Devereaux (Walter Hampden), Maum Maria (Louise Beavers), Mrs. Claiborne (Elisabeth Risdon), Mrs. Mottram (Janet Beecher), Aunt Henrietta Beresford (Hedda Hopper), Ivy Devereaux (Martha O'Driscoll), Widgeon (Victor Kilian), Salt Meat (Oscar Polk), Chinkapin (Ben Carter), The Lamb (William Davis), Sam (Lane Chandler), Judge Marvin (Davidson Clark), _Pelican_ captain (Lou Merrill), Dr. Jepson (Frank M. Thomas), Captain Carruthers (Keith Richards), Lubbock (Victor Varconi), Port captain (J. Farrell Macdonald), Mace (Harry Woods), Master shipwright (Raymond Hatton), Lieutenant Farragut (Milburn Stone), "Claiborne" Lookout (Dave Wengren), Cadge (Tony Paton), Charleston ladies (Barbara Britton, Julia Faye, Ameda Lambert), Charleston beaux (D'Arcy Miller, Bruce Warren).

The Revengers (National General, 1972; 110 min.) Producer, Martin Rackin. Director, Daniel Mann. Assistant Directors, Robert Goldstein, Felipe Palomino. Screenplay, Wendell Mayes. Story, Steven W. Carabatsos. Photography, Gabriel Torres. Color by DeLuxe. Editors, Walter Hannemann, Juan Jose Marino. Music, Pino Calvi. Sound, Jesus Gonzalez Gancy, Angel Trejo. Art Direction, Jorge Fernandez. Cast: John Benedict (William Holden), Hoop (Ernest Borgnine), Elizabeth (Susan Hayward), Job (Woody Strode), Quiberon (Roger Hanin), Zweig (Rene Koldehoff), Chamaco (Jorge Luke), Cholo (Jorge Martinez de Hoyos), Free State (Arthur Hunnicutt), Tarp (Warren Vanders), Arny (Larry Pennell), Whitcomb (John Kelly), Lieutenant (Scott Holden), Morgan (James Daughton), Mrs. Benedict (Lorraine Chanel), Warden (Raul Prieto).

The Saxon Charm (Universal-International, 1948; 88 min.) Producer, Joseph Sistrom. Director, Claude Binyon. Assistant Director, Frank Shaw. Screenplay, Claue Binyon. Based on the novel by Frederic Wakeman. Editor, Paul Weatherwax. Photography, Milton Krasner. Music, Walter Scharf. Orchestrations, David Tamkin. Dance Director, Nick Castle. Sound, Leslie I. Carey, Glenn E. Anderson. Art Direction, Alexander Golitzen. Set Decoration, Russell A. Gausman, Ted Offenbecker. Production Coordinator, John Hambleton. Makeup, Bud Westmore. Gowns, Mary K. Dodson. Hairstyles, Carmen Dirigo. Special Photography, David S. Horsley. Cast: Matt Saxon (Robert Montgomery), Janet Busch (Susan Hayward), Eric Busch (John Payne), Alma Wragge (Audrey Totter), Hermy (Henry Morgan), Zack Humber (Harry Von Zell), Dolly Humber (Cara Williams), Captain Chatham (Chill Wills), Vivian Saxon (Heather Angel), Peter Stanhope (John Baragrey), Abel Richman (Addison Richards), Ingenue (Barbara Challis), Jack Bernard (Curt Conway), Mrs. Noble (Fay Baker), Chris (Philip Van Zandt), Manager (Martin Garralaga), Proprietor (Max Willenz), Headwaiter (Fred Nurney), Mrs. Maddox (Archie Twitchell), Mrs. Maddox (Barbara Billingsley), Harassed secretary (Eula Guy), Bald man (Al Murphy), Mr. McCarthy (Clarence Straight), Mr. Noble (Bert Davidson), Mrs. McCarthy (Maris Wrixon), Cyril Leatham (Peter Brocco), Flower girl (Donna Martell), Designer (Mauritz Hugo), Agent (Anthony Jochim), Nurse (Kathleen Freeman), Soubrette (Blanche Obronska), Buxom nurse (Laura Kasley Brooks), Blonde (Vivian Mason), Leading man (Robert Spencer), Character man (Basil Tellou), Waiter (Paul Rochin), Headwaiter (Lomax Study), Bus boy (Robert Cabal).

Say Goodbye, Maggie Cole (ABC TV movie, Spelling/Goldberg Productions; ABC Circle Films, 9/27/1972; 90 min.) Producers, Aaron Spelling, Leonard Goldberg. Associate Producer, Robert Monroe. Director, Jud Taylor. Assistant Director, Fred Giles. Teleplay, Sandor Stern. Script Supervisor, Doris DeHerdt. Photography, Tim Southcott. Editor, Bill Mosher. Music Supervision, Rocky Moriana. Theme Song: "Learn to Say Goodbye" by Bradford Craig, Hugo Montenegro; Sung by Dusty Springfield. Sound Engineer, Glen Anderson. Art Direction, Tracy Bousman. Set Decoration, Don Webb. Costumes, Bob Fuca, Madeline Sylos. Hairstyles, Joyce Morrison. Makeup, Howard Smit. Property Master, Bob Henderson. Casting Supervisor, Bert Remsen. Production Manager, Norman Henry. Unit Manager, Phil Bondrelli. Miss Hayward's Wardrobe, Nolan Miller. Makeup, Gene Hibbs. Hairstyle, Sherry Wilson, Costumer, Evelyn Caruth. Cast: Dr. Maggie Cole (Susan Hayward), Dr. Lou Grazzo (Darren McGavin), Dr. Sweeney (Michael Constantine), Lisa Downey (Michelle Nichols), Hank Cooper (Dane Clark), Myrna Anderson (Beverly Garland), Grandma Downey (Jeanette Nolan), Dr. Benjamin Cole (Richard Anderson), Mr. Allessandro (Frank Puglia), Nurse Ferguson (Maidie Norman), Isadore Glass (Harry Basch), Anderson (Richard Carlyle), Pathologist (Peter Hobbs), Ivan Dvorsky (Jan Peters), Night nurses (Leigh Adams, Mira Martinez), Brig (Robert Cleaves), Policeman (Guy Remsen), First day nurse (Virginia Hawkins), Second day nurse (Jerrie Wollen), Waiter (Bob Bennett), Barney (Scott Edmonds).

Sis Hopkins (Republic, 1941; 98 min.) Producer, Robert North. Director, Joseph Santley. Screenplay, Jack Townley, Milt Gross, Ed Eliscu. Based on a play by F. McGrew Willis. Editor, Ernest Nims. Photography, Jack Marta. Musical Direction, Cy Feuer. Songs, Frank Loesser, Jule Styne. Songs: "Cracker Barrel Country," "If You're in Love," "Well! Well!", "It Ain't Hay (It's the USA)," "Look at You, Look at Me," "Wait for the Wagon," "Some of These Days." Choreography, Ada Broadbent. Art Direction, John Victor Mackay. Cast: Sis Hopkins (Judy Canova), Jeff Farnsworth (Bob Crosby), Horace Hopkins (Charles Butterworth), Professor (Jerry Colonna), Carol Hopkins (Susan Hayward), Clara Hopkins

(Katherine Alexander), Ripple (Elvia Allman), Cynthia (Carol Adams), Phyllis (Lynn Merrick), Vera de Vere (Mary Ainslee), Butler (Charles Coleman), Mayor (Andrew Tombes), Rollo (Charles Lane), Joe (Byron Foulger), Mrs. Farnsworth (Betty Blythe), Jud (Frank Darien). Joe Devlin, Elliot Sullivan, Hal Price, Anne O'Neal, Bob Crosby Orchestra with the Bobcats (Bit Parts).

Smash-Up: The Story of a Woman (Universal-International, 1947; 103 min.) Producer, Walter Wanger. Assistant Producer, Martin Gabel. Director, Stuart Heisler. Assistant Director, Fred Frank. Screenplay, John Howard Lawson. Based on a story by Dorothy Parker and Frank Cavett. Additional Dialogue, Lionel Wiggam. Director of Photography, Stanley Cortez. Editor, Milton Carruth. Music, Frank Skinner. Orchestrations, David Tamkin. Sound, Charles Felstead. Songs, "Hushabye Island," "I Miss That Feeling," "Life Can Be Beautiful," Music, Jimmy McHugh; Lyrics, Harold Adamson. "A Cowboy's Never Lonesome" by Jack Brooks. "Lonely Little Ranch House," Music, Edgar Fairchild; Lyrics, Jack Brooks. Technician, Joe Lapis. Art Direction, Alexander Golitzen. Set Decoration, Russell Gausman, Ruby Levitt. Make-up, Jack Pierce. Gowns, Travis Banton. Hairstyles, Carmen Dirigo. Special Photography, David S. Horsley. Cast: Angie Evans (Susan Hayward), Ken Conway (Lee Bowman), Martha Gray (Marsha Hunt), Steve (Eddie Albert), Dr. Lorenz (Carl Esmond), Fred Elliott (Carleton Young), Mike Dawson (Charles D. Brown), Miss Kirk (Janet Murdoch), Edwards (Tom Chatterton), Angelica (Sharyn Payne), Mr. Gordon (Robert Shayne), Wolf (George Meeker), Emcee (Larry Blake), Farmer (Erville Alderson).

The Snows of Kilimanjaro (20th Century–Fox, 1952; 114 min.) Producer, Darryl F. Zanuck. Director, Henry King. Screenplay, Casey Robinson. Based on the story by Ernest Hemingway. Editor, Barbara McLean. Photography, Leon Shamroy. Technicolor Color Consultant, Leonard Doss. Music, Bernard Herrmann. Sound, Bernard Freericks, Roger Heman. Art Direction, Lyle Wheeler, John De Cuir. Set Decoration, Thomas Little, Paul S. Fox. Wardrobe Direction, Charles LeMaire. Makeup, Ben Nye. Special Photographic Effects, Ray Kellogg. Cast: Harry Street (Gregory Peck), Helen (Susan Hayward), Cynthia (Ava Gardner), Countess (Hildegarde Neff), Uncle Bill Swift (Leo G. Carroll), Johnson (Torin Thatcher), Beatrice (Ava Norring), Connie (Helene Stanley), Emile (Marcel Dalio), Guitarist (Vicente Gomez), Spanish dancer (Richard Allan), Dr. Simmons (Leonard Carey), Witch doctor (Paul Thompson), Molo (Emmett Smith), Charles (Victor Wood), American soldier (Bert Freed), Margot (Agnes Laury), Annette (Janine Grandel), Compton (John Dodsworth), Harry age 17 (Charles Bates), Venduse (Lisa Ferraday), Princess (Maya Van Horn), Marquis (Ivan Lebedeff).

Soldier of Fortune (20th Century–Fox, 1955; 96 min.) Producer, Buddy Adler. Director, Edward Dmytryk. Assistant Director, Hal Herman. Screenplay, Ernest K. Gann. Based on his novel. Editor, Dorothy Spencer. Photography, Leo Tover. CinemaScope. Color by DeLuxe. Color Consultant, Leonard Doss. Music, Hugo Friedhofer. Orchestration, Edward B. Powell. Vocal Supervision, Ken Darby. Art Direction, Lyle Wheeler, Jack Martin Smith. Set Decoration, Walter M. Scott, Stuart A. Reiss. Wardrobe Direction, Charles LeMaire. Makeup, Ben Nye. Hair Styles, Helen Turpin. Special Photographic Effects, Ray Kellogg. Cast: Hank Lee (Clark Gable), Jane Hoyt (Susan Hayward), Inspector Merryweather (Michael Rennie), Louis Hoyt (Gene Barry), Rene Chevalier (Alex D'Arcy), Tweedie (Tom

Tully), Mme. Dupree (Anna Sten), Icky (Russell Collins), Big Matt (Leo Gordon), Poilin (Richard Loo), Daklai (Soo Yong), Ying Fai (Frank Tang), Austin Stoker (Jack Kruschen), Fernand Rocha (Mel Welles), Major Leith Phipps (Jack Raine), Gunner (George Wallace), Australian airman (Alex Finlayson), Luan (Noel Toy), Chinese clerk (Beal Wong), Father Xavier (Robert Burton), Frank Stewart (Robert Quarry), Hotel desk clerk (Charles Davis), Goldie (Victor Sen Yung), Maxine Chan (Frances Fong), Billy Lee (Danny Chang).

Star Spangled Rhythm (Paramount, 1942; 99 min.) Producer, Joseph Sistrom. Director, George Marshall. Screenplay, Harry Tugend. Sketches, George Kaufman, Arthur Ross, Melvin Frank, Norman Panama. Editor, Paul Weatherwax. Photography, Leo Tover, Theodor Sparkuhl. Music, Robert Emmett Dolan. Musical Assistant, Arthur Franklin. Vocal Arrangements, Joseph J. Lilley. Sound Recording, Harry Mills, John Cope. Dances, Danny Dare. Vera Zorina's dance staged by George Balanchine. Songs: Lyrics, Johnny Mercer; Music, Harold Arlen. Songs: "That Old Black Magic," "Hit the Road to Dreamland," "Old Glory," A Sweater, a Sarong and a Peekaboo Bang," "I'm Doing It for Defense," "Sharp as a Tack," "On the Swing Shift," "He Loved Me Till the All-Clear Came." Art Direction, Hans Dreier, Ernst Fegte. Set Decoration, Steve Seymour. Costumes, Edith Head. Makeup, Wally Westmore. Cast: Pop "Bronco Billy" Webster (Victor Moore), Johnny Webster (Eddie Bracken), Polly Judson (Betty Hutton), G. B. De Soto (Walter Abel), Sarah (Anne Revere), Mimi (Cass Daley), Hi-Pockets (Gil Lamb), Mr. Fremont (Edward Fielding), Mac (Edgar Dearing), Duffy (William Heade), Ramrod (James Millican), Sailor (Maynard Holmes), Tommy (Eddie Johnson), Casey (Arthur Loft), Captain Kingsley (Boyd Davis), Petty Officers (Eddie Dew, Rod Cameron), Master of Ceremonies (Bob Hope), "Old Glory" Number (Bing Crosby), "Dreamland" Number (Mary Martin, Dick Powell, Golden Gate Quartette), Men playing cards (Fred MacMurray, Franchot Tone, Ray Milland, Lynne Overman), "Sweater, Sarong and Peekaboo Bang" Number (Dorothy Lamour, Paulette Goddard, Veronica Lake), "Black Magic" Number (Vera Zorina), Scarface (Alan Ladd), "Smart as a Tack" Number (Rochester), Motorcycle Chauffeur for Rochester (Woodrow W. [later Woody] Strode), Herman [Husband] in Bob Hope Skit (William Bendix), Wife in Bob Hope Skit (Marion Martin), Air Raid Warden in Bob Hope Skit (Chester Clute), Introduces Bob Hope Skit (Jerry Colonna), Louis the Lug (Macdonald Carey), Genevieve in "Priorities" Number (Susan Hayward), "Swing Shift" Number (Marjorie Reynolds, Betty Rhodes, Dona Drake, Don Castle), Himself (Gary Crosby), "Black Magic" Number (Johnnie Johnston), Murgatroyd in "Priorities" Number (Ernest Truex), "Smart as a Tack" Number Dancers (Katherine Dunham, Slim and Slam), Comics in "Sweater, Sarong and Peekaboo Bang" Number (Arthur Treacher, Walter Catlett, Sterling Holloway), "Sweater, Sarong and Peekaboo Bang" Number Hitler (Tom Dugan), Mussolini (Paul Porcasi), Hirohito (Richard Loo), Specialty Act (Walter Dare Wahl and Company), Themselves (Cecil B. DeMille, Preston Sturges, Ralph Murphy, Barney Dean, Jack Hope). Finale: Veronica Lake, Dorothy Lamour, Paulette Goddard, Albert Dekker, Marjorie Reynolds, Cecil Kellaway, Lynne Overman, Alan Ladd, Ellen Drew, Jimmy Lydon, Charles Smith, Frances Gifford, Susanna Foster, Robert Preston, Louise LaPlanche, Donivee Lee, Christopher King, Alice Kirby, Marcella Phillips).

Stolen Hours (United Artists/Mirisch Films-Barbican Films-Millar/Turman Productions, 1963; 100 min.) Producer, Denis Holt. Executive Producers, Stuart Millar, Lawrence Turman. Assistant to the Producer, Rose Tobias Shaw. Production Assistant, Marion Rosenberg. Director, Daniel Petrie. Assistant Directors, Colin Brewer, Scott Wodehouse, Barry Langley, Kit Lambert. Screenplay, Jessamyn West. Story Adaptation, Joseph Hayes. Photography, Harry Waxman. Camera Operator, Gerry Turpin. Focus Operator, Gerry Anstiss. Editor, Geoffrey Foot. First Assistant Film Editor, Graham Shipham. Second Assistant Film Editor, Roy Deverall. Music, Mort Lindsey. Song Lyrics, Marilyn Keith, Alan Bergman. Sound Mixer, Cecil Mason. Sound Camera Operator, Desmond Edwards. Dubbing Editor, Gordon Daniel. Art Direction, Tony Woollard. Set Decoration, John Hoesli. Scenic Artist, Peter Melrose. Draughtsmen, Fred Carter, Brian Ackland-Snow. Production Design, Wilfred Shingleton. Production Supervisor, Teddy Joseph. Unit Production Manager, John Peverall. Continuity, Pamela Davies. Main Titles, Maurice Binder. Boom Operator, Charles Wheeler. Wardrobe Mistress, Beatarice Dawson. Miss Hayward's Costumes, Fabiani. Makeup, George Partleton, Tony Sforzini. Hairstyles, Joan Smallwood. Property Buyer, George Durant. Still Photographer, Ted Reed. Construction Manager, Leon Davis. Grip, Frank Howard. Property, J. Hayward. Electrical Supervision, Maurice Gillett. Cast: Laura Pember (Susan Hayward), Dr. John Carmody (Michael Craig), Ellen Pember (Diane Baker), Mike Bannerman (Edward Judd), Dr. Eric McKenzie (Paul Rogers), Peter (Robert Bacon), Dalporto (Paul Stassino), Colonel (Jerry Desmonde), Miss Kendall (Ellen McIntosh), Hospital sister (Gwen Nelson), Reynolds (Peter Madden), Mrs. Hewitt (Joan Newell), Himself (Chet Baker).

Tap Roots (Universal-International, 1948; 109 min.) Producer, Walter Wanger. Director, George Marshall. Assistant Director, Aaron Rosenberg. Second Unit Director, George Templeton. Screenplay, Alan LeMay. Based on the novel by James Street. Additional Dialogue, Lionel Wiggam. Editor, Milton Carruth. Photography, Lionel Lindon, Winton C. Hoch. Technicolor Color Director, Natalie Kalmus. Associate, Morgan Padelford. Music, Frank Skinner. Orchestrations, David Tamkin. Sound, Leslie I. Carey, Glenn E. Anderson. Art Direction, Frank A. Richards. Set Decoration, Russell A. Gausman, Ruby R. Levitt. Production Design, Alexander Golitzen. Makeup, Bud Westmore. Costumes, Yvonne Wood. Hair Stylist, Carmen Dirigo. Cast: Keith Alexander (Van Heflin), Morna Dabney (Susan Hayward), Tishomingo (Boris Karloff), Aven Dabney (Julie London), Clay MacIvor (Whitfield Connor), Hoab Dabney (Ward Bond), Bruce Dabney (Richard Long), Reverend Kirkland (Arthur Shields), Dr. MacIntosh (Griff Barnett), Shellie (Sondra Rodgers), Dabby (Ruby Dandridge), Sam Dabney (Russell Simpson).

They Won't Believe Me (RKO, 1947; 95 min.) Producer, Joan Harrison. Director, Irving Pichel. Assistant Director, Harry D'Arcy. Screenplay, Jonathan Latimer. Based on a story by Gordon McDonnell. Editor, Elmo Williams. Photography, Harry J. Wild. Music, Roy Webb. Music Director, C. Bakaleinikoff. Sound, John Tribby. Art Direction, Albert S. D'Agostino, Robert Boyle. Set Decoration, Darrell Silvera, William Matinetti. Special Effects, Russell A. Cully. Cast: Lawrence Ballentine (Robert Young), Verna Carlson (Susan Hayward), Gretta Ballentine (Rita Johnson), Janice Bell (Jane Greer), Defense attorney Cahill (Frank Ferguson), Thomason (Don Beddoe), Lieutenant Carr (George Tyne),

Trenton (Tom Powers), Judge Fletcher (Harry Harvey), Patric Gold (Wilton Graff), Susan Haines (Janet Shaw), Parking lot attendant (Glen Knight), Tough patient (Anthony Caruso), Highway policeman (George Sherwood), Police stenographer (Perc Launders), Mortician (Byron Foulger), Nick (Hector Sarno), Chauffeur (Carl Kent), Detective (Lee Frederick), Maid (Jean Andren), Mr. Bowman (Paul Maxey), Mrs. Bowman (Elena Warren), Sheriff (Herbert Haywood), Mrs. Hines (Lillian Bronson), Sailor (Martin Wilkins), Emma (Dot Farley), Court clerk (Milton Parsons), Bailiff (Lee Phelps), Patrick Collins (Frank Pharr), Screaming woman (Ellen Corby), Tiny old man (Matthew McHugh), Officer guarding Larry (Bob Pepper), Waiter (Ira Buck Woods), Woman (Irene Tedrow), Untidy woman (Berta Ledbetter), Newsstand girl (Lida Durova), Hotel clerk (Bob Thom), Bartenders (Ivan Browning, Jack Gargan), Mrs. Roberts (Madam Borget), Rancher (Harry Strang), Driver (Bud Wolfe), Gus (Sol Gorss), Miss Jorday (Lovyss Bradley), Fisherman (Harry D'Arcy), Tour conductor (Jack Rice), Spinster (Netta Packer).

Thunder in the Sun (Paramount, 1959; 81 min.) Producer, Clarence Greene. Director, Russell Rouse. Second Unit Director, Winston Jones. Screenplay, Russell Rouse. Based on an original story by Guy Trosper. Editor, Chester Schaeffer. Photography, Stanley Cortez. Music, Cyril Mockridge. Song "Mon Petit," Music, Cyril Mockridge; Lyrics, Ned Washington; Sung by Jacques Bergerac. Choreography, Pedro de Cordoba. Art Direction, Boris Leven. Miss Hayward's Costumes, Charles LeMaire. Cast: Gabrielle Dauphin (Susan Hayward), Lon Bennett (Jeff Chandler), Pepe Dauphin (Jacques Bergerac), Louise Dauphin (Blanche Yurka), Andre Dauphin (Carl Esmond), Fernando (Fortunio Bonanova), Danielle (Felix Locher), Duquette (Bertrand Castelli), Marie (Veda Ann Borg), Gabrielle's dance partner (Pedro de Cordoba).

Top Secret Affair (Warner Bros., 1957; 100 min.) Producer, Martin Rackin. Supervising Producer, Milton Sperling. Director, H. C. Potter. Assistant Director, Russell Saunders. Screenplay, Roland Kibbee, Allan Scott. Based on characters from *Melville Goodwin, U.S.A.* by John P. Marquand. Editor, Folmar Blangsted. Photography, Stanley Cortez. Music, Roy Webb. Orchestrations, Gus Levene, Maurice de Packh. Sound, Stanley Jones. Art Direction, Malcolm Bert. Set Decoration, William Wallace. Costume Design, Charles LeMaire. Makeup, Gordon Bau. Technical Adviser, Lieutenant Colonel Frederick J. Bremerman. Cast: Dottie Peale (Susan Hayward), Major General Melville Goodwin (Kirk Douglas), Phil Bentley (Paul Stewart), Colonel Gooch (Jim Backus), General Grimshaw (John Cromwell), Senator Burwick (Roland Winters), Butler (A. E. Gould-Porter), Lotzie (Michael Fox), Sergeant Kruger (Frank Gerstle), Bill Hadley (Charles Lane).

Tulsa (Eagle-Lion, 1949; 90 min.) Producer, Walter Wanger. Associate Producer, Edward Lasker. Director, Stuart Heisler. Assistant Director, Howard W. Koch. Screenplay, Frank Nugent, Curtis Kenyon. Suggested by a story by Richard Wormser. Editor, Terrell Morse. Photography, Winton Hoch. Technicolor Director, Natalie Kalmus. Associate Color Director, Richard Mueller. Musical Director, Irving Friedman. Music Conductor, Charles Previn. Orchestrations, David Tamkin. Song "Tulsa," Music, Allie Wrubel; Lyrics, Mort Greene. Sound, Howard Fogetti. Art Direction, Nathan Juran. Set Decoration, Armor Marlowe, Al Orenbach. Costume Design, Herschel. Makeup, Ern Westmore, Del Armstrong. Hair

Styling, Joan St. Oegger, Helen Turpin. Production Supervision, James T. Vaughn. Special Photographic Effects, John Fulton. Cast: Cherokee Lansing (Susan Hayward), Brad Brady (Robert Preston), Jim Redbird (Pedro Armendariz), Bruce Tanner (Lloyd Gough), Pinky Jimpson (Chill Wills), Johnny Brady (Ed Begley), Steve (Roland Jack), Nelse Lansing (Harry Shannon), Homer (Jimmy Conlin), Tooley (Paul E. Burns), Charlie Lightfoot (Chief Yowlachie), Winters (Pierre Watkin), Cab driver (Tom Dugan), Mr. Kelly (Lane Chandler), Candy Williams (Lola Albright), Osage Indian (Iron Eyes Cody), Joker (Dick Wessel), Oilmen (John Dehner, Selmer Jackson), Oil worker (Fred Graham), Governor (Larry Keating), Judge McKay (Joseph Crehan), Man with newspaper (Nolan Leary), Winslow (Thomas Browne Henry).

Untamed (20th Century–Fox, 1955; 111 min.) Producers, Bert E. Friedlob, William A. Bacher. Director, Henry King. Assistant Director, Stanley Hough. Screenplay, Talbot Jennings, Frank Fenton, Michael Blankfort. Adaptation, Talbot Jennings, William A. Bacher. Based on the novel by Helga Moray. Editor, Barbara McLean. Photography, Leo Tover. CinemaScope. Color by DeLuxe. Color Consultant, Leonard Doss. Music, Franz Waxman. Orchestration, Edward B. Powell. Choreography, Stephen Papich. Art Direction, Lyle Wheeler, Addison Hehr. Set Decoration, Walter M. Scott, Chet Bayhi. Wardrobe Direction, Charles LeMaire. Costume Design, Renie. Makeup, Ben Nye. Hair Styles, Helen Turpin. Special Photographic Effects, Ray Kellogg. Cast: Paul Van Riebeck (Tyrone Power), Katie O'Neill/Kildare (Susan Hayward), Kurt Hout (Richard Egan), Shawn Kildare (John Justin), Aggie (Agnes Moorehead), Julia (Rita Moreno), Maria De Groot (Hope Emerson), Christian (Brad Dexter), Squire O'Neill (Henry O'Neill), Tschaka (Paul Thompson), Jan (Alexander D. Havemann), Joubert (Louis Mercier), Jantsie (Emmett Smith), Simon (Jack Macy), Mme. Joubert (Trude Wyler), Bani (Louis Pollimon Brown), Maria's children (Brian Corcoran, Linda Lowell, Tina Thompson, Gary Diamond, Bobby Diamond), Grandfather Joubert (Edward Mundy), Miss Joubert (Catherine Pasques), Young Joubert (Christian Pasques), York (Robert Adler), Captain Richard Eaton (John Dodsworth), Driver in Bree Street (Alberto Morin), Schuman (Philip Van Zandt), Young Paul (Kevin Corcoran), Sir George Gray (Charles Evans), Cornelius (John Carlyle), Lady Veron (Eleanor Audley).

Valley of the Dolls (20th Century–Fox, 1967; 123 min.) Producer, David Weisbart. Director, Mark Robson. Screenplay, Helen Deutsch, Dorothy Kingsley. Based on the novel by Jacqueline Susann. Photography, William H. Daniels. Editor, Dorothy Spencer. Music Adapt & Cond, Johnny Williams. Orchestrations, Herbert Spencer. Songs: "Theme from Valley of the Dolls," Andre Previn, Dory Previn; Sung by Dionne Warwick. "Give a Little More," "It's Impossible," Andre Previn, Dory Previn; Sung by Patty Duke. "Come Live with Me," Andre Previn, Dory Previn; Sung by Tony Scotti. "I'll Plant My Own Tree," Andre Previn, Dory Previn; Sung by Margaret Whiting. Choreography, Robert Sidney. Sound, Don Bassman, David Dockendorf. Music Editor, Kenneth Wannberg. Art Direction, Jack Martin Smith, Richard Day. Set Decoration, Walter M. Scott, Raphael Bretton. Assistant Director, Eli Dunn, Richard Lang. Unit Production Manager, Francisco Day. Production Manager, Dave Silver. Gowns Design, Travilla. Makeup, Ben Nye. Miss Parkins' Hairstyles, Kenneth. Hairstyles Supervision, Edith Lindon. Special Photographic Effects, L. B. Abbott, Art Cruickshank, Emil Kosa,

Jr. Cast: Anne Welles (Barbara Parkins), Neely O'Hara (Patty Duke), Lyon Burke (Paul Burke), Jennifer North (Sharon Tate), Helen Lawson (Susan Hayward), Tony Polar (Tony Scotti), Mel Anderson (Martin Milner), Kevin Gillmore (Charles Drake), Ted Casablanca (Alexander Davion), Miriam (Lee Grant), Miss Steinberg (Naomi Stevens), Henry Bellamy (Robert H. Harris), Reporter (Jacqueline Susann), Director (Robert Viharo), Man in hotel room (Mikel Angel), Man in bar (Barry Cahill), Claude Chardot (Richard Angarola), Telethon MC (Joey Bishop), Grammy Awards MC (George Jessel), Stage call boy (Richard Dreyfuss).

Where Love Has Gone (Paramount, 1964; 114 min.) Producer, Joseph E. Levine. Director, Edward Dmytryk. Assistant Director, D. Michael Moore. Screenplay, John Michael Hayes. Dialogue Director, Frank London. Based on a novel by Harold Robbins. Photography, Joseph MacDonald. Technicolor. Editor, Frank Bracht. Music, Walter Scharf. Title Song, Sammy Cahn, James Van Heusen; Sung by Jack Jones. Sound, John Carter, Charles Grenzbach. Art Direction, Hal Pereira, Walter Tyler. Set Decoration, Sam Comer, Arthur Krams. Production Manager, Frank Caffey. Costumes, Edith Head. Makeup, Wally Westmore, Gene Hibbs. Special Photographic Effects, Paul K. Lerpae. Process Photography, Farciot Edouart. Cast: Valerie Hayden Miller (Susan Hayward), Mrs. Gerald Hayden (Bette Davis), Luke Miller (Michael Connors), Danielle Valerie "Dani" Miller (Joey Heatherton), Marian Spicer (Jane Greer), Sam Corwin (DeForest Kelley), Gordon Harris (George Macready), Dr. Sally Jennings (Anne Seymour), Judge Murphy (Willis Bouchey), George Babson (Walter Reed), Mrs. Geraghty (Ann Doran), Mr. Coleman (Bartlett Robinson), Professor Bell (Whit Bissell), Rafael (Anthony Caruso).

White Witch Doctor (20th Century–Fox, 1953; 96 min.) Producer, Otto Lang. Director, Henry Hathaway. Assistant Director, Gerd Oswald. Screenplay, Ivan Goff, Ben Roberts. Based on the novel by Louise A. Stinetorf. Editor, James B. Clark. Photography, Leon Shamroy. Technicolor Color Consultant, Leonard Doss. Music, Bernard Herrmann. Sound, Eugene Grossman, Harry M. Leonard. Art Direction, Lyle Wheler, Mark-Lee Kirk. Set Decoration, Stuart Reiss. Wardrobe Direction, Charles LeMaire. Costume Design, Dorothy Jeakins. Makeup, Ben Nye. Special Photographic Effects, Ray Kellogg. Cast: Ellen Burton (Susan Hayward), Lonni Douglas (Robert Mitchum), Huysman (Walter Slezak), Jacques (Mashood Ajala), Utembo (Joseph C. Narcisse), Kapuka (Elzie Emanuel), Jarrett (Timothy Carey), Bakuba boy (Otis Green), Gorilla (Charles Gemora), Witch doctors (Paul Thompson, Naaman Brown), Aganza (Myrtle Anderson), Bakuba king (Everett Brown), Chief's wife (Dorothy Harris), De Gama (Michael Ansara), Paul (Michael Granger), Council member (Leo C. Aldridge-Milas), Councilman (Louis Polliman Brown), Chief (Floyd Shackleford).

With a Song in My Heart (20th Century–Fox, 1952; 117 min.) Producer, Lamar Trotti. Director, Walter Lang. Screenplay, Lamar Trotti. Editor, J. Watson Webb, Jr. Photography, Leon Shamroy. Technicolor. Technicolor Color Consultant, Leonard Doss. Music, Alfred Newman. Orchestration, Herbert Spencer, Earle Hagen. Vocal Direction, Ken Darby. "Montparnase" music, Alfred Newman. Lyrics, Eliot Daniel. "Jim's Toasty Peanuts," Ken Darby. Dance Staging, Billy Daniel. Sound, Arthur L. Kirbach, Roger Heman. Art Direction, Lyle

Wheeler, Joseph C. Wright. Set Decoration, Thomas Little, Walter M. Scott. Wardrobe Direction, Charles LeMaire. Makeup, Ben Nye. Special Photographic Effects, Fred Sersen, Ray Kellogg. Technical Adviser, Jane Froman. Cast: Jane Froman (Susan Hayward), John Burn (Rory Calhoun), Don Ross (David Wayne), Clancy (Thelma Ritter), G.I. paratrooper (Robert Wagner), Jennifer March (Helen Westcott), Sister Marie (Una Merkel), Tenor (Richard Allan), Guild (Max Showalter), Radio director (Lyle Talbot), General (Leif Erickson), Diplomat (Stanley Logan), USO man (Eddie Firestone), USO girl (Beverly Thompson), Texas (Frank Sully), Muleface (George Offerman).

Woman Obsessed (20th Century–Fox, 1959; 103 min.) Producer, Sidney Boehm. Director, Henry Hathaway. Assistant Director, David Hall. Screenplay, Sydney Boehm. Based on the novel by John Mantley. Editor, Robert Simpson. Photography, William C. Mellor, Leon Shamroy. Color Consultant, Leonard Doss. Color by DeLuxe. CinemaScope. Music, Hugo Friedhofer. Conductor, Lionel Newman. Orchestration, Earle Hagen. Sound, W. D. Flick, Harry M. Leonard. Art Direction, Lyle Wheeler, Jack Martin Smith. Set Decoration, Walter M. Scott, Stuart A. Reiss. Executive Wardrobe Design, Charles LeMaire. Makeup, Ben Nye. Hair Styles, Helen Turpin. Special Photographic Effects, L. B. Abbott. Cast: Mary Sharron (Susan Hayward), Fred Carter (Stephen Boyd), Mayme Radzevitch (Barbara Nichols), Robbie (Dennis Holmes), Dr. Gibbs (Theodore Bikel), Sergeant Le Moyne (Ken Scott), Tom Sharron (Arthur Franz), Henri (James Philbrook), Mrs. Gibbs (Florence MacMichael), Ian Campbell (Jack Raine), Mrs. Campbell (Mary Carroll), Officer Follette (Fred Graham), Ticket taker (Mike Lally).

Young and Willing (United Artists, 1943; 82 min.) Producer and director, Edward H. Griffith. Screenplay, Virginia Van Upp. Based on a play by Francis Swann. Editor, Eda Warren. Photography, Leo Tover. Sound Recording, Harold Lewis, Don Johnson. Art Direction, Hans Dreier, Ernst Fegte. Costumes, Edith Head. Makeup, Wally Westmore. Cast: Norman Reese (William Holden), George Bodell (Eddie Bracken), Arthur Kenny (Robert Benchley), Kate Benson (Susan Hayward), Dottie Coburn (Martha O'Driscoll), Marge Benson (Barbara Britton), Tony Dennison (James Brown), Muriel Foster (Florence MacMichael), Mrs. Garnet (Mabel Paige), Mr. Coburn (Jay Fassett), Phillips (Billy Bevan), Cops (Paul Hurst, Olin Howlin).

Notes

Preface

1. Bronte Woodward, "Susan Hayward: She Always Came Back," *Los Angeles Times Calendar*, April 27, 1975.

Introduction

1. Dick Williams, "The Hayward Mystery," *Los Angeles Mirror–News*, April 27, 1955, Part II, p. 4.

2. Robin Wood in Amy L. Unterburger, ed., *International Dictionary of Films and Filmmakers—3: Actors and Actresses*, 3rd ed., Detroit and New York: St. James Press, 1996, p. 534. The case is rather overstated. Directors Joseph L. Mankiewicz and Robert Wise would seem to merit the appellation "distinguished."

3. Ian and Elisabeth Cameron, *Dames*, New York: Praeger, 1969, pp. 47–49.

4. David Shipman, *The Great Movie Stars: The International Years*, London: Angus & Robertson, 1972, p. 241.

5. Joyce Haber, "It's Tomorrow, but Susan Hayward's Not Crying," *Los Angeles Times*, September 3, 1972, p. 11.

6. Christopher P. Andersen, *A Star, Is a Star, Is a Star! The Life and Loves of Susan Hayward*, Garden City, NY: Doubleday, 1980, p. 112.

7. "Susan's Life Full of Storm," *Los Angeles Herald Express*, April 7, 1959.

Chapter 1

1. Beverly Linet, *Portrait of a Survivor: Susan Hayward*, New York: Berkley, 1984, p. 11.

2. Linet, p. 11; Robert LaGuardia and Gene Arceri, *Red: The Tempestuous Life of Susan Hayward*, New York: Macmillan, 1985, p. 5.

3. LaGuardia and Arceri, p. 5; Linet, p. 12.

4. Linet, pp. 12, 13.

5. LaGuardia and Arceri, p. 4.

6. Sidney Skolsky, "Hollywood Is My Beat: Tintypes," *Hollywood Citizen–News*, June 30, 1949.

7. Kirk Crivello, "Carrollton, Georgia, Remembers Lovely Susan Hayward," *Hollywood Studio Magazine*, March 1976, p. 6.

8. *Susan Hayward Collectors' Club Newsletter*, July-August 1985, p. 4.

9. Thomas Wood, "If You Knew Susie," 20th Century–Fox publicity release biography, ca. 1951, p. 3.

10. Susan Hayward, 20th Century–Fox *Press Release*, 1955, p. 2.

11. LaGuardia and Arceri, p. 12.

12. Linet, p. 19.

13. Florence Marrenner, "My Sister, Susan Hayward, Has Millions—But I'm on Relief," *Confidential*, May 1961, p. 10.

14. Ron Nelson in LaGuardia and Arceri, p. 203.

15. Timothy Barker in *Susan Hayward: The Brooklyn Bombshell*, Arts & Entertainment TV network *Biography*, 1998.

16. Andersen, p. 9.

17. Florence Marrenner in LaGuardia and Arceri, p. 10.

18. Wally Marrenner in LaGuardia and Arceri, p. 10.

19. LaGuardia and Arceri, p. 10.

20. *Susan Hayward: The Brooklyn Bombshell*, Arts & Entertainment TV network *Biography*, 1998.

21. Eduardo Moreno, *The Films of Susan Hayward*, Secaucus, NJ: Citadel Press, 1979, p. 36.

Chapter 2

1. *Time* review of *The Hairy Ape*, June 19, 1944, p. 94.

2. Andersen, *A Star*, p. 25.

3. "Walter Thornton, the Merchant of Venus," *Saturday Evening Post*, October 30, 1937, pp. 20–21, 43, 46, 48.

4. "Biography of Susan Hayward," Paramount Biographies, August 1958, p. 1. The *SEP* cover that people were thinking of was October 7, 1939. As before, Ivan Dimitri took the color portrait. And again, Edythe is not identified by name. Even a 1951 Fox press release says Susan was on a 1937 cover: "It's [*I'd Climb the Highest Mountain*] her 25th film since David O. Selznick discovered her, then a model, on the cover of the *Saturday Evening Post* and tested her for the role of Scarlett O'Hara in *Gone with the Wind*." Johnson, 20th Century–Fox, ca. 1951, p. 2. If not disingenuous, Hayward herself had a hazy memory: "It was a magazine cover that got me my first movie bid. David O. Selznick saw me as a redhead on a *Saturday Evening Post* at the time when he was searching for someone to play Scarlett O'Hara in *Gone with the Wind*. He tested me but I was a 'green' redhead without any training and flunked out." Gordon, 20th Century–Fox press release, ca. 1949, pp. 1–2. In 1949 Susan told columnist Hedda Hopper, "People have helped me and taught me, ever since the first time, when David Selznick saw my picture in a magazine and brought me out to be tested, and George Cukor, the

director, took me aside very kindly and said, 'You must try to project yourself.'" Hedda Hopper, "Hayward of the Wayward Roles," *Chicago Sunday Tribune*, June 19, 1949. Later still, Hayward maintained that, "It was the *Saturday Evening Post* cover which brought me to Hollywood, David O. Selznick saw it and thought my red hair and hazel eyes might qualify me for the coveted role of a 'Scarlett O'Hara' in *Gone with the Wind*. He tested me and, rather pointedly, I thought, suggested I needed more experience. But I liked orange trees and decided to stay. My mother and sister were with me and we cashed Mr. Selznick's return tickets for sustenance." Susan Hayward, Press Release, ca. 1955, p. 2. Accounts have it that after cashing in her tickets, Susan and her sister survived on shredded wheat. Thomas Wood, "If You Knew Susie," p. 5.

5. Linet, p. 37; club newsletter, September-October 1986, p. 6.

6. Thomas Wood, "If You Knew Susie," p. 4.

7. Linet, p. 38.

8. Linet, p. 37.

9. *Memo from David O. Selznick*, New York: Viking, 1972, p. 176.

10. *Memo from David O. Selznick*, memo to Daniel T. O'Shea, p. 177.

11. "The Last Time Susan Hayward was Directed by George Cukor....," *Los Angeles Examiner*, February 27, 1951.

12. Cobina Wright, "Susan Hayward Wrests Fame from 'Taboo Roles,'" *Los Angeles Examiner*, September 24, 1950, Sec. III.

13. Favius Friedman, "You Wouldn't Know Susie Now," *Pageant*, June 1961, p. 100.

14. Linet, p. 39.

15. Thomas Wood, "If You Knew Susie," p. 5.

16. "Susan Hayward Termed at WB; Gets 2 Spots," *Hollywood Reporter*, February 19, 1938.

17. "Biography of Susan Hayward (Paramount Contract Player)," July 1940, p. 2.

18. Andersen, *A Star*, p. 37.

19. LaGuardia and Arceri, p. 30.

20. Doug McClelland, *The Complete Life Story of Susan Hayward...Immortal Screen Star*, New York: Pinnacle Books, 1975, p. 17.

21. Andersen, *A Star*, p. 45.

22. McClelland, p. 19.

23. Eduardo Moreno, *The Films of Susan Hayward*, Secaucus, NJ: Citadel Press, 1979, p. 41.

24. Moreno, p. 41.

25. *Campus Cinderella*, released on December 23, 1938, was directed by Noel Smith, produced by George Ade, and had a screenplay by Lee Katz. Besides Hayward (no longer Marrenner), it featured Johnnie Davis, Penny Singleton, Anthony Averill and Peggy Moran.

26. Bosley Crowther, *New York Times*, October 21, 1938, p. 27.

27. Paramount Press Release, ca. 1939.

28. Thomas Wood, "If You Knew Susie," p. 6.

29. Andersen, *A Star*, p. 48.

30. B. R. Crisler, *New York Times*, August 3, 1939, p. 15.

31. *Newsweek*, August 7, 1939, pp. 40–41.

32. Arts & Entertainment TV network *Biography*, 1998.

33. Andersen, p. 50.

34. LaGuardia and Arceri, p. 18. They argue that her standoffishness made her a victim of "psychological isolation," and hence nearsightedness was not why she ignored people.

35. Frank S. Nugent, *New York Times*, August 24, 1939, p. 17.

36. Frank S. Nugent, *New York Times*, October 5, 1939, p. 27.

37. Moreno, p. 58.

38. "Biography of Susan Hayward (Paramount Contract Player)," July 1940, p. 3.

39. Bosley Crowther, *New York Times*, March 28, 1941, p. 26.

40. *Screen Album*, Summer 1942.

41. Susan Hayward, "The Role I Liked Best..." *Saturday Evening Post*, April 6, 1946, p. 126.

42. Hayward, "The Role," p. 126.

43. Elizabeth Wilson, "Brown-Eyed Susan," *Liberty*, May 10, 1947, p. 23.

44. Patricia Morrison on *Susan Hayward: The Brooklyn Bombshell*.

45. Bosley Crowther, *New York Times*, May 1, 1941, p. 27.

46. Nino Frank is credited with first using the term "film noir" in 1946. Alain Silver and Elizabeth Ward, *Film Noir: An Encyclopedic Reference to the American Style*, 3rd ed., Woodstock, NY: Overlook Press, 1992, p. 1.

47. Theodore Strauss, *New York Times*, December 13, 1941, p. 25.

48. Bob Porfirio in Alain Silver and Elizabeth Ward, *Film Noir: An Encyclopedia Reference to the American Style*, p. 11.

49. McClelland, p. 27.

50. Bosley Crowther, *New York Times*, March 27, 1942, p. 27.

51. *Newsweek*, April 6, 1942, p. 65.

52. McClelland, p. 43.

53. Andersen, p. 65.

54. Theodore Strauss, *New York Times*, October 22, 1942, p. 25.

55. *Time*, November 2, 1942, p. 97.

56. Thomas Wood, "If You Knew Susie," p. 8.

57. Moreno, p. 75.

58. *Screen Album*, Summer 1942.

59. *Time*, November 9, 1942, p. 94.

60. Bosley Crowther, *New York Times*, November 20, 1942, p. 27.

61. McClelland, p. 49.

62. Bosley Crowther, *New York Times*, December 31, 1942, p. 20.

63. Manny Farber, *New Republic*, March 1, 1943, p. 284.

64. *A Letter from Bataan*, released in September 1942, was produced by William C. Thomas, directed by William H. Pine, and had a screenplay by Maxwell Shane. Daniele Amfitheatrop composed the score, and Howard A. Smith edited. Besides Hayward, the cast included Richard Arlen, Janet Beecher, Jimmy Lydon, Joe Sawyer, Keith Richards, Esther Dale, and Will Wright.

65. Moreno, p. 49. Charles Brackett scripted this one for the U.S. Office of War Information.

66. Other Hayward radio credits include the Orson Welles–hosted 1943–44 *Radio Almanac; Lux Radio Theatre* ("Hold Back the Dawn," 11/10/41, with Edgar Barrier, Charles Boyer, Paulette Goddard. "The Petrified Forest," 4/23/45, with Ronald Colman, Thomas Mitchell, Lawrence Tierney; "Tap Roots," 9/27/48, with Van Heflin; "My Foolish Heart," 8/28/50, with Dana Andrews; "I'd Climb the

Highest Mountain," 10/29/51, with William Lundigan; "With a Song in My Heart," 2/9/53, with Thelma Ritter, Robert Wagner, David Wayne); *Philip Morris Playhouse* ("The Crystal Ball," 3/19/43); the Hedda Hopper–hosted *This Is Hollywood* ("Canyon Passage," 10/19/46, with John Hodiak; "The Magnificent Obsession," 5/24/47, with Lew Ayres); *Suspense* ("The Dead Sleep Lightly," 3/30/43, with Lee Bowman, Walter Hampden; "Dame Fortune," 10/24/46, with Hans Conried, William Johnstone, Wally Maher); *The Harold Lloyd Comedy Theater* ("Take a Letter, Darling," 12/3/44, with John Hodiak; "Hold Back the Dawn," 2/8/43, with Charles Boyer, Margaret Lindsay; "Heaven Can Wait," 5/7/45, with John Carradine, Walter Pidgeon; "Gaslight," 2/3/47, with Charles Boyer); *The Cavalcade of America* ("Breakfast at Nancy's," 3/25/52).

67. Andersen, *A Star*, pp. 68–69.

68. Andersen, *A Star*, p. 69.

69. Andersen, *A Star*, p. 69.

70. Leonard Maltin, *TV Movies: 1975 Edition*, New York: Signet, 1974, p. 664.

71. Thomas M. Pryor, *New York Times*, April 16, 1943, p. 24.

72. A. H. Weiler, *New York Times*, March 3, 1944, p. 19.

73. *Newsweek*, March 6, 1944, p. 80.

74. Bosley Crowther, *New York Times*, March 20, 1944, p. 14.

75. Philip K. Scheuer, *Los Angeles Times*, January 30, 1944.

76. *Time*, June 19, 1944, p. 94.

77. Paul P. Kennedy, *New York Times*, July 3, 1944, p. 8.

78. Bosley Crowther, *New York Times*, November 23, 1944, p. 38.

79. Louella Parsons, "Susan Hayward, Jess Barker to Wed," *Los Angeles Examiner*, July 19, 1944.

80. "Actor to Wed Susan Hayward Tomorrow," *Los Angeles Times*, July 22, 1944.

81. "Miss Hayward Wed to Actor," *Los Angeles Times*, July 24, 1944.

82. Andersen, *A Star*, p. 70.

83. As early as September 1944 marital problems were reported in the newspapers: "It was just a gag," Jess said of his separation after a Beverly Hills house party that was also famous for a confrontation between Lana Turner's ex-husband, Stephen Crane, and actor Turhan Bey. According to Barker, he couldn't open the car door as he and Susan were leaving. She disappeared and "I went on home expecting her to come home with friends. Yesterday morning, when she didn't return, someone asked me what action Miss Hayward was taking. Frankly, I don't know." Hayward had sought advice from Paramount attorney Sidney Justin. Barker said he wasn't sure if there would be a reconciliation. ("Susan Hayward Mate's Gag Put Him on Spot," *Los Angeles Times*, September 19, 1944.) Reconciliation did occur. Louella Parsons reported that the pair were back together, with Susan due to become a mother the following April. Susan told Louella that, "we love each other so we have decided to give our marriage another chance and see if we cannot work out our troubles. I suppose...much of our unhappiness was due to our living in my small apartment. We will rent a house and it will be Jess' home—the one he selects. He will be head of the house." Louella concluded that Jess' lack of work might have contributed to the duo's problems. (Louella Parsons, "Susan Hayward and Jess Barker Reconciled," *Los Angeles Examiner*, September 30, 1944.)

84. Eleanor Harris, "She Does as She Pleases," *Motion Picture Magazine*, September 1944, pp. 56, 106.

85. Andersen, *A Star*, pp. 71–72.

Chapter 3

1. Marsha Hunt in James Bawden, "Marsha Hunt," *Films in Review*, November 1989, p. 518.

2. Andersen, p. 80.

3. Bosley Crowther, *New York Times*, April 4, 1946, p. 33.

4. Bob Porfirio in Silver and Ward, *Film Noir*, pp. 86–87.

5. Andersen, *A Star*, p. 88.

6. Tourneur had helmed the critically acclaimed Val Lewton–produced low-key horror films *Cat People* (1942) and *I Walked with a Zombie* (1943), and in 1947 would direct the classic noir *Out of the Past,* with Robert Mitchum. In *Canyon Passage* Tourneur had quality material from master western novelist Ernest Haycox, among whose other stories transferred to the screen would be *Bugles in the Afternoon* (1952).

7. *Time*, August 5, 1946, pp. 98, 101.

8. Thomas M. Pryor, *New York Times*, August 8, 1946, p. 18.

9. Brian Garfield, *Western Films: A Complete Guide*, New York: Rawson Associates, 1982, p. 132.

10. LaGuardia and Arceri, pp. 55–56.

11. Like Victor Mature, another Fox leading man, Dana Andrews was often overlooked by critics. Like Mature, Andrews left a body of work of which some "great stars" could be envious (e.g., *The Ox-Bow Incident, The Purple Heart, Laura, A Walk in the Sun, State Fair, The Best Years of Our Lives, Boomerang, Where the Sidewalk Ends, Night of the Demon).*

12. "Eviction Woes Hit Jess Barker, Susan Hayward," *Los Angeles Times*, November 2, 1946.

13. "Film Couple Evicted from Home," *Los Angeles Daily News*, November 2, 1946.

14. "Susan Hayward Homeless; Blasts Black Mart Housing," *Los Angeles Examiner*, November 2, 1946.

15. Hermine Rich Isaacs, *Theatre Arts*, April 1947, p. 54.

16. Bosley Crowther, *New York Times*, April 11, 1947, p. 31.

17. McClelland, pp. 74–75.

18. Thomas Wood, "If You Knew Susie," p. 11.

19. McClelland, p. 76.

20. Dewitt Gilpin, "A Drink with Susan Hayward," *Salute*, June 1947.

21. Gilpin.

22. James Bawden, "Marsha Hunt," *Films in Review*, November, 1989, p. 518.

23. Cameron Shipp, "Susan Hayward," *Redbook Magazine*, February 1956, p. 33.

24. Elizabeth Wilson, "Brown-Eyed Susan," *Liberty*, May 10, 1947, p. 23.

25. A. H. Weiler, *New York Times*, July 17, 1947, p. 16.

26. *Theatre Arts*, September 1947, p. 14.

27. Bob Porfirio in Silver and Ward, p. 286.

28. "Susan Hayward, Startling Hollywood, Asks Divorce," *Los Angeles Times*, October 1, 1947.

29. "Miss Hayward, Mate Reunited," *Los Angeles Examiner*, November 27, 1947.

30. Andersen, *A Star*, p. 96.

31. Bosley Crowther, *New York Times*, November 22, 1947, p. 10.

32. *Newsweek*, January 5, 1948, p. 69.

33. Don Lee Keith, "Susan Hayward: Flame-Haired Blizzard from Brooklyn," *After Dark*, January 1973, p. 42.

34. *Newsweek*, August 16, 1948, p. 76.

35. Thomas M. Pryor, *New York Times*, August 26, 1948, p. 16.

36. *Newsweek*, September 27, 1948, p. 88.

37. Thomas M. Pryor, *New York Times*, September 30, 1948, p. 32.

Chapter 4

1. Hortense Powdermaker, *Hollywood: The Dream Factory*, New York: Universal Library/Grosset & Dunlap, 1950, p. 248.

2. "Film Actress Cited Most Beautiful," *Los Angeles Daily News*, January 18, 1949.

3. *Newsweek*, April 25, 1949, p. 91.

4. Bosley Crowther, *New York Times*, May 27, 1949, p. 25.

5. John L. Scott, "Susan Hayward Likes 'Vital' Roles to Fit That Redhead Temperament," *Los Angeles Times*, April 3, 1949, p. 3.

6. Andersen, *A Star*, p. 97.

7. Her only mention in Leo Guild's *Zanuck: Hollywood's Last Tycoon* is that she was one of the flock considered for *Cleopatra* (*Zanuck: Hollywood's Last Tycoon*, Los Angeles, CA: Holloway House, 1970, p. 201). The only substantive sections in the Zanuck memos selected by Rudy Behlmer concern Susan's promotion by Joseph L. Mankiewicz for the starring role in *All About Eve* (Rudy Behlmer, ed., *Memo from Darryl F. Zanuck: The Golden Years at Twentieth Century–Fox*, New York: Grove Press, 1993, p. 165), and Zanuck's decision to turn down *I'll Cry Tomorrow*, which became an MGM film (*Memo*, p. 257). Hayward is not mentioned at all in Marlys J. Harris' *The Zanucks of Hollywood: The Dark Legacy of an American Dynasty* (New York: Crown, 1989), nor in Mel Gussow's *Don't Say Yes Until I Finish Talking: A Biography of Darryl F. Zanuck* (Garden City, NY: Doubleday, 1971). None of these books are definitive biographies or studio histories, however. Their authors have specific agendas, which rarely encompass the moviemaking process, bur rather concentrate on love affairs, Marilyn Monroe, and *Cleopatra*. The only reference in Leonard Mosley's *Zanuck: The Rise and Fall of Hollywood's Last Tycoon* is that Hayward co-starred with Gregory Peck in *David and Bathsheba* (*Zanuck: The Rise and Fall of Hollywood's Last Tycoon*, Boston: Little, Brown, 1984, p. 241).

8. Thomas Wood, "If You Knew Susie," p. 2.

9. Hedda Hopper, "Hayward of the Wayward Roles," June 19, 1949.

10. Bosley Crowther, *New York Times*, July 2, 1949, p. 8.

11. Blake Lucas and Alain Silver in Silver and Ward, p. 134.

12. *Manchester Guardian*, August 27, 1949, in Kenneth L. Geist, *Pictures Will Talk: The Life and Films of Joseph L. Mankiewicz*, New York: Charles Scribner's Sons, 1978, p. 150.

13. Gordon, "Press Releases," Twentieth Century–Fox, 1949.

14. Sidney Skolsky, "Hollywood Is My Beat: Tintypes," *Hollywood Citizen-News*, June 30, 1949.

15. *Variety Movie Guide*, New York: Prentice Hall, 1992, p. 412.

16. John McCarten, *The New Yorker*, January 28, 1950, p. 75.

17. Bosley Crowther, *New York Times*, January 20, 1950, p. 29.

18. *Newsweek*, January 23, 1950, p. 80.

19. Andrew Sarris, "The Heart is a Lonely Hunter," *Film Comment*, January/February 1991, pp. 42.

20. A. Scott Berg in *Goldwyn: A Biography*, New York: Knopf, 1989, quoted in Sarris, p. 43.

21. Sarris, pp. 43–44.

22. "Miss Hayward Gets Glamour Queen Title," *Los Angeles Times*, July 11, 1950.

23. Behlmer, *Memo from Darryl F. Zanuck*, p. 165.

24. Thomas M. Pryor, *New York Times*, March 26, 1951, p. 19.

25. Garfield, p. 265.

26. LaGuardia and Arceri, p. 75.

27. Thomas M. Pryor, *New York Times*, April 5, 1951, p. 34.

28. Earle F. Walbridge, *Library Journal*, April 15, 1951, p. 720.

29. McClelland, p. 106.

30. Edith H. Crowell, *Library Journal*, February 15, 1951, p. 343.

31. Bosley Crowther, *New York Times*, May 10, 1951, p. 38.

32. Susan Hayward Collectors' Club Newsletter, May-June 1989, p. 3; James Robert Parish, *The Fox Girls*, New Rochelle, NY: Arlington House, 1971, p. 569.

33. Johnson, Press Release, 20th Century–Fox, ca. 1951, p. 1.

34. "Miss Hayward Misses Death," *Los Angeles Examiner*, June 1, 1950.

35. Dorothy Manners, "Brooklyn's Child Is Full of Faith," *Photoplay*, July 1955.

36. Wolfson, 20th Century–Fox press release, ca. 1951.

37. Arthur Knight, "SRL Goes to the Movies," *Saturday Review*, September 8, 1951, p. 36.

38. *Variety Movie Guide*, p. 139.

39. A. H. Weiler, *New York Times*, August 15, 1951, p. 23.

40. *Christian Century*, September 26, 1951, p. 1111.

41. "Plane Causes Stampede of Film Camels," *Los Angeles Times*, December 2, 1950.

42. Darr Smith, "Darr Smith," *Los Angeles Daily News*, August 28, 1951.

43. Mendelsohn, 20th Century–Fox Press Release, ca. 1951, p. 1.

44. Mendelsohn, p. 2.

45. Louis Berg, "Bathsheba Takes a Bath," *Los Angeles Times This Week Magazine*, August 19, 1951.

46. Behlmer, *Memo* [July 25, 1952] *from Darryl F. Zanuck*, p. 221.

47. Ed Colbert letter to author, September 9, 2000.

48. Susan Sackett, *The Hollywood Reporter Book of Box Office Hits*, New York: Billboard Books, 1990, p. 96.

49. John Griggs, *The Films of Gregory Peck*, Secaucus, NJ: Citadel, 1984, p. 109.

50. Sackett, p. 92.

51. Cobbett Steinberg, *Reel Facts: The Movie Book of Records*, updated ed., New York: Vintage, 1982, c1981, p. 20.

52. "Now Actress Gets Brush-off from Canada," *Los Angeles Times*, September 15, 1951.

53. Wolfson, 20th Century–Fox press release, ca. 1951.

54. Bosley Crowther, *New York Times*, April 5, 1952, p. 20.

55. *Variety Movie Guide*, p. 678.

56. *Theatre Arts*, May 1952, p. 104.

57. "Look Movie Review: With a Song in My Heart," *Look*, April 8, 1952, p. 98.

58. "Look Movie Review: With a Song in My Heart," p. 100.

59. Molly Haskell on *Susan Hayward: The Brooklyn Bombshell*, 1998.

60. Andersen, *A Star*, p. 120.

61. LaGuardia and Arceri, p. 74.

62. Wolfson, 20th Century–Fox press release, ca. 1952.

63. Thomas Wood, "If You Knew Susie," p. 9.

64. Wolfson, "Tintype of Susan Hayward," 20th Century–Fox press release, ca. 1952, p. 1.

65. Susan Hayward on *The Joey Bishop Show*, ABC-TV, February 1968.

66. Wolfson, "Tintype," p. 2.

67. Wolfson, ca. 1952. *Gilda* (1946) featured the famous Rita Hayworth "Put the Blame on Mame" number.

68. Wolfson, ca. 1952.

69. LaGuardia and Arceri, p. 79.

70. LaGuardia and Arceri, pp. 79–80.

71. "Susan Hayward," *PIX*, July 17, 1954, p. 37.

72. Wolfson, "Tintype," p. 4.

73. Wolfson, "Tintype," p. 7.

74. Markson, 20th Century–Fox press release, ca. 1951, p. 2.

75. "$ucce$$ for $ultry $u$an," *People Today*, February 27, 1952.

76. Hedda Hopper, "Susan Hayward—Beauty with a Brain," *Chicago Sunday Tribune*, March 9, 1952, p. 6.

77. Hopper, "Susan Hayward—Beauty," p. 15.

78. "Susan Hayward Makes Big School Comeback," *New York Journal–American*, March 12, 1952.

79. "Susan Hayward Advises Stars to Stay Off Stump in Political Campaigns," *Daily Variety*, October 27, 1952.

80. Ida Zeitlin, "Three Loves Has Susan," *Photoplay*, November 1952, p. 82.

81. Zeitlin, p. 86.

82. John McCarten, *The New Yorker*, September 20, 1952, p. 120.

83. Bosley Crowther, *New York Times*, September 19, 1952, p. 19.

84. *Newsweek*, September 29, 1952, p. 94.

85. *Variety Movie Guide*, p. 556.

86. Johnson, 20th Century–Fox press release by Susan Hayward.

87. Steinberg, *Reel Facts*, pp. 20–21.

88. "All-Time Boxoffice Champs," *Variety*, January 3, 1973, p. 30. On p. 32 *Snows* is listed as having taken in $6,500,000.

89. Bosley Crowther, *New York Times*, October 25, 1952, p. 12.

90. Garfield, p. 223.

91. Quite a few rodeo films have provided fine entertainment. Amazingly, four interesting, sometimes excellent ones were released in 1972: *When the Legends Die*, *The Honkers*, *Junior Bonner*, *J W Coop*.

92. Howard Thompson, *New York Times*, May 22, 1953, p. 31.

93. *Variety Movie Guide*, p. 474.

94. Charlton Heston, *In the Arena: An Autobiography*, New York: Simon & Schuster, 1995, p. 123.

95. Heston, *In the Arena*, p. 125.

96. "Susan Hayward, Gary Cooper Win Fan Poll," *Los Angeles Times*, February 3, 1953.

97. "Susan Hayward, Gary Cooper Get Special Honors," *Los Angeles Daily News*, February 10, 1953.

98. "Foreign Press Honors Susan Hayward, Wayne," *Los Angeles Times*, February 15, 1953.

99. "It Was Fun But...," *Movie Life*, August 1953.

100. A. H. Weiler, *New York Times*, July 2, 1953, p. 19.

101. "Guest Column for Dorothy Kilgallen by Susan Hayward," Press Release, ca. 1954, pp. 1–2.

102. *The Times* [U.K.], September 13, 1954, p. 3.

103. *Variety Movie Guide*, p. 148.

104. Bosley Crowther, *New York Times*, June 19, 1954, p. 9.

105. Campbell, 20th Century–Fox press release, ca. 1954, p. 1.

106. LaGuardia and Arceri, p. 84.

107. Martin S. Dworkin, *New Republic*, September 6, 1954, p. 20.

108. John McCarten, *The New Yorker*, July 17, 1954, p. 57.

109. A. H. Weiler, *New York Times*, July 10, 1954, p. 7.

110. *Time*, July 19, 1954, p. 76.

111. Garfield, *Western Films*, p. 170.

112. *Garden of Evil* Exhibitor's Campaign Book, New York: Twentieth Century–Fox, 1954, p. 5.

113. Johnson, 20th Century–Fox press release, ca. 1954.

114. Susan Hayward in "Stay-at-Homes Lift Wings to Circle Globe for Film," *Garden of Evil* Exhibitor's Campaign Book, p. 10.

115. Linet, p. 154.

116. Nineteen fifty-four was a year of personal upheaval for Hayward. Divorce from Jess Barker loomed, despite a reconciliation meeting. Attorney S. S. Hahn said, "Every time Barker said he'd forgive her for having done something, she'd remember something she wouldn't forgive. Barker told her he'd forget about the time she stuck a lighted cigarette in his eye and the time she bit his arm....Then she said she'd never forgive him for throwing her in their swimming pool with her clothes on and for spanking her in a tender spot. ("Susan Hayward, Hubby Call Calling Off Off," *Los Angeles Daily News*, February 25, 1954.) Naturally the press had a field day. Hayward told a Superior Court judge that she made $17,000 a month and had $240,000 in assets but that Barker wouldn't get out of bed and find a job. She said the first instance of violence occurred on the night of July 16–17, 1953, when Barker tossed her in the swimming pool and her terry-cloth bathrobe pulled her down. Furthermore, Barker pushed her under when she did come up. Barker countered that Hayward and he had had a few drinks and that she insulted his mother. He admitted to slapping her. She bit his arm and he spanked her "reasonably hard." She screamed when he put her in the bedroom, and to cool her off dropped her in the shallow end of the pool. "I did not try to kill her." Howard Hughes' name came up. He'd been to the house when Barker was out. Hayward explained that she was making *The Conqueror* for Hughes. She sought to keep Barker out of the house for fear of molestation. She was willing to grant visitation rights to the children. ("Susan Hayward, Barker Tell Story of Clashes," *Los Angeles Times*, February 26, 1954.) The next-door maid, Lodee Hazel

Swain, told the judge she saw "Miss Hayward's nude dash to the house. ("Susan's friend Martha Little appeared in the middle of the fracas. "Susan Sobs, Says Jess Spanked Her," *Los Angeles Examiner*, February 26, 1954.) Court appearances continued for months. On March 15, 1954, Hayward was granted temporary custody of her sons. Barker got visitation rights for each Wednesday and alternate weekends. He was restrained from "annoying, molesting or harassing" his wife and denied access to their home at 3737 Longridge Avenue, Sherman Oaks. Neither party was to take the twins out of state without the written consent of the other. ("Susan Hayward Wins Custody Case Point," *Los Angeles Times*, March 16, 1954.) Burbank Superior Judge Herbert V. Walker warned the duo against condemning each other in front of the children. ("Susan Gets Tots' Custody," *Los Angeles Examiner*, March 16, 1954.) On April 7, 1954, a predivorce conference aimed at avoiding a trial came to naught when neither Susan nor Jess could agree on major points. Barker maintained he wanted the marriage to continue. Hayward sought divorce on the grounds of mental cruelty. Barker thought their prenuptial agreement invalid. ("Barker, Susan Hayward Agreement Move Fails," *Los Angeles Times*, April 8, 1954.) The divorce hearing commenced. Barker complained about the prenuptial agreement. Susan's assets were cited: $106,742 in stock, $23,501 in bonds, $66,947 in cash, $45,757 payment toward their home, $46,302 insured value of furs, jewelry and personal property, and $4,570 cash surrender value of an insurance policy. Barker asserted that he'd assisted Hayward with her career by helping her study lines at home and on the set, consulting on costumes and makeup and lip-synching, and with contract negotiations with Fox. "She's a great actress....I am very proud of her. I feel a part of it." ("Jess Barker Vows Love for Wife in Courtroom," *Los Angeles Times*, April 18, 1954.) Barker disputed Hayward's wish to take the twins to St. George, Utah, June 4 to July 4, where she was making *The Conqueror*. ("Susan Hayward Mate Balks at Trip for Twins," *Los Angeles Times*, May 9, 1954.) Hayward won after indicating that she'd take a tutor. ("Susan Hayward Gets OK to Take Sons from State," *Los Angeles Times*, May 20, 1954.) The actual divorce trial started on June 14. Hayward returned from location. ("Susan Hayward and Barker in Court Today," *Los Angeles Times*, June 14, 1954.) The trial was juicy, with Lodee Hazel Swain providing more detail about Susan's nude flight from the pool to the house. "She was nude and her hair was red. I wouldn't swear that it was Miss Hayward. But that's who was living next door." Barker's attorney disputed the fact that Mrs. Swain could have seen the incident at about 3 a.m., July 17, 1953, especially as a foliage-covered fence could have interfered with her view. Barker reiterated that if a reconciliation were not possible, he wanted a division of community property despite the prenuptial agreement. Barker's attorney alleged that community property included $1,000,000 left on Hayward's unexpired contract, in addition to over $250,000 in negotiable assets. ("Susan Hayward's Screams of 'Don't Kill Me' Described," *Los Angeles Times*, June 15, 1954.) The *Los Angeles Times*, *Los Angeles Examiner* and the *Daily News* included pictures of Susan and Jess beside the infamous swimming pool.

Hayward became upset after the reading of a Barker deposition on the 15th, and the judge granted a continuance until the 16th. The deposition told of past separations in 1944 and 1947. Marriage counselors had been seen. Barker indicated that Hayward had been more fortunate in the business. While he stayed at home, "She became a star." ("Susan Hayward Breaks Down at Divorce Trial," *Los Angeles Times*, June 16, 1954.) Barker alleged that Susan's attorney had approached him with a settlement offer of $100,000. Hayward's attorney, Martin Gang, denied it. (Years later Gang and his firm would be embroiled with Hayward in another legal battle. In 1965 Gang et al. claimed Hayward owed money for work from 1949 to 1969, including movie contracts and the Barker divorce. Hayward counter sued, claiming the attorneys' advice resulted in paying extra taxes. The suit was settled out of court. ["Accord Ends Movie Star Hayward Suit," *Hollywood Citizen–News*, July 7, 1965.]) Barker said he'd refused the offer. There was dispute over taxes. They'd filed jointly, so Barker insisted half of Susan's property was rightfully his. ("Susan's Divorce Offer of $100,000 Reported," *Los Angeles Daily News*, June 16, 1954, p. 3.)

Barker continued protestations of love for his wife and a desire for reconciliation. A deposition from Hayward read in court indicated that she told Barker that before they married she'd always be able to take care of herself. He wasn't ready for marriage and responsibilities, he'd said. She'd said he'd felt marriage would harm his career as a young actor. Hayward admitted to biting Barker on the arm before he'd tossed her into the pool. ("Barker Pleads 'Let's Reconcile,'" *Los Angeles Examiner*, June 18, 1954.)

When the trial ended, Judge Herbert V. Walker said he'd make his decision after considering the effects on the twins. Barker's attorney, S.S. Hahn, pleaded with the judge not to grant a divorce. "Melt the ice in the heart of that woman with a legal whip.... A river of gold has blinded that woman to her responsibilities to her children and to her husband." ("Lawyers End Case in Susan Hayward Divorce," *Los Angeles Times*, June 19, 1954.)

"But despite her domestic difficulties, Susan Hayward has gone from strength to strength as an actress. She has established herself, not only as one of the most beautiful and popular, but as one of the most versatile of stars." ("Susan Hayward," *PIX*, July 17, 1954, p. 37.)

On August 17, 1954, Hayward was granted an interlocutory divorce decree. She received custody of the twins. Barker received visitation rights on Wednesdays and every other weekend. He also got a station wagon, and his attorney was to receive $3,500 from Hayward. Susan and Jess were ordered not to harass each other. ("Divorce Granted to Susan Hayward," *Los Angeles Times*, August 18, 1954, Part I, p. 28.)

On August 18 Barker's attorney said he would appeal the decision on the grounds that the "ante-nuptial agreement" was against public policy; that even if legal, it had been canceled by Hayward when she made out tax returns signing that her earnings were community property; that California law entitles each spouse to half the earnings accumulated during the marriage; and, "That the evidence upon which the divorce was granted her was insufficient because she provoked the quarrel which culminated in the dunking in the swimming pool." ("Barker Lawyer to Appeal Susan Hayward Divorce," *Los Angeles Times*, August 19, 1954.)

Later that month, while working on *Untamed*, Hayward said she'd doubtless try marriage again. "My two boys are my life. I would love to have a little girl or two or three to go with them." (Dorothy Manners, "Susan Hayward Thinks She'll Remarry," *Los Angeles Examiner*, August 29, 1954, p. 12.)

117. "New Hayward-Barker Divorce Trial Asked," *Los Angeles Times*, October 5, 1954.

118. "Rule Susan Hayward Sons to Stay in U.S.," *Los Angeles Herald Express*, October 13, 1954.

119. Bosley Crowther, *New York Times*, March 12, 1955, p. 11.

120. George G. Goodwin, *Natural History*, April 1955, p. 221.

121. Garfield, p. 335.

122. "Susan Hayward, From Harry Brand, Director of Publicity, "20th Century–Fox Studio, ca. 1955, pp. 1–2.

123. Campbell, "Notes on Susan Hayward for Dorothy Manners," 20th Century–Fox, ca. 1955, p. 1.

124. "Susan Hayward Ordered to Finance Mate's Appeal," *Los Angeles Times*, December 14, 1954.

Chapter 5

1. Thomas Wiseman, *The Seven Deadly Sins of Hollywood*, London: Oldbourne Press, 1957, p. 47.

2. I.Z. [Ida Zeitlin?], "Actress Around the World," *Cue*, April 16, 1955.

3. "Film Actress Rushed to Hospital; 2 Pill Bottles Discovered," *Los Angeles Times*, April 26, 1955.

4. Dick O'Connor, et al., "Save Star; Blame Row with Ex-Mate," *Los Angeles Herald Express*, April 26, 1955, pp. 1, 5. Another article said the reported suicide occurred a few days after a secret meeting between Susan and Jess at an Ambassador Hotel bungalow. Hayward's mother said that Susan had phoned to say, "Mother, you will be well taken care of." Brother Wally said, "I don't know why she did it. You can assume anything. She seemed happy when I saw her about a week ago. She was always close-mouthed about her trouble with Barker, even with relatives." ("Police Kick in Door, Find Actress Unconscious, Rush Her to Hospital," *Los Angeles Mirror–News*, April 26, 1955, Part I, pp. 1, 10.)

A separate article quoted an unnamed acquaintance to the effect that Hayward bottled up her emotions and didn't broadcast her troubles. "That's why Hollywood has always called her withdrawn and cold." (Kendis Rochlen, "Emotion Explodes in Susan," *Los Angeles Mirror–News*, April 26, 1955, pp. 1, 10.)

As for Barker, who was in New Orleans promoting *Kentucky Rifle* (1955), co-star Chill Wills said, "Barker was hit hard by the divorce and he's been trying hard to make a comeback in films. He always felt that he was sort of overshadowed by his wife's name. He was working hard and getting along fine. Now this thing has him all broken up." ("Miss Hayward Rallies After Pill Overdose," *Hollywood Citizen–News*, April 26, 1955.)

By April 27 the East Coast was reporting on the suicide: how two detectives broke down the patio door and found Hayward unconscious in a housedress on the living room floor, how they decided an ambulance would take too long so they carried her to the squad car and took her to North Hollywood Receiving Hospital where her stomach was pumped, that brother Wally said she was despondent over a "tiff" with her ex-husband plus overwork. ("Film Star Tries Suicide," *New York Times*, April 27, 1955, p. 27.)

On the 27th it was reported that Barker's attorney said Barker would press for custody of the twins since Susan had attempted suicide and that until she returned from the hospital he had a right to move back into the Longridge Avenue house to care for them. Barker disputed his attorney's comments and also denied that he'd collapsed in New Orleans upon hearing the news of his ex-wife's suicide attempt and had said he loved her. She had refused his attempt to see her in the hospital. ("Sue May Lose Two Children as New Court Fight Looms," *Los Angeles Mirror–News*, April 27, 1955, p. 1.)

Others echoed Hayward's brother's remarks that she was exhausted from overwork and concern about Barker and her sons. (Dick Williams, "The Hayward Mystery," *Los Angeles Mirror–News*, April 27, 1955, Part II, p. 4.)

Hayward rejected the possibility of reconciliation from her hospital room. "There is not the slightest possibility of a reconciliation.... If Mr. Barker can discuss the future of our children in a rational manner, I shall always be willing to confer with him on the subject." ("Miss Hayward, On Mend, Spurns Barker's Offer," *Los Angeles Times*, April 28, 1955.)

A studio photographer was allowed into her hospital room on the 29th. ("Susan Hayward Expected to Leave Hospital Today," *Los Angeles Times*, April 29, 1955.) She left the hospital the same day, encountering a legion of reporters who wanted to know if she was still through with Barker. "That's what the lady said!" she responded, adding that she'd be back at MGM on Monday working on *I'll Cry Tomorrow*. "I have to get this show back on the road." She embraced Nurse Mary Ann Thompson before leaving. ("Susan Hayward Leaves Hospital to Go Home," *Los Angeles Times*, April 30, 1955.)

No sooner was Hayward home than Barker's attorney, S.S. Hahn, filed briefs for a motion to dismiss Hayward's appeal concerning payment of additional attorney's fees. ("Susan Home, Faces Suit," *Los Angeles Examiner*, May 1, 1955.)

The newspapers had more grist when Police Chief William H. Parker revealed that the manner in which his officers saved Hayward's life was technically illegal because they had violated her property and personal rights. There was no prohibition against suicide in California. ("Actress' Life Illegally Saved," *Hollywood Citizen–News*, June 1, 1955.)

A month later Barker claimed that Hayward had a weakness for sleeping pills and had taken an overdose during their vacation in Rome in April 1953. This was part of his plan to gain total custody of his sons and countered her petition to take them to the Pacific Northwest and Canada for an August vacation. Barker wanted them for part of August and September. Barker's petition was denied by Burbank Superior Court on the grounds that Barker's appeal of the interlocutory decree was even then before the District Court of Appeals. ("Two Suicide Tries by Susan Hayward Claimed," *Los Angeles Times*, July 21, 1955, Part I, p. 5.)

Damage control was supplied in July and August when three major film magazines ran articles on Hayward. Susan spoke of her willingness to take professional criticism ("Don't forget that an actress takes criticism and help every day from her directors"), her sons ("My boys and I have a lot of fun together. We go to most of the football and baseball games, we love to go fishing, I attend most of their club meetings at school, and we have many long talks about anything and everything," her sentimentality ("I like mood music too—and that's pure sentiment"), her temper ("I have had moments when I have lost my temper with the boys—and when they have blown at me"), money ("Money is nice if you have it, but it's far from being all there is"), and marriage ("I doubt, though, that I'll ever marry a man in the motion picture field"). (Jack Holland, "Susan Hayward—Fact and Fiction," *Screenland*, July 1955, pp. 41, 68.)

Hayward spoke at length of faith, how her father's words helped her through difficult times. She called faith "passionate intuition." (Dorothy Manners, "Brooklyn's Child Is Full of Faith," *Photoplay*, July 1955, p. 83.)

She talked of her teachers at Girls' Commercial High in Brooklyn, of a happy family life, of shyness and of "pretty stinky" clothes. (Frank Degan, "When They Hit You—BOUNCE!" *Silver Screen*, August 1955, p. 63.)

Hayward won in the District Court of Appeal. She didn't have to pay Barker's attorney's fees, and the district court turned down Barker's appeal that the property should be divided equally. ("Susan Hayward Wins Twice; Ex-Mate Loses Fees, Appeal," *Los Angeles Examiner*, February 16, 1956.) In April the California State Supreme Court refused to hear appeals from both Susan and Jess. ("High Court Won't Hear Susan Hayward Appeal," *Los Angeles Times*, April 12, 1956.)

In July 1956 Hayward petitioned the Superior Court to drop Barker from her name so she could become Edythe Marrenner once more. ("Susan Hayward Would Drop Ex-Mate's Name," *Los Angeles Times*, July 26, 1956.) This was granted in September. ("Susan Hayward Gets Old Name Back," *Los Angeles Herald Express*, September 4, 1956.)

5. Bosley Crowther, *New York Times*, May 28, 1955, p. 7.

6. *Time*, June 13, 1955, pp. 100, 102.

7. Linet, pp. l 177–178.

8. Edward Dmytryk, *It's a Hell of a Life but Not a Bad Living*, New York: Times Books, 1978, p. 190.

9. *Hollywood Studio Magazine*, April 1978.

10. Dmytryk, *It's a Hell*, p. 190.

11. "Actress Susan Hayward Flies to Honolulu," *Los Angeles Times*, September 8, 1955.

12. Harrison Carroll, "Lost Her Temper; Susan Sorry," *Los Angeles Herald Express*, November 4, 1955, pp. 1, 4.

13. Louella O. Parsons, "Susan Tells of Slapping," *Los Angeles Examiner*, November 4, 1955. In another account, Hayward was said to have "attacked and mauled" Jarmyn. ("Movie Queen Blows Top, Swings Clothes Brush," *Los Angeles Mirror News*, November 4, 1955.)

Jarmyn signed a request for a battery complaint, and Deputy City Attorney C. R. Powers, Jr. set November 16 for a hearing to determine if a complaint would be issued. ("Susan Hayward Whacked Her, Actress Charges," *Los Angeles Times*, November 5, 1955.)

In some accounts, Hayward was accosted while in Barry's bed. ("Susan to Face Court," *Los Angeles Herald Express*, November 5, 1955, p. A-4.) The incident was to be used by Barker's lawyer to help him get custody of the twins. (Florabel Muir, "Susan Hayward in Brawl with Blonde in Actor's Bedroom," *Daily News* [Los Angeles], November 5, 1955, pp. 3, 6.)

Newspapers kept up the story about Jarmyn's battery complaint, about which she was said to have had second thoughts. "Jil Jarmyn, the blonde who said she came off second best in a boudoir hair-snatching match with Susan Hayward, indicated today that she won't file a battery complaint against the red-haired actress." ("Hayward Tiff to End in Draw," *Los Angeles Mirror News*, November 7, 1955, Part I, p. 5.) On the 16th Jarmyn formally dropped the complaint. ("Actress Drops Charges Against Sue Hayward," *Los Angeles Examiner*, November 16, 1955.)

The funniest take on the incident can be found in Kendis Rochlen's column: "Both Susan and Jil said they dropped in at Barry's place to enjoy a cup of his java. Now when you find a big star like Susie so fond of Barry's mocha that she trots over without stopping to change from her blue polka-dot pajamas, or throw on that pink terrycloth bathrobe, you just have to figure the guy's pretty good with a percolator…. Since he's been riding around in western films all these years it figures that Barry just might have picked up a few cowboy tricks. My guess is he brews the stuff in an old tomato can over a fire of buffalo chips." (Kendis Rochlen, "Candid Kendis: Have Silex—Will Travel," *Los Angeles Mirror–News*, November 7, 1955.)

14. Van Spear, "Spearheads," *Boxoffice*, December 3, 1955.

15. Hollis Alpert, *Saturday Review*, January 7, 1956, p. 56.

16. Alpert, p. 56.

17. Bosley Crowther, *New York Times*, January 13, 1956, p. 18.

18. David Shipman, *The Great Movie Stars: The International Years*, London: Angus & Robertson, 1972, p. 214.

19. "Movie Review: Susan Hayward Bids for an Academy Award," *Look*, December 13, 1955, p. 104.

20. Charlotte Bilkey Speicher, *Library Journal*, February 1, 1956, p. 360.

21. Jon Whitcomb, "Songbird Susan," *Cosmopolitan*, February 1956, pp. 62–63.

22. Philip K. Scheuer, "Susan Hayward Awes MGM with Her Polished Singing," *Los Angeles Times*, July 3, 1955, Part IV, p. 2.

23. Scheuer, "Susan Hayward Awes MGM," p. 2.

24. "Movie Review: Susan Hayward Bids," p. 106.

25. Timothy Barker in *Susan Hayward: The Brooklyn Bombshell*.

26. Rudy Behlmer, *Memo from Darryl F. Zanuck*, December 12, 1955, p. 257.

27. "All-Time Boxoffice Champs," *Variety*, January 3, 1973, p. 32.

28. Earl Wilson, "Susan Hayward Speaks Up," *Los Angeles Mirror–News*, January 18, 1956.

29. "*Look* Movie Awards: Fifteenth Anniversary," *Look*, March 20, 1956, p. 86.

30. "Air Force Salute Opens at Pershing Square," *Los Angeles Times*, March 8, 1956.

31. "Susan Hayward's First Television Appearance," http://community-2.webtv.net/GINBOB/SUSANHAYWARDSFIRST; 4/25/00.

32. McClelland, p. 180.

33. "Camera Targets," *Los Angeles Times*, April 30, 1956.

34. "Susan Hayward Wins Top Acting Prize at Cannes," *Hollywood Citizen–News*, May 10, 1956; "Susan Hayward Only American Cannes Winner," *Hollywood Reporter*, May 11, 1956.

35. W.R. Wilkerson, "Trade[press]," *Hollywood Reporter*, May 11, 1956.

36. A. H. Weiler, *New York Times*, March 31, 1956, p. 13.

37. *Time*, April 9, 1956, p. 112.

38. The time was not yet right for actress navels in American movies. Neither Joan Collins in *Land of the Pharaohs* (1955) nor Gina Lollobrigida in *Solomon and Sheba* (1959) could show a navel minus a precious gem. Surviving footage of Marilyn Monrie in the aborted *Something's Got to Give* (1961) reveals navel and more, but she was fired and the production halted. The first major American leading lady to expose an undiluted midriff is probably Shirley MacLaine in *What a Way to Go!* (June 1964), beating by a half year Kim Novak in *Kiss Me, Stupid* (December 1964).

39. "This story, though fiction, is based on fact." But not much fact or RKO would have made it longer, acquired thousands more horsemen, and filmed on grassland, not desert. *The Conqueror* is a slightly elevated version of the mini-epics

with which Universal-International had been countering TV, and in which ... groomed for stardom Rock Hudson, Tony Curtis, Janet Leigh, Jeff Chandler, Barbara Rush, Martha Hyer and Piper Laurie. Chandler and Jack Palance co-starred in another saga of the barbarians from the east, *Sign of the Pagan,* with Palance as Attila the Hun. As befit its major studio status, MGM had entered with more grandiose projects such as *Quo Vadis?* (1950). Fox had made *The Robe* (1953) and its sequel, *Demetrius and the Gladiators* (1954). Warner Bros. had *Land of the Pharaohs* (1955). The same year as *The Conqueror* the "roadshow" era was truly launched with Biblical and other epics such as *The Ten Commandments.* In 1959 came *Ben-Hur.* The epics were invariably filmed in Spain (*El Cid*) or Argentina (*Taras Bulba*) or Italy (*War and Peace*) with those countries' armies, caballeros or low-paid extras.

40. "All-Time Boxoffice Champs," *Variety,* January 3, 1973, p. 34.

41. Pilar Wayne and Alex Thorleifson, *John Wayne: My Life with the Duke,* New York: McGraw-Hill, 1987, p. 102. Although Pilar noted the coincidence of death by cancer of principal players in *The Conqueror,* she provided an equally valid cause to counter those who blamed nuclear fallout from Nevada A-bomb tests: smoking. "But I was there on location day in and out, as were many other people who never became ill. The real culprit in the deaths of my husband, Susan Hayward, Agnes Moorehead, Pedro Armendariz, and Dick Powell was their constant, incessant smoking. They all had a two-pack-per day (or more) habit. Duke never smoked fewer than three packs a day." (Pilar Wayne, p. 103.)

The possibility of radiation continued to come up, linked to the "Dirty Harry" atomic bomb exploded on May 19, 1953. ("Stars' Cancer Deaths Linked to '53 A-Test," *Los Angeles Times,* August 6, 1979.) In 1980 *People* magazine gave credence to the A-bomb theory for the 1953 Yucca Flat, Nevada, test affecting St. George, Utah, 137 miles away. Tim Barker, one of Susan's sons, then 35, was considering a negligence suit against the government. He'd had a benign tumor removed from his mouth in 1968. Yet even he admitted, "I still smoke a pack a day." (Karen G. Jackovich and Mark Sennet, "The Children of John Wayne, Susan Hayward and Dick Powell Felt That Fallout Killed Their Parents," *People,* November 10, 1980, pp. 42, 44.)

But Pilar Wayne is probably correct. Smoking, not radioactive fallout, most likely caused her husband's death. John Wayne had a lung removed in 1963 but didn't die until 1979 and was very active in between. Director Dick Powell died of cancer at age 58 in 1963. Pedro Armendariz learned he had neck cancer and killed himself at age 51 in 1963. Agnes Moorehead died of lung cancer at age 73 in 1974. Thomas Gomez died following a car accident at the age of 65 in 1971. Except for Lee Van Cleef, who died of an apparent heart attack at age 64 in 1989, the film's major character actors lived average life spans. Ted de Corsia died at age 69 in 1973, John Hoyt from lung cancer at age 85 in 1991, William Conrad from cardiac arrest at age 73 in 1994, Leo Gordon at age 78 in 2000.

42. Bosley Crowther, *New York Times,* January 31, 1957, p. 21.

43. *Time,* February 4, 1957, p. 92.

44. "Biographies," Warner Bros. Studios, Burbank, Calif., November 21, 1956, p. 2.

45. "Susan Hayward Married to Georgia Attorney," *Los Angeles Times,* February 9, 1957.

46. Louella A. Parsons, "Susan Hayward Weds," *Los Angeles Examiner,* February 9, 1957.

47. Vincent X. Flaherty, "An Ungainly Cupid Bares Confession," *Los Angeles Examiner*, February 11, 1957.

48. Vincent X. Flaherty, "That Little 'If' Makes World Move 'Round," *Los Angeles Examiner*, April 12, 1959.

49. "Susan Hayward to Take Twin Sons to Georgia," *Los Angeles Times*, April 27, 1957.

50. "Susan Hayward to Play Babs Graham Biopic," *Daily Variety*, October 9, 1957.

51. Campbell, "20th Century–Fox Press Release," ca. 1957.

52. Bob Thomas, "Susan Hayward Happy with Life in Georgia Hills," *Hollywood Citizen–News*, April 7, 1958.

53. Vernon Scott, "Susan Hayward Returns for Film," *Hollywood Citizen–News*, April 7, 1958.

54. Erskine Johnson, "Susan Hayward Has Found Happiness in the Deep South," *Los Angeles Mirror-News*, April 19, 1958.

55. "Susan Hayward Mother Dies of Heart Ailment," *Los Angeles Mirror–News*, April 16, 1958.

56. "Susan Flies to Stricken Husband," *Los Angeles Examiner*, July 25, 1958.

57. Bosley Crowther, *New York Times*, November 22, 1958, p. 45.

58. Arthur Knight, *Saturday Review*, November 29, 1958, p. 25.

59. Mary Hatch, *Library Journal*, December 1, 1958, pp. 3418–3419.

60. Sidney Skolsky, "Hollywood Is My Beat: Tintypes," *Hollywood Citizen–News*, December 24, 1958.

61. Trace the course of Wanger's trial and imprisonment via the *New York Times*: "Temporary Insanity Pleaded by Wanger," January 8, 1952, p. 28; "Wanger Victim May Be Crippled," January 20, 1952, p. 34; "Wanger Trial Postponed," February 8, 1952, p. 18; "Wanger Trial Postponed," February 27, 1952, p. 14; "Wanger to Ask Mercy," April 15, 1952, p. 30; "Jury Trial Waived by Wanger on Coast," April 16, 1952, p. 31; "Wanger Is Sentenced to 4 Months in Jail," April 23, 1952, p. 18; "Wanger Loses Plea," August 6, 1952, p. 17; "Wanger Ends Jail Term," September 14, 1952, p. 49. Wanger's prison experiences probably inspired his decision to produce *Riot in Cell Block 11*.

62. Sergio Leemann, *Robert Wise on His Films: From Editing Room to Director's Chair*, Los Angeles: Silman-James Press, 1995, p. 153.

63. Peary, *Close-Ups*, p. 460.

64. Peary, *Close-Ups*, p. 460.

65. Peary, *Close-Ups*, p. 462.

66. Peary, *Close-Ups*, p. 463.

67. Leemann, *Robert Wise*, p. 154.

68. Johnny Mandel to John Tynan, reproduced from *Down Beat Magazine* on *I Want to Live!* 1958 soundtrack album. New York: United Artists Records, 1958. UA-LA271-G.

69. Moreno, p. 213.

70. "Miss Hayward Wins Award for Film Role," *Los Angeles Times*, March 22, 1959. Victor Sjostrom won best actor for *Wild Strawberries*, which also garnered the best film award.

71. "City Film Critics Give Awards to 7," *New York Times*, January 25, 1959, p. 80.

72. Mason Wiley and Damien Bona, *Inside Oscar: The Unofficial History of the Academy Awards*, New York: Ballantine Books, 1986, p. 301.

73. Louella O. Parsons, "Oscar Leaves a Turbu [lence]: Susan Hayward's Dream of '39 Reality in '59," *Los Angeles Examiner*, April 8, 1959, Sec. 1, p. 2.

74. Don Lee Keith, "Susan...Brooklyn," p. 45.

75. Vincent X. Flaherty, "Susan—The New Champion," *Los Angeles Examiner*, April 9, 1959.

76. Erskine Johnson, "Susan's Tranquilizer," *Los Angeles Mirror–News*, June 4, 1959.

77. Jim Murphy, "Susan Hayward's Georgia Years," *Films of the Golden Age*, Spring 2001, pp. 89–90.

Chapter 6

1. Don Rickles on *The Joey Bishop Show*, ABC-TV, February 1968.

2. Hayward was said to have been asked to co-star with Burt Lancaster in *Elmer Gantry* (1960). Jean Simmons ended up the female lead. Don Lee Keith, "Susan...Brooklyn," p. 45.

3. Howard Thompson, *New York Times*, April 9, 1959, p. 37.

4. Garfield, p. 321.

5. *Newsweek*, June 15, 1959, p. 105.

6. Bosley Crowther, *New York Times*, May 28, 1959, p. 34.

7. Arlene Dahl, "Fads Don't Appeal to Miss Hayward," *Hollywood Citizen–News*, March 31, 1959.

8. Claudette Colbert had starred in Cecil B. Demille's lavish 1934 Paramount production. Vivien Leigh essayed the queen in the George Bernard Shaw–based 1945 *Caesar and Cleopatra*. Various lesser productions featured Cleopatra, such as *Serpent of the Nile* (1953) with Rhonda Fleming.

9. Walter Wanger and Joe Hyams, *My Life with Cleopatra*, New York: Bantam, 1963, p. 13.

10. Wanger and Hyams, p. 16.

11. LaGuardia and Arceri, p. 145.

12. Bosley Crowther, *New York Times*, January 7, 1961, p. 12.

13. Moira Walsh, *America*, January 14, 1961, p. 480.

14. Bob Thomas, "Susan Hayward Has No Regrets About Leaving 20th Century–Fox," *Los Angeles Mirror*, August 9, 1960.

15. Lee Belser, "Sister of Film Star Fights for Her Baby," *Los Angeles Mirror*, January 23, 1961, Part 2, p. 4.

16. Dean Jennings, "Hollywood's Late-Blooming Redhead," *Saturday Evening Post*, July 11, 1959, p. 79.

17. "Letters," *Saturday Evening Post*, August 15, 1959, p. 4.

18. Dick Williams, "Week-End Wrap-up," *Los Angeles Mirror–News*, July 10, 1959.

19. Peary, *Close-ups*, pp. 462–63.

20. Florence Marrenner, "My Sister, Susan Hayward, Has Millions—But I'm on Relief," *Confidential*, May 1961, pp. 13, 56–57.

21. Bosley Crowther, *New York Times*, August 26, 1961, p. 15.

22. *Time*, September 8, 1961, p. 89.

23. James Robert Parish, *Prostitution in Hollywood Films*, p. 4.

24. Parish, *Prostitution*, p. 5.

25. Bosley Crowther, *New York Times*, October 13, 1961, p. 27.

26. *Time*, November 3, 1961, p. 75.

27. Scott Macdonough, "Carol Burnett: 'I want to be Susan Hayward!'" *Show*, December 1971, p. 42.

28. Not Bogart, Cagney, DeNiro, Eastwood, Hoffman, McQueen, Robinson, Wayne, or Widmark.

29. Gavin was such a good sport that he parodied himself in *Thoroughly Modern Millie* (1967). To give him his due, he was fine in *Psycho* (1960), a film in which he also chaperoned Vera Miles.

30. *Newsweek*, September 17, 1962, p. 60.

31. *Times* [U.K.], July 20, 1962, p. 10.

32. Bosley Crowther, *New York Times*, September 15, 1962, p. 15.

33. Moira Walsh, *America*, November 2, 1963, p. 533.

34. Bosley Crowther, *New York Times*, October 17, 1963, p. 39.

35. *Times* [U.K.], April 9, 1964, p. 16.

36. Bosley Crowther, *New York Times*, November 3, 1964, p. 26.

37. *Newsweek*, November 16, 1964, p. 103.

38. "Suitor of Lana Turner Is Killed by Her Daughter, 14, with Knife," *New York Times*, April 6, 1958, pp. 1, 70.

39. Mike Connors in Lawrence J. Quirk, *Fasten Your Seat Belts: The Passionate Life of Bette Davis*, New York: Signet, 1990, p. 430.

40. Dmytryk, p. 264.

41. Dmytryk, pp. 264–65.

42. Alexander Walker, *Sex in the Movies: The Celluloid Sacrifice*, Baltimore, MD: Penguin Books, 1969, c1966, p. 196.

43. LaGuardia and Arceri, p. 156.

44. Hawk, *Variety*, March 22, 1967, pp. 6, 26.

45. Bosley Crowther, *New York Times*, May 23, 1967, p. 52.

46. Moreno, p. 49.

47. Hiram Bray, "Hollywood Movie Star Made Her Home in Carrollton," *Times-Georgian*, July 27, 1986, p. 1B.

48. Linet, p. 245.

49. "Susan Hayward's Husband Dies," *Los Angeles Times*, January 10, 1966.

50. Linet, p. 245.

51. Andersen, *A Star*, p. 218.

52. LaGuardia and Arceri, p. 160.

53. Don Lee Keith, "Susan Hayward...Brooklyn," p. 46.

54. Sheilah Graham, "Susan Takes Over Judy's 'Doll' Role," *Hollywood Citizen-News*, May 27, 1967.

55. Bob Freund, "'Restless' Susan Hayward Heading for *Valley of the Dolls*," *Ft. Lauderdale News*, May 8, 1967.

56. "Susan Hayward," *Stage & Cinema*, August 4, 1967.

57. *Time*, December 22, 1967, p. 78.

58. Murf, *Variety*, December 20, 1967, p. 6.

59. Bosley Crowther, *New York Times*, December 16, 1967, p. 51.

60. LaGuardia and Arceri, p. 175.

61. Douglas Brode, *The Films of the Sixties*, Secaucus, NJ: Citadel Press, 1980, p. 200.

62. Tate was being given the glamour treatment, married director Roman Polan-

ski, and might have been a new Monroe had not Charles Manson and his "family" ended her life in 1969. Parkins was using her role as Betty on TV's *Peyton Place* to launch what proved to be a fairly short film career. As a child, Patty Duke had mesmerized moviegoers in *The Miracle Worker* (1962) and had a successful TV series in which she played twins (*The Patty Duke Show*). As with Parkins, a major theatrical film career never really materialized, but she carved out a successful career in TV movies.

63. "Big Rental Films of 1968,"*Variety*, January 8, 1969, p. 15.

64. Jacqueline Susann in Joyce Haber, "It's Tomorrow, But Susan Hayward's Not Crying," *Los Angeles Times*, September 3, 1972, p. 11.

65. Robert Sidney on *Backstory: Valley of the Dolls*, 20th Century–Fox/AMC, 2001.

66. Patty Duke on *Backstory: Valley of the Dolls*.

67. Linet, p. 251.

68. Bob Sidney in LaGuardia and Arceri, p. 174.

69. Susan Hayward on *The Joey Bishop Show*, ABC-TV, February 1968.

70. Abe Greenberg, "Of Susan Hayward & *Mame*," *Hollywood Citizen–News*, December 27, 1968.

71. Earl Wilson, "Susan's Turn at *Mame*," *Los Angeles Herald–Examiner*, January 6, 1969.

72. LaGuardia and Arceri, pp. 179–180.

73. Loretta Swit on *Mysteries and Scandals: Susan Hayward*, E! TV network ,

74. C. Robert Jennings, "Susan's Finally in the Theatre," *Los Angeles Times*, February 1969.

75. "Celeste Holm in *Mame*," *Hollywood Citizen–News*, February 20, 1969.

76. Don Lee Keith, "Susan...Brooklyn," p. 46.

77. LaGuardia & Arceri, p. 188.

78. LaGuardia & Arceri, p. 192.

Chapter 7

1. Hank Grant, *Hollywood Reporter*, April 17, 1969.

2. "Susan Hayward Rescued in Fire," *Los Angeles Herald–Examiner*, January 22, 1971.

3. "Susan Hayward Unhurt as Fire Hits Apartment," *Los Angeles Times*, January 23, 1971, Part I, p. 10.

4. *Hollywood Reporter*, July 16, 1971.

5. Whit, *Variety*, June 7, 1972, p. 18.

6. Howard Thompson, *New York Times*, June 22, 1972, p. 47.

7. Bill Davidson, "Just Like Paramount in 1945!" *TV Guide*, February 26, 1972, p. 20.

8. Nancy Anderson, "Susan's Looking for Work," *Philadelphia Bulletin* [Copley News Service], September 26, 1971.

9. Nancy Anderson.

10. Nancy Anderson.

11. "Susan Hayward in *Fitzgerald* Role," *Hollywood Reporter*, November 30, 1971.

12. Polly Terry, "Susan Hayward Steps Back Into Movies," *Photoplay* [U.K.], May 1972, p. 26.

13. Leonard Maltin, *TV Movies: 1975 Edition*, New York: Signet, 1974, p. 240.

14. "Susan Hayward Replaces Stanwyck in *Fitzgerald* Role," *Hollywood Reporter*, November 30, 1971.

15. Vernon Scott, "Susan Hayward Set for Film Return," *Los Angeles Herald–Examiner*, December 30, 1971.

16. Davidson, "Just like Paramount," p. 18.

17. Army Archerd, "Hollywood Style," *Daily Variety*, April 17, 1972.

18. Mary Murphy, "Dr. Cole as a Vehicle for Susan," *Los Angeles Times*, September 27, 1972, Part IV, p. 20.

19. Leonard Maltin, *TV Movies: 1975 Edition*, New York: Signet, 1974, p. 497.

20. Don Lee Keith, "Susan Hayward: Flame-Haired Blizzard from Brooklyn," *After Dark*, January 1973, p. 46.

21. Dianne Thomas, "Maggie Cole—15 Years," *Susan Hayward Collectors' Club Newsletter*, September-October, 1987, p. 5.

22. Robert Osborne, "The ABC's of Susan Hayward," *Sky* [Delta Airlines], November 1972, pp. 24–25.

23. Dorothy Manners, "Susan Hayward Still Ill but Home from Hospital," *Los Angeles Herald–Examiner*, June 19, 1973.

24. Rambling Reporter, *Hollywood Reporter*, August 24, 1973.

25. Nolan Miller in Wiley and Bona, p. 488.

26. Frank Westmore in Westmore, pp. 239, 242.

27. Linet, p. 292.

28. Osborne, pp. 18–19.

29. Hal Wallis and Charles Higham, *Starmaker: The Autobiography of Hal Wallis*, New York: Macmillan, 1980, p. 177.

30. John J. Miller, *San Francisco Sunday Examiner & Chronicle*, April 21, 1974.

31. *Los Angeles Times*, July 19, 1974.

32. "Susan Hayward Leaves Hospital," *Los Angeles Herald–Examiner*, July 24, 1974.

33. "Actress Ailing," *Los Angeles Herald–Examiner*, October 12, 1974.

34. *Boxoffice*, November 18, 1974.

35. Her sometime companion Ron Nelson might or might not have been with her.

36. "Body of Susan Hayward Flown to Ga. for Burial," *Daily Variety*, March 17, 1975, p. 6.

37. "Susan Hayward Buried Near Her Home in Georgia," *Los Angeles Times*, March 17, 1975.

38. *Hollywood Reporter*, March 20, 1975.

39. Kirk Crivello, "Carrollton, Georgia Remembers Lovely Susan Hayward," *Hollywood Studio Magazine*, March, 1976, p. 6.

40. "Susan Hayward Estate Estimated at $950,000," *Daily Variety*, April 14, 1975; "Susan Hayward Leaves Almost $1 Mil Estate," *Hollywood Reporter*, April 14, 1975.

41. "Last Will and Testament of Edythe Marrenner Chalkley Known As: Susan Hayward." Beverly Hills, CA. Clarence E. Cabell, County Clerk, Los Angeles County, CA. 6 December 1973, pp. 1–3.

42. "Codicil to Will of Susan Chalkley." Clarence E. Cabell, County Clerk, County of Los Angeles. November 7, 1974.

43. "Creditor's Claim. Case Number P 612 200. Superior Court of California. March 19, 1976.

44. "Rejection of Claim." No. P 612200. Superior Court of California. County of Los Angeles. March 24, 1976.

45. "Broadway Ballyhoo," *Hollywood Reporter*, October 15, 1984.

46. In spite of achieving a measure of fame at Paramount and the status of major star at 20th Century–Fox, Hayward made many of her best films on loanouts from those home studios. At RKO she appeared in *Deadline at Dawn*, *My Foolish Heart* and *The Lusty Men*. At MGM, *I'll Cry Tomorrow*. For United Artists, *I Want to Live!* Three of her five Academy Award nominations, including her win, derived from these films.

47. Bronte Woodward, "Susan Hayward: She Always Came Back," *Los Angeles Times Calendar*, April 27, 1975.

Bibliography

Articles

"Academy Award-winning actress Susan Hayward was released from Emory University Hospital in Atlanta..." *Los Angeles Times*, October 28, 1974.

"Accord Ends Movie Star Hayward Suit." *Hollywood Citizen–News*, July 7, 1965.

"Actor to Wed Susan Hayward Tomorrow." *Los Angeles Times*, July 22, 1944.

"Actress Drops Charges Against Sue Hayward." *Los Angeles Examiner*, November 16, 1955.

"Actress Hopes to Drop Susan Hayward Charge." *Los Angeles Times*, November 7, 1955.

"Actress Susan Hayward Flies to Honolulu." *Los Angeles Times*, September 8, 1955.

"Actress Susan Hayward Given 'Youth Oscar.'" *Los Angeles Times*, March 23, 1952.

"Actress Susan Hayward was admitted to Atlanta's Emory University Hospital..." *Boxoffice*, August 5, 1974.

"Actress Susan Hayward, who re-entered Emory University Hospital here October 7..." *Boxoffice*, November 18, 1974.

"Actress Susan Hayward's Mother Dies." *Los Angeles Times*, April 16, 1958.

"After Bedroom Battle with Jil: Susan to Face Court." *Los Angeles Herald & Express*, November 5, 1955, p. A-4.

Agan, Patrick. "Susan Hayward—The Rebellious Survivor." *Hollywood Studio Magazine*, August 1980, pp. 8–12, 33

"Air Force Salute Opens at Pershing Square: Actress Susan Hayward Cuts Ribbon for Display of Various Types of Equipment." *Los Angeles Times*, March 8, 1956.

Alpert, Hollis. "Tragedy, Happy Ending Style." *Saturday Review*, January 7, 1956, p. 56.

Arthur B. Goode auction ad in *Los Angeles Times*, June 6, 1976.

"Arthur Goode will auction..." *Daily Variety*, May 27, 1976.

"At some point..." *Hollywood Studio Magazine*, April 1978,. [re Susan's stand-in Dale Logue].

"Barker Asks for Reconciliation but Susan Says 'No.'" *Los Angeles Herald Express*, April 27, 1955, pp. 1, 4.

"Barker Lawyer to Appeal Susan Hayward Divorce." *Los Angeles Times*, August 19, 1954.

"Barker Pleads 'Let's Reconcile.'" *Los Angeles Examiner*, June 18, 1954.

"Barker Raps Miss Hayward." *Los Angeles Examiner*, July 21, 1955.

"Barker, Susan Hayward Agreement Move Fails." *Los Angeles Times*, April 8, 1954.

Bawden, James. "Marsha Hunt." *Films in Review*, November 1989, pp. 514–525.

"Beauticians Pick Susan Hayward." *Los Angeles Examiner*, January 18, 1949.

Berg, Louis. "Bathsheba Takes a Bath." *Los Angeles Times This Week Magazine*, August 19, 1951.

Bernstein, Jay. "To Tell the Truth." *TV Guide*, October 8, 1983.

"Biblical Bath." *Life*, August 27, 1951, pp. 77, 79, 82, 85.

"Body of Susan Hayward Flown to Ga. for Burial." *Daily Variety*, March 17, 1975, pp. 1, 6.

Brand, Harry [20th Century–Fox Director of Publicity]. "By Susan Hayward." 20th Century–Fox press release, ca. 1955. 5 pages.

"Broadway Ballyhoo: Susan Hayward's 'magnificent jewelry' collection..." *Hollywood Reporter*, October 15, 1984.

"Camera Box: Bonzo Was Busy That Night." *Los Angeles Herald–Examiner*, August 9, 1980 [circa 1938 photo of Susan with Ronald Reagan].

"Camera Targets" [Susan and Kim Novak at Cannes Film Festival]. *Los Angeles Times*, April 30, 1956.

Campbell [Publicity director]. "Susan Hayward must have heard..." [20th Century–Fox press release]. ca. 1954, 4 pages.

_____. "Notes on Susan Hayward for Dorothy Manners" [20th Century–Fox press release]. ca. 1955, 4 pages.

_____. "News" [20th Century–Fox press release]. ca. 1957. 1 page.

Candee, Marjorie Dent, ed. *Current Biography 1953*. New York: H. W. Wilson, c1954, pp. 258–59 with photo.

Carroll, Harrison. "Susan Hayward Beat Me Up, Charges Film Beauty." *Los Angeles Herald Express*, November 4, 1955, pp. 1, 4.

"Cotton for Christmas." *Photoplay*, December 1947.

Crivello, Kirk. "Carrollton, Georgia Remembers Lovely Susan Hayward." *Hollywood Studio Magazine*, March 1976, pp. 5–6.

Cronin, Jeff. "Susan Hayward's Walk with God." *Screen Stories*, March 1975, pp. 38–39, 58.

Dahl, Arlene. "Fads Don't Appeal to Miss Hayward." *Hollywood Citizen–News*, March 31, 1959.

Davidson, Bill. "Just Like Paramount in 1945!" *TV Guide*, February 26, 1972, pp. 18–21.

Degan, Frank. "Susan Hayward Says: 'When They Hit You—Bounce!'" *Silver Screen*, August 1955, pp. 62–63.

"Divorce Granted to Susan Hayward." *Los Angeles Times*, August 18, 1954, Part I, p. 28.

Drew, Janice. "Wool Gathering." *Screen Stories*, June 1943.

Dreyfuss, John. "Susan Hayward Dies at 55; Received Oscar in 1958." *Los Angeles Times*, March 15, 1975, pp. 1, 24.

Duncan, Angela Fox. "Every Inch an Actress." *American Movie Classics* (August 1990).

"Eviction Woes Hit Jess Barker, Susan Hayward." *Los Angeles Times*, November 2, 1946.

Ferguson, Ken. "Susan Hayward: One of the Great Fighters." *Photoplay* [U.K.], June 1975, pp. 22–24.

"Film Actress Cited Most Beautiful." *Los Angeles Daily News*, January 18, 1949.

"Film Couple Evicted from Home." *Los Angeles Daily News*, November 2, 1946.

"Film Star Tries Suicide." *New York Times*, April 27, 1955, p. 27.

Flaherty, Vincent X. "An Ungainly Cupid Bares Confession." *Los Angeles Examiner*, February 11, 1957.

"Foreign Press Honors Susan Hayward, Wayne." *Los Angeles Times*, February 15, 1953.

Friedman, Favius. "You Wouldn't Know Susie Now." *Pageant*, June 1961, pp. 97–103.

Gilpin, Dewitt. "A Drink with Susan Hayward." *Salute*, June 1947.

Goldwyn, Samuel, Productions, Inc. "Biography of Susan Hayward" [press release]. ca. 1949, 5 pages.

Gordon [Publicity director]. 20th Century–Fox press release. ca. 1949.

Haber, Joyce. "It's Tomorrow, but Susan Hayward's Not Crying." *Los Angeles Times*, September 3, 1972, p. 11.

Harris, Eleanor. "She Does as She Pleases." *Motion Picture*, September 1944, pp. 56, 106.

"Hayward Divorce Move Postponed." *Los Angeles Times*, November 18, 1954.

Hayward, Susan. "The Role I Liked Best." *Saturday Evening Post*, April 6, 1946, p. 126.

_____."By Susan Hayward" [Johnson; 20th Century–Fox press release]. ca. 1952, 3 pages.

_____. "Guest Column for Dorothy Kilgallen" [20th Century–Fox press release]. ca. 1954, 6 pages

"Hayward Tiff to End in Draw." *Los Angeles Mirror-News*, November 7, 1955, p. 5.

"Hayward Trial Attorneys Clash." *Los Angeles Times*, June 18, 1954.

"High Court Won't Hear Susan Hayward Appeal." *Los Angeles Times*, April 12, 1956.

Holland, Jack. "Susan Hayward—Fact and Fiction." *Screenland*, July 1958, pp. 38, 41, 68.

"Hong Kong Trip Denied Actress Sons." *Los Angeles Examiner*, October 14, 1954.

Hopper, Hedda. "Hayward of the Wayward Roles." *Chicago Sunday Tribune*, June 19, 1949.

_____. "Susan Hayward—Beauty with a Brain." *Chicago Sunday Tribune*, March 9, 1952, pp. 6, 15.

"If You Knew Susan." *Look*, July 14, 1953, pp. 64–68.

I. Z. [Ida Zeitlin?] "Actress Around the World." *Cue*, April 16, 1955.

Jackovich, Karen G., and Mark Sennet. "The Children of John Wayne, Susan Hayward and Dick Powell Fear That Fallout Killed Their Parents." *People*, November 10, 1980, pp. 42–47.

"Jess Barker Asks Susan to Pay Costs." *Los Angeles Times*, November 9, 1954.

"Jil Asks Her Charges on Sue Hayward Be Dropped." *Los Angeles Herald Express*, November 15, 1955.

"Jil Jarmyn Drops Action Against Susan Hayward." *Los Angeles Times*, November 16, 1955.

"Jil Jarmyn May Drop Susan Hayward Charge." *Los Angeles Examiner*, November 6, 1955.

"Jil Jarmyn Wants to Drop Susan Hayward Complaint." *Los Angeles Examiner*, November 7, 1955.

Johnson [Publicity director]. "One Minute Interview with Susan Hayward" [20th Century–Fox press release]. ca. 1954, 1 page.

Johnson, Erskine. "Susan Hayward Has Found Happiness in the Deep South." *Los Angeles Mirror–News*, April 19, 1958.

"Jury Trial Waived by Wanger on Coast." *New York Times*, April 16, 1952, p. 31.

Keith, Don Lee. "Susan Hayward: Flame-Haired Blizzard from Brooklyn." *After Dark*, January 1973, pp. 40, 42, 45–46.

King [Publicity Director]. "Biography of Susan Hayward" [Paramount press release]. July 1940.

"The last time Susan Hayward was directed by George Cukor..." *Los Angeles Examiner*, February 27, 1951.

"Lawyers End Case in Susan Hayward Divorce." *Los Angeles Times*, June 19, 1954.

"Letters." *Saturday Evening Post*, August 15, 1959, p. 4.

Lieber, Perry [Publicity Director]. "Susan Hayward: Biography" [RKO Radio Studios press release]. January 13, 1955, 3 pages.

Ludwig, Jerry [Publicity Director] "Susan Hayward" [Mirisch Company press release]. October 1962, 6 pages.

McClelland, Douglas. "Susan Hayward: Made a Career Out of the Chip Poverty Put on Her Shoulder." *Films in Review*, May 1962, pp. 266–276.

_____."The Brooklyn Bernhardt." *Films and Filming*, March 1965, pp. 11–15.

_____. "Susan Hayward, 1919–1975." *After Dark*, June 1975, p. 72.

Manners, Dorothy. "Susan Hayward Thinks She'll Remarry." *Los Angeles Examiner*, August 29, 1954, pp. 9, 12.

_____. "Susan Hayward Still Ill but Home from Hospital." *Los Angeles Herald–Examiner*, June 19, 1973.

Manning, Dorothy. "Brooklyn's Child Is Full of Faith." *Photoplay*, July 1955. pp 49–50, 83-86.

Markson [Publicity director]. [20th Century–Fox Press release regarding *I Can Get It for You Wholesale*]. ca. 1951.

Marrenner, Florence. "My Sister, Susan Hayward, Has Millions–But I'm on Relief." *Confidential*, May, 1961, pp. 10–13, 56–57.

Mendelsohn [Publicity director] [20th Century–Fox Press release re *David and Bathsheba*. ca. 1951, 2 pages.

_____."Comely Susan Hayward become [sic] Darryl F. Zanuck's box-office champion among women..." [20th Century–Fox press release]. ca. 1953, 1 page.

_____. "Susan Hayward tintype—for Skolsky" [20th Century–Fox press release]. ca. 1953, 5 pages.

"Milestones" [obituary]. *Time*, March 24, 1975, p. 59.

"Miss Hayward Gets Glamour Queen Title." *Los Angeles Times*, July 11, 1950.

"Miss Hayward Gets OK to Take Sons from State." *Los Angeles Times*, April 20, 1954.

"Miss Hayward, Mate Reunite." *Los Angeles Examiner*, November 27, 1947.

"Miss Hayward Misses Death." *Los Angeles Examiner*, June 1, 1950.

"Miss Hayward Moves to Ease Custody Curb." *Los Angeles Times*, May 8, 1954.

"Miss Hayward, on Mend, Spurns Barker's Offer." *Los Angeles Times*, April 28, 1955.

"Miss Hayward Rallies After Pill Overdose." *Hollywood Citizen–News*, April 26, 1955.

"Miss Hayward to Be Buried in Carrollton, Ga." *Los Angeles Times*, March 16, 1975.
"Miss Hayward Wed to Actor." *Los Angeles Times*. July 24, 1944.
"Miss Hayward Weds Lawyer." *Hollywood Citizen–News*, February 9, 1957, p. 2.
"Miss Hayward Wins Award for Film Role." *Los Angeles Times*, March 22, 1959.
"Miss Hayward's Nude Dash Told." *Los Angeles Examiner*, June 15, 1954.
Moritz, Charles, ed. *Current Biography 1975*. New York: H. W. Wilson, c1975, 1976. "Necrology," p. 467.
"Movie Queen Blows Top, Swings Clothes Brush." *Los Angeles Mirror–News*, November 4, 1955, pp. 1, 2.
Muir, Florabel. "Susan Hayward in Brawl with Blonde in Actor's Bedroom." *Los Angeles Daily News*, November 5, 1955, pp. 3, 6.
Murphy, Jim. "Susan Hayward's Georgia Years." *Films of the Golden Age*, Spring 2001, pp. 88–91.
"New Hayward-Barker Divorce Trial Asked." *Los Angeles Times*, October 5, 1954.
"No Reconciliation, Says Susan, Still in Hospital." *Los Angeles Examiner*, April 28, 1955, pp. 1, 5.
"Now Actress Gets Brush-off from Canada." *Los Angeles Times*, September 15, 1951.
O'Connor, Dick, and M. Himmel. "Actress Susan Hayward Tries Sleep Pill Suicide," *Los Angeles Herald Express*, April 26, 1955, pp. 4–5.
Osborne, Robert. "The ABC's of Susan Hayward." *Sky* [Delta Airlines], November 1972, pp. 23–25.
"Oscar Takes Over." *Movie Life*, June 1948, pp. 21–26.
Paramount. "Biography of Susan Hayward" [press release]. August 1958, 4 pages.
Parsons, Louella O. "Susan Hayward and Jess Barker Reconciled." *Los Angeles Examiner*, September 30, 1944.
_____. "Susan Tells of Slapping." *Los Angeles Examiner*, November 4, 1955.
_____. "Susan Flies to Stricken Husband." *Los Angeles Examiner*, July 25, 1958.
"Plane Causes Stampede of Film Camels." *Los Angeles Times*, December 2, 1950.
"Police Paradox: Actress' Life Illegally Saved." *Hollywood Citizen–News*, June 1, 1955.
"Posing for Hubby." *Movies Magazine*, February 1951, pp. 16–17.
"Rambling Reporter." *Hollywood Reporter*, August 24, 1973.
"Remembering a Redhead." *Courier–Journal Magazine*, January 31, 1988, p. 5.
Rochlen, Kendis. "Emotion Explodes in Susan." *Los Angeles Mirror–News*, April 26, 1955, pp. 1, 10.
_____."Candid Kendis: Have Silex—Will Travel." *Los Angeles Mirror–News*, November 7, 1955.
Royce, Bill. "Susan: A Great Lady—And a Real One!" *Rona Barrett's Hollywood Magazine*, November 1972.
"Rule Susan Hayward Sons to Stay in U.S." *Los Angeles Herald Express*, October 13, 1954.
Scheuer, Philip K. "Producers Blindly Neglect Another Scarlett O'Hara." *Los Angeles Times*, January 30, 1944, pp. 1, 5.
_____. "Susan Hayward Awes MGM with Her Polished Singing." *Los Angeles Times* (Sunday), July 3, 1955, Sec. IV, p. 2.
Scott, John L. "Susan Hayward Likes 'Vital' Roles to Fit That Redhead Temperament." *Los Angeles Times*, April 3, 1949, pp. 1, 3.
Scott, Vernon. "Beats the Measles: Susan Hayward Returns for Film." *Hollywood Citizen–News*, April 7, 1958.

"Services Pending for Oscar Winner Susan Hayward." *Hollywood Reporter*, March 17, 1975.

"She Wanted to Win: Susan Hayward." *New York Times*, April 8, 1959, p. 41.

Shipp, Cameron. "Susan Hayward." *Redbook Magazine*, February 1956, pp. 31, 33–35, 96–98.

Skolsky, Sidney. "Hollywood Is My Beat: Tintypes." *Hollywood Citizen–News*, June 30, 1949.

_____. "Hollywood Is My Beat: Tintypes." *Hollywood Citizen–News*, December 24, 1958.

Sloan, Lloyd L. "Interested in Astrology? Talk to Susan Hayward." *Hollywood Citizen-News*, March 7, 1949.

Smith, Darr. "Darr Smith" [columnist]. *Los Angeles Daily News*, January 24, 1951, [re *David and Bathsheba*].

_____. *Los Angeles Daily News*, August 28, 1951, [re *David and Bathsheba*].

Spear, Van. "Spearheads." *Boxoffice*, December 3, 1955.

"Star Susan Hayward Tries Suicide with Sleeping Pills." *Los Angeles Mirror–News*, April 26, 1955, pp. 1, 10.

"Stars' Cancer Deaths Linked to '53 A-Test." *Los Angeles Times*, August 6, 1979.

"State High Court Denies Hayward Divorce Appeals." *Los Angeles Examiner*, April 12, 1956.

"$ucce$$ for $ultry $u$an." *People Today*, February 27, 1952.

"Sue May Lose 2 Children as New Court Fight Looms." *Los Angeles Mirror–News*, April 27, 1955, pp. 1, 13.

Susan Autographs Forecourt in Gold Flakes." *Hollywood Citizen-News*, August 23, 1951.

"Susan Faces Decree Wait." *Los Angeles Examiner*, June 20, 1954.

"Susan Gets Tots' Custody." *Los Angeles Examiner*, March 16, 1954.

"Susan Hayward." *PIX*, July 17, 1954, pp. 35–37.

"Susan Hayward." *Screen Greats Vol. V: Legendary Ladies*. New York: Starlog Press, 1981, 15 pages.

"Susan Hayward Advises Stars to Stay Off Stump in Political Campaigns." *Daily Variety*, October 27, 1952.

"Susan Hayward and Barker in Court Today." *Los Angeles Times*, June 14, 1954.

"Susan Hayward Awarded Divorce from Jess Barker." *Los Angeles Examiner*, August 18, 1954.

"Susan Hayward, Barker Tell Story of Clashes." *Los Angeles Times*, February 26, 1954.

"Susan Hayward Believes Crises Are Stimulating." *Desert News* [Salt Lake City], April 11, 1952.

"Susan Hayward Bids for an Academy Award." *Look*, December 13, 1955, pp. 104, 106.

"Susan Hayward Breaks Down at Divorce Trial." *Los Angeles Times*, June 16, 1954, pp. 1, 2.

"Susan Hayward Buried Near Her Home in Georgia." *Los Angeles Times*, March 17, 1975.

"Susan Hayward Dead." *Philadelphia Daily News*, March 15, 1975, p. 6.

"Susan Hayward Denies Offering Mate $100,000." *Los Angeles Times*, June 17, 1954.

"Susan Hayward Dies at 55." *Los Angeles Herald–Examiner*, March 15, 1975.

"Susan Hayward Dies at 55; Oscar-Winning Movie Star." *New York Times*, March 15, 1975, p. 30.

"Susan Hayward Estate Estimated at $950,000." *Daily Variety*, April 14, 1975.

"Susan Hayward Expected to Leave Hospital Today." *Los Angeles Times*, April 29, 1955.

"Susan Hayward Found Unconscious in Home." *Los Angeles Times*, April 26, 1955.

"Susan Hayward, Gary Cooper Get Special Honors." *Los Angeles Daily News*, February 10, 1953.

"Susan Hayward, Gary Cooper Win Fan Poll." *Los Angeles Times*, February 3, 1953.

"Susan Hayward Gets OK to Take Sons from State." *Los Angeles Times*, May 20, 1954.

"Susan Hayward Gets Her Original Name Restored." *Los Angeles Times*, September 5, 1956.

"Susan Hayward Gets Old Name Back." *Los Angeles Herald Express*, September 4, 1956.

"Susan Hayward Given Custody of Twin Sons." *Los Angeles Times*, May 11, 1957.

"Susan Hayward Gives Birth to Twin Boys." *Los Angeles Times*, February 20, 1945.

"Susan Hayward Happy with Life in Georgia's Hills." *Hollywood Citizen–News*, April 7, 1958.

"Susan Hayward Homeless; Blasts Black Mart Housing." *Los Angeles Examiner*, November 2, 1946.

"Susan Hayward, Hubby Call Calling Off Off." *Los Angeles Daily News*, February 25, 1954.

"Susan Hayward, Jess Barker to Wed." *Los Angeles Examiner*, July 19, 1944.

"Susan Hayward Leaves Almost $1 Mil Estate." *Hollywood Reporter*, April 14, 1975.

"Susan Hayward Leaves Hospital." *Los Angeles Herald–Examiner*, July 24, 1974.

"Susan Hayward Leaves Hospital to Go Home." *Los Angeles Times*, April 30, 1955.

Susan Hayward Makes Big School Comeback." *New York Journal–American*, March 12, 1952.

"Susan Hayward Married to Georgia Attorney." *Los Angeles Times*, February 9, 1957.

"Susan Hayward Mate Balks at Trip for Twins." *Los Angeles Times*, May 9, 1954.

"Susan Hayward Mate's Gag Puts Him on Spot." *Los Angeles Times*, September 19, 1944.

"Susan Hayward Mother Dies of Heart Ailment." *Los Angeles Mirror–News*, April 16, 1958.

"Susan Hayward Okay" [unspecified minor surgery]. *Hollywood Citizen–News*, November 30, 1956.

"Susan Hayward Only American Cannes Winner." *Hollywood Reporter*, May 11, 1956.

"Susan Hayward Ordered to Finance Mate's Appeal." *Los Angeles Times*, December 14, 1954.

"Susan Hayward Quits Hospital." *New York Times*, April 30, 1955, p. 10.

"Susan Hayward Quits Hospital, Goes Home." *Los Angeles Examiner*, April 30, 1955.

"Susan Hayward Recovering After Suicide Attempt." *Los Angeles Daily News*, April 26, 1955, pp. 1, 2.

"Susan Hayward Sole U.S. Prize at Cannes Fest." *Variety*, May 16, 1956.

"Susan Hayward, Startling Hollywood, Asks Divorce." *Los Angeles Times*, October 1, 1947.

"Susan Hayward, 'Strong Gal' Role Specialist, Dies." *Variety*, March 19, 1975, pp. 4, 46.

"Susan Hayward Suit: Barker Names Hughes as Visitor to Home." *Hollywood Citizen–News*, February 26, 1954.

"Susan Hayward Target in New Legal Action." *Los Angeles Herald Express*, May 4, 1955.

"Susan Hayward Termed at WB; Gets 2 Spots." *Hollywood Reporter*, February 19, 1938.

"Susan Hayward to Play Babs Graham Biopic." *Daily Variety*, October 9, 1957.

"Susan Hayward to Take Twin Sons to Georgia." *Los Angeles Times*, April 27, 1957.

"Susan Hayward Wants Name Back." *Los Angeles Herald Express*, July 26, 1956.

"Susan Hayward Weds." *Los Angeles Examiner*, February 9, 1957.

"Susan Hayward Whacked Her, Actress Charges." *Los Angeles Times*, November 5, 1955.

"Susan Hayward Wins Custody Case Point." *Los Angeles Times*, March 16, 1954.

"Susan Hayward Wins Top Acting Prize at Cannes." *Hollywood Citizen–News*, May 10, 1956.

"Susan Hayward Wins Twice; Ex-Mate Loses Fees, Appeal." *Los Angeles Examiner*, February 16, 1956.

"Susan Hayward Would Drop Ex-Mate's Name." *Los Angeles Times*, July 26, 1956.

"Susan Hayward's Screams of 'Don't Kill Me' Described." *Los Angeles Times*, June 15, 1954.

"Susan Hayward's Sons Willed Bulk of 950G Estate." *Variety*, April 16, 1975.

"Susan Home, Faces Suit." *Los Angeles Examiner*, May 1, 1955.

"Susan in the Cement." *Los Angeles Daily News*, August 24, 1951.

"Susan Loses Her Dog" [London quarantine]. *Los Angeles Times*, May 14, 1956.

"Susan Sobs, Says Jess Spanked Her." *Los Angeles Examiner*, February 26, 1954, cover, Part I, pp. 2, 6.

"Susan Weeps at Testimony." *Los Angeles Examiner*, June 16, 1954.

"Susan's Divorce Offer of $100,000 Reported." *Los Angeles Daily News*, June 16, 1954, pp. 3, 50.

"Susan's Life Full of Storm." *Los Angeles Herald Express*, April 7, 1959.

"Susan's Nude Flight Told by Eyewitness." *Los Angeles Daily News*, June 15, 1954, pp. 1, 33.

"Temporary Insanity Pleaded by Wanger." *New York Times*, January 8, 1952, p. 28.

Terry, Polly. "Susan Hayward Steps Back into Movies." *Photoplay* [U.K.], May 1972, pp. 24, 26.

"Transitions." [obituary] *Newsweek*, March 24, 1975, p. 61.

Turner, Marjorie. "An Authentic Red Head Speaks." *Syracuse Herald-Journal*, April 11, 1952.

"Two Suicide Tries by Susan Hayward Claimed." *Los Angeles Times*, July 21, 1955, p. 5.

Universal-International. "Susan Hayward—Biography" [press release]. May 27, 1947.

_____. "Susan Hayward—Biography" [press release]. March 12, 1948.

Van Gelder, Lawrence. "A Life Like the Movies." *New York Times*, March 15, 1975, p. 30.

"Wanger Ends Jail Term." *New York Times*, September 14, 1952, p. 49.

"Wanger Is Sentenced to 4 Months in Jail." *New York Times*, April 23, 1952, p. 18.

"Wanger Loses Plea." *New York Times*, August 6, 1952, p. 17.

"Wanger to Ask Mercy." *New York Times*, April 15, 1952, p. 30.

"Wanger Trial Postponed." *New York Times*, February 8, 1952, p. 18.

"Wanger Trial Postponed." *New York Times*, February 27, 1952, p. 14.

"Wanger Victim May Be Crippled." *New York Times*, January 20, 1952, p. 34.

Warner Bros. Studios. "Biography of Susan Hayward" [press release]. November 21, 1956. 2 pages.

"What Every Starlet Dreams." *Quick*, September 3, 1951, p. 31.

Whitcomb, Jon. "Songbird Susan." *Cosmopolitan*, February 1956, pp. 61–63.

Wilkerson, W. R. "Trade[ ]." *Hollywood Reporter*, May 11, 1956.

Williams, Dick. "The Hayward Mystery." *Los Angeles Mirror-News*, April 27, 1955, Part II, p. 4.

Wilson, Earl. "Earl Wilson" [Hayward in New York making *House of Strangers* and buying a mink]. *Los Angeles Daily News*, March 15, 1949.

_____. "Susan Hayward Speaks Up." *Los Angeles Mirror-News*, January 18, 1956.

Wilson, Elizabeth. "Brown-Eyed Susan." *Liberty*, May 10, 1947, p. 23.

Wilson, Lisa. "The Harder You're Hit…" *American Weekly*, August 1, 1954

Wolfson [Publicity director]. "Do You Know That" [20th Century–Fox press release]. ca. 1951.

_____. "Susan Hayward's Pre-Christmas 'Give a G.I. a Lift with a Gift…'" [20th Century–Fox press release]. ca. 1951.

_____. "Three Hundred Extras…*With a Song in My Heart*" [20th Century–Fox press release]. ca. 1952.

_____. "Susan Hayward, the Red-Tressed Beauty…." [20th Century–Fox press release]. ca. 1953. 5 pages.

_____. "Susan Hayward Was…Voted the Most Popular Actress of Egypt" [20th Century–Fox press release]. ca. 1953. 1 page.

"Women: Privilege of the Podium." *Time*, November 30, 1953, p. 26.

Wood, Thomas. "If You Knew Susie" [press release]. ca. 1951. 14 pages.

Woodard, Bronte. "Susan Hayward: She Always Came Back." *Los Angeles Times Calendar*, April 27, 1975.

Wright, Comena. "Susan Hayward Wrests Fame from 'Taboo Roles.'" *Los Angeles Examiner*, September 24, 1950.

Zeitlin, Ida. "Three Loves Has Susan." *Photoplay*, November 1952, pp. 41–43, 82, 84, 86.

Books

Andersen, Christopher P. *A Star, Is a Star, Is a Star! The Lives and Loves of Susan Hayward*. Garden City, NY: Doubleday, 1980.

Behlmer, Rudy, ed. *Memo from Darryl F. Zanuck: The Golden Years at Twentieth Century–Fox*. New York: Grove Press, 1993.

Cameron, Ian and Elisabeth. *Dames*. New York: Praeger, 1969.

Dmytryk, Edward. *It's a Hell of a Life but Not a Bad Living*. New York: Times Books, 1978.

Garfield, Brian. *Western Films: A Complete Guide*. New York: Rawson Associates, 1982.

Geist, Kenneth L. *Pictures Will Talk: The Life and Films of Joseph L. Mankiewicz*. Introduction by Richard Burton. New York: Charles Scribner's Sons, 1978.

Grams, Martin, Jr. *Radio Drama: A Comprehensive Chronicle of American Network Programs, 1932–1962.* Jefferson, NC: McFarland, 2000.

Heston, Charlton. *In the Arena: An Autobiography.* New York: Simon & Schuster, 1995.

LaGuardia, Robert, and Gene Arceri. *Red: The Tempestuous Life of Susan Hayward.* New York: Macmillan, 1985.

Leeman, Sergio. *Robert Wise on His Films: From Editing Room to Director's Chair.* Los Angeles: Silman-James Press, 1995.

Linet, Beverly. *Portrait of a Survivor: Susan Hayward.* New York: Berkley, 1984 [originally published by Atheneum, 1980].

Matthews, Charles. *Oscar A to Z: A Complete Guide to More Than 2,400 Movies Nominated for Academy Awards.* New York: Main Street Books (Doubleday), 1995.

McClelland, Doug. *Susan Hayward: The Divine Bitch.* New York: Pinnacle, 1973.

_____. *The Complete Life Story of Susan Hayward...Immortal Screen Star.* New York: Pinnacle, 1975 [revised ed. of McClelland's 1973 biography, with details of her death].

Moreno, Eduardo. *The Films of Susan Hayward.* Secaucus, NJ: Citadel, 1979.

Osborne, Robert. *Academy Awards 1974 Oscar Annual.* La Habra, CA: ESE California, 1974.

Parish, James Robert. *The Fox Girls.* New Rochelle, NY: Arlington House, 1971.

_____. *Prostitution in Hollywood Films: Plots, Critiques, Casts and Credits for 389 Theatrical and Made-for-Television Releases.* Jefferson, NC: McFarland, 1992.

_____, and Don E. Stanke. *The Forties Gals.* Westport, CT: Arlington House, 1980.

Peary, Danny, ed. *Close-Ups: Intimate Profiles of Movie Stars by Their Costars, Directors, Screenwriters, and Friends.* New York: Fireside, 1988, c1978. [Robert Wise on Susan Hayward].

Roberts, Randy, and James S. Olson. *John Wayne: American.* New York: Free Press, 1995.

Roth, Lillian, with Mark Connolly and Gerold Frank. *I'll Cry Tomorrow.* New York: Frederick Fell, 1954.

Sackett, Susan. *The Hollywood Reporter Book of Box Office Hits.* New York: Billboard Books, 1990.

Scagnetti, Jack. *Movie Stars in Bathtubs.* Middle Village, NY: Jonathan David Publishers, 1975.

Shipman, David. *The Great Movie Stars: The International Years.* London: Angus & Robertson, 1972.

Silver, Alain, and Elizabeth Ward. *Film Noir: An Encyclopedic Reference to the American Style.* 3rd ed. Woodstock, NY: Overlook Press, 1992.

Selznick, David O. *Memo from David O. Selznick.* Selected and Edited by Rudy Behlmer. New York: Viking Press, 1972.

Steinberg, Cobbett. *Reel Facts: The Movie Book of Records.* Updated ed. New York: Vintage, 1982, c1981.

Unterberger, Amy L., ed. *International Dictionary of Films and Filmmakers—3: Actors and Actresses.* 3rd ed. Detroit and New York: St. James Press, 1996.

Wallis, Hal, and Charles Higham. *Starmaker: The Autobiography of Hal Wallis.* New York: Macmillan, 1980.

Wanger, Walter, and Joe Hyams. *My Life with Cleopatra.* New York: Bantam, 1963.

Wayne, Pilar, with Alex Thorleifson. *John Wayne: My Life with the Duke.* New York: McGraw-Hill, 1987.

Westmore, Frank, and Muriel Davidson. *The Westmores of Hollywood*. Philadelphia and New York: J. B. Lippincott, 1976.

Wiley, Mason, and Damien Bona. *Inside Oscar: The Unofficial History of the Academy Awards*. New York: Ballantine Books, 1986.

Wiseman, Thomas. *The Seven Deadly Sins of Hollywood*. London: Oldbourne Press, 1957.

Index